A Shell Guide

STAFFORDSHIRE

by Henry Thorold

Mariae Alexandrae Herbert
hunc librum auctor, nepos, dedicat

A Shell Guide

STAFFORDSHIRE

by Henry Thorold

Faber & Faber   3 Queen Square   London

First published in 1978
by Faber and Faber Limited
3 Queen Square London WC1
Printed in Great Britain by
Butler & Tanner Ltd, Frome and London
All rights reserved

St George & The Dragon by Thomas Wright, 1958. Darlaston

British Library Cataloguing in Publication Data

Thorold, Henry
    Staffordshire. – (A Shell guide).
    1. Staffordshire – Description and travel – Guide books
    I. Title   II. Series
    914.24′6′04857   DA670.S7

    ISBN 0–571–10516–5

Acknowledgements

The idea of a *Shell Guide to Staffordshire* I owe to my friend, the Rev. T. B. Williams, Rector of Hougham-cum-Marston; indeed he hoped to collaborate with me in the task. But the demands of an extensive country parish unfortunately made this impossible, and I have had to content myself with his company on a number of explorations, and the savour of a few of his sentiments in the text. But it was he who introduced me to Staffordshire.

Great gratitude I owe once again to Mr John Piper, Editor of the *Shell Guides*, for allowing me to write another volume in the series, and to him and Mr Edward Piper for their help and their photographs. Many other friends, in Staffordshire and elsewhere, have also given me much help: Mr Dennis Birch, Mr Howard Colvin, Mr John Cornforth, Mr Patrick Cormack, M.P., Mr Edward Croft Murray, the Provost of Denstone, Mr Peter Fleetwood-Hesketh, Dr A. H. Gomme, Mr Peter Howell, the Rev. Gerard Irvine, His Honour Judge Irvine, Mr John Readett-Bayley, Miss Mary Stanley-Smith, and Mr E. J. Thompson. Mr John Barratt, Mr J. de C. Stevens-Guille and the Rev. Basil Wilks (with his camera) were my frequent companions on expeditions; Mr Jasper More, M.P., once again helped me with much railway history, and the Rt Hon Enoch Powell, M.P., treated me to a memorable tour of Wolverhampton. I am also most grateful to all those who so kindly took me round their houses, or their churches, and often entertained me so generously.

Finally I must mention that the *Shell Guide to Staffordshire* (in common with other volumes in the series) treats of the historic County of Stafford. It therefore includes various places which were unfortunately transferred, for administrative purposes, to another, newly invented, authority in 1974. But, historically and spiritually, these are part of Staffordshire.

Marston Hall,   Henry Thorold
Grantham
September 1977

Tutbury

Illustrations

Note: Captions to the photographs include place names in **bold type**. These refer to entries in the gazetteer, pages 51–189.

Introduction

Of all the counties of England Staffordshire is the most intriguing. 'A book on Staffordshire?' people will say. 'You're writing a book on Staffordshire?' They look puzzled. 'One of your northern counties, is it? What do you find of interest there? Is it all Potteries? Or is it the Black Country? Or are they the same thing? Is there much to see?'

◁ Near **Longnor** *(top)* and **Alstonfield** *below* Goldsitch Moss

Except to the initiated, Staffordshire remains a mystery. Even to the initiated it reveals its secrets slowly. For Staffordshire is neither north nor south, neither east nor west. It is neither the largest of counties, nor is it the smallest. It is a great manufacturing county—yet its greatest industry is agriculture. No English county is farther from the sea—yet it has produced two of England's greatest sailors. It is one of the most

Hollington

The Weaver Hills near **Wootton**

The Dove near **Ellastone**

populous of counties—yet four-fifths of it are wholly rural. Some of its finest country is thought to be in Derbyshire. One of its finest country houses is thought to be in Shropshire. Its cathedral is under-estimated, its parish churches unknown. Its castles are unheard of, its great houses and gardens too little visited. Its countryside is maligned. Primitive Methodism was founded in the county, yet in Staffordshire are to be found more old pockets of Roman Catholicism than anywhere else in England. It is a county of contrasts.

How to see Staffordshire

Staffordshire is divided into two unequal halves by the great river Trent. Rising on the grim moorland of Biddulph, the river makes its way through Stoke, past pottery and power station, on through countryside typically Staffordshire, towards Lichfield and the south. Lichfield it never reaches; instead it turns east, makes its way between the highlands of Cannock Chase to the north, the highlands of Needwood Forest to the south, on to Burton, to Nottingham, to Newark; to divide Nottinghamshire from Lincolnshire, the Province of Canterbury from the Province of York, northern England from southern England; and finally flows into the great estuary of Humber.

NW Staffordshire is dominated by industry, the Potteries, the coal mines, the steelworks, and the bleak moors where Mow Cop divides Staffordshire from Cheshire.

The NE embraces some of the loveliest and wildest Peakland, limestone country of singular beauty, the remote world of stone walls and dales—Milldale, Dovedale, the Valley of the Manifold. Here Staffordshire meets Derbyshire. Here London and the outside world seem a thousand miles away.

p12 The Manifold near **Wetton** *(top)* and The ▷ Roaches, **Meerbrook**

p13 **Wychnor** *(top)* and **Hamstall Ridware**

Most of Staffordshire's southern frontier is Black Country: Wolverhampton, Walsall, West Bromwich dominate this borderland; cooling towers, chimneys, canals, railways, motorways command this industrial scene—which extends to the coalfields on the southern face of Cannock Chase.

The middle country is rich farmland, green pastures, mellow brick villages, woods of oak and beech, hedgerows of ash and holly, the farms presided over by those tall red farmhouses so characteristic of Staffordshire. Here is rural England, unsophisticated, unvisited, unknown. In this middle country are Stafford, the county town, and Lichfield, the cathedral city.

And where better to start a tour of Staffordshire than Lichfield? Here a visitor will find hotels, quiet streets of old houses not yet ruined by the 20th century, a glorious little-known cathedral, and the birthplace of Dr Johnson. All these will absorb and delight him. From here he can spend a day in Needwood Forest, find Hoar Cross and Blithfield, smell the rich aroma of beer at Burton. From here he can make a sortie into the Black Country, savour the special quality of Walsall, of Bilston, of Wednesbury and Tipton, of Brierley Hill and Rowley Regis, of Dudley Castle and Wolverhampton. From here he can visit Stafford, examine the William Salt Library (if he has a taste for local history), see Shugborough, the gate-house at Tixall, the church at Ingestre.

Staffordshire is a large county, and the visitor may choose to go farther north and stay in Dovedale. Here he can explore the Dales and Valleys, that wild country of stone walls and remote villages, and can also visit

11

Rugeley   Black Country near **West Bromwich** *(top)* and near **Wednesbury** ▷

St Mary's, **Bilston**

Hollington

the Potteries; above all, he can penetrate that most mysterious region, the Churnet Valley, and see Checkley, Cheadle, Croxden Abbey, Alton.

The long western frontier of Staffordshire, the quiet land where Staffordshire meets Shropshire, is again a world apart. Here the visitor will wish to stay. The scenery is undramatic, green, restful; the villages secluded, rewarding: Whitmore, Maer, Mucklestone, Ashley. Here he can visit Weston Park, and enjoy Lord Bradford's great collection of pictures. West of Eccleshall is the woodland quarter, with its thick woods, mysterious narrow lanes, remote hamlets, the rare church of Broughton, Eccleshall itself. Here the Shropshire Union Canal makes its way along the borderland, with straight silent stretches of dark water—between high, wooded banks, or raised up on lofty embankments with the roads running through tunnels underneath. Adbaston, High Offley, Norbury, Gnosall, Forton, Weston-under-Lizard—the villages follow one another as far as Boscobel and Chillington, the romantic country for ever associated with Charles II. Unspoiled rural England stretches on, for all the proximity of

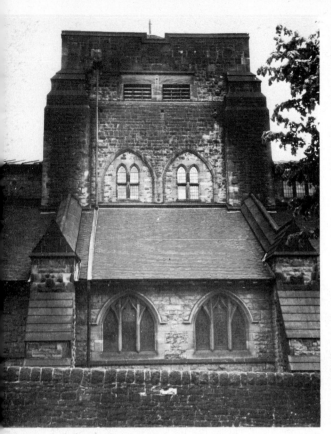

All Saints', **Leek**

Denstone

Churches

As for architecture, the early crosses at Ilam, Leek and Wolverhampton speak of Anglo-Saxon Christianity. There is the great Norman nave at Tutbury, the Norman transept at Gnosall and the little Norman church of St Chad at Stafford. Norman fonts in Staffordshire are notable too—such as those at St Mary's, Stafford, at Ilam, at Armitage, and Pipe Ridware.

Wolverhampton, right down to Enville and Kinver Edge, where Staffordshire merges with Worcestershire. So in a week, or more probably a month, the visitor will have passed through a county rich in varied scenery, rich in architecture, rich in history.

Of the Early English period, the finest work is to be found in the choir of Lichfield Cathedral, with the crossing and the transepts; in the ruins of Croxden Abbey, with its long, narrow, lancet windows; in the miniature church of Coppenhall; in the chancels at Pattingham and Brewood; and the tower at Weston-on-Trent.

The nave and Lady Chapel at Lichfield are superb examples of the Decorated period; Clifton Campville, the finest village church in Staffordshire, is almost wholly of this period; the great church at Tamworth, the chancels at Checkley and Norbury—all these display the elegant and flowing style of the late 13th and early 14th centuries.

Of the Perpendicular period the grand collegiate churches at Wolverhampton and

Detail of the altar rails, **Elford**

Penkridge are splendid examples; of the very latest Gothic, the singularly complete church of Barton-under-Needwood (1533), and Broughton (1633), most charming of little family shrines, with its glass, its furnishings and its monuments, are remarkable too.

Only forty years separate the Gothic survival of Broughton from the accomplished Classical church at Ingestre (perhaps by Wren, 1676); the tower of Abbots Bromley is of 1688. And thereafter there is a long procession of 18th-century churches: Burton-on-Trent by William and Francis Smith (1726); Shareshill (1740); Marchington by Richard Trubshaw (1742); Patshull by James Gibbs (1743); Bradley-in-the-Moors (1750); Stone—an early essay in Georgian Gothick—by William Robinson (1753); St John's Wolverhampton by William Baker (1758); Brierley Hill (1765); Mavesyn Ridware (1782); St John's Hanley (1788); St John's Longton (1792); nor must we forget the endearing little churches of Elkstone (1786) and Cotton (1795).

The 19th-century churches of Staffordshire are among its greatest glories: St

Lichfield: west front

Lichfield: chancel ▷

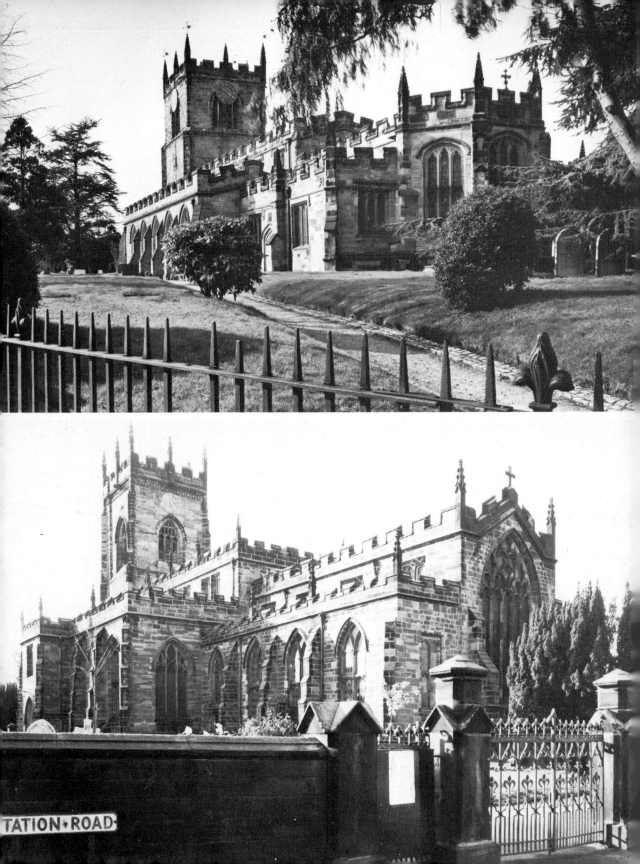

Broughton

Matthew's Walsall (1820) and St Leonard's Bilston (1826), both by Francis Goodwin; the Roman Catholic churches at Walsall and Wolverhampton by Joseph Ireland (both 1826); magnificent Commissioners' churches, like St Mark's Hanley by Pickersgill and Oates (1830), and St James-the-Less Longton by Thomas Johnson (1832), lead on to Wordsley by Lewis Vulliamy (1830), Hartshill by Gilbert Scott (1842), and Butterton near Newcastle by Thomas Hopper (1844). Then masterpiece follows masterpiece: the Roman Catholic church at Cheadle by Pugin (1841); Sheen by Burleigh and Butterfield (1850); Hollington (1859), Denstone (1860), and Little Aston (1870); all by Street; Glascote by Basil Champneys (1880); Hopwas by John Douglas (1881); All Saints Leek by Norman Shaw (1887); Hoar Cross (1876–1906) and St Chad's Burton-on-Trent (1903–1910), both by Bodley;

p24 **Burslem** *(top)* and **Longton**

p25 top & bottom **Burton-on-Trent**

Barton-under-Needwood *(top)* and **Penkridge**

Bilston Town Hall

Bilston church

Walsall

Eccleshall *(top)* and **Uttoxeter** ▷

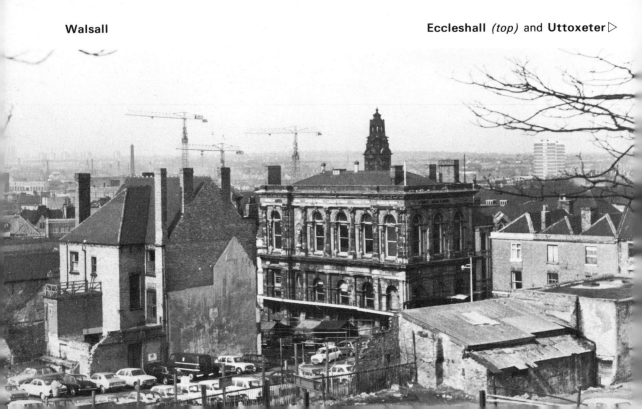

St Paul's Walsall by Pearson (1891); Stretton near Burton, by Micklethwaite and Somers Clarke (1897): the list seems unending. And as a postscript must be added Longsdon by Gerald Horsley (1905), and Canwell by Temple Moore (1911). There is no need to comment on the influence of the Industrial Revolution on Staffordshire churches.

Towns

The Industrial Revolution has moulded the towns of Staffordshire too. Lichfield retains its 18th-century charm, its cathedral city atmosphere. The centre of Stafford is attractive too. Uttoxeter and Stone are old market towns. Burton retains some good 18th-century houses; and the Breweries and Victorian public buildings, and its position by the Trent, give it character. Newcastle preserves some of the air of a country town, but its industries, and its proximity to the Potteries, give it a dour industrial air. Leek, though not large, is a decidedly North-country town, with its mills and steep streets and cobbles; but it has its fine 18th-century houses.

The Black Country has a fascination all its own. Wolverhampton is an ancient town, but for the most part is redolent of 19th-century prosperity. Walsall, with its church-crowned hill, has unexpected character. Bilston has an air. But for the most part the Black Country is a conglomeration of little towns that have grown together during the 19th century. Canals and railways and warehouses and sidings and factories and chimneys and furnaces and power stations and shoddy streets and patches of derelict land quite often—as at Tipton or Rowley Regis or Brierley Hill—prove fascinating. In many places, such as in the neighbourhood of Cradley Heath, the industrial sites go back

p30 **Tamworth** castle ▷
p31 **Chartley** *(top)* and **Tutbury**

to the 17th century, when Dud Dudley, illegitimate son of the 5th Lord Dudley, first used coal for smelting. Indeed the Dudleys and the Wards owe their wealth to industrial pioneering, as do the Foleys; the 1st Lord Paget of Beaudesert established what was perhaps the first furnace at his ironworks on Cannock Chase in about 1560, and the earliest slitting mill was worked by Thomas Chetwynd half a century earlier.

As for the Potteries, they are disappointing architecturally. The Six Towns grew up during the 18th and 19th centuries from a string of villages. Now that so many bottle kilns have disappeared, their most striking architectural feature is missing. But some fine early 19th-century premises remain, long brick ranges bordering the streets, often punctuated by an arched entrance with a Venetian window over. There are a few imposing public buildings (often badly sited), and some grand 19th-century churches.

Of the small towns and villages, several call for special mention: Eccleshall with its wide street, Brewood with its many charming houses surrounding the church, Kinver with its long winding street. There are little market towns like Abbots Bromley and Cheadle, industrial villages like Tean, estate villages like Sandon, Enville and Ilam, remote villages like Longnor. All are delightful for their medley of houses, or their setting, or both.

Castles

As with everything else in Staffordshire, its castles—and its country houses—are

mysterious, romantic and unknown. Little remains of Stafford Castle, originally built soon after the Conquest, and rebuilt by the 1st Earl of Stafford about 1350. It was slighted in the Civil War, partially rebuilt in the early 19th century, and is now reduced to the base of its walls and bastions, crouching on a wooded hill. But it still belongs to Lord Stafford, descendant of the builder, though the title has been at different times forfeited and revived, and has passed through the female line.

Chartley is a romantic, crumbling ruin on the hillside close to the Stafford–Uttoxeter road. Built by Ralph Blundeville, Earl of Chester, in the 13th century, it was abandoned as a place of residence in the 16th, in favour of Chartley Hall, where Mary Queen of Scots was imprisoned for nine months in 1586. Chartley belonged to the Ferrers family, descendants of the builder, until 1907.

Tutbury is a ruin too, prominent above its little town. Most of what we see—it is an impressive ruin—was built in the 14th or 15th centuries, though the origins of the castle date back to the 11th. Mary Queen of Scots was imprisoned here four times; the place was dismantled by the Parliamentarians in the Civil War, and the ruins are maintained by the Duchy of Lancaster, whose property it has been since the reign of Henry III.

One more ruined castle is Dudley, aloof and detached on its hilltop in the Black Country. Built between the 11th and the 16th centuries, burnt and abandoned in the 18th, surrounded now by the factories of an industrial town, it has one more Staffordshire surprise for us: it houses a zoo. So our visitor today can combine the usual pleasures of medieval architecture—with the unexpected pleasures of penguins and polar bears.

Unlike all these, Tamworth Castle, with its memories of the Mercian kings, stands intact above the river Tame. Originally a motte-and-bailey castle, it was rebuilt soon after the Conquest by Robert de Marmion; later a Jacobean Great Hall was built within the keep. Abandoned as a residence, later used as a factory, it was at the end of the last century acquired by the borough from Lord Townshend, descendant of the Marmions, and is now a museum.

And quite unlike anything else is Alton Castle, standing in the spectacular scenery of the Churnet Valley. Alton, on its precipitous, craggy hillside, is the perfect fairy castle. It was built in the middle of the 19th century by Pugin for the 16th Earl of Shrewsbury, whose forbear Theobold de Verdun had built the original 14th-century castle, of which so little survives. It could not rival what Pugin and Shrewsbury have bequeathed to us.

Country Houses

One moated quadrangular 15th-century country house remains, partly ruined, in a lonely stretch of meadowland to the west of Cannock Chase: Pillaton Hall. Built by the Littletons, whose tombs adorn Penkridge church, it was deserted by the family, who built a grander 18th-century house at Teddesley, not far away. But Teddesley has been pulled down, Pillaton remains their property—and is now (1977) being restored for family occupation. With its gatehouse and medieval chapel it is a rare and precious gem.

Of the 16th and 17th centuries a number of notable houses survive. The gatehouse of Tixall stands intriguing and magnificent above the river Sow. Built by Sir Walter Aston in 1580, its great house has gone. But it must be the finest gatehouse in England, and it is now being restored by Mr John Smith for his Landmark Trust.

Wootton Lodge, which stands in dramatic country close to the Churnet Valley, was built about twenty years later by Sir Richard Fleetwood. It was almost certainly designed by Robert Smythson; tall and of amazing beauty, it is like a smaller sister of Hardwick and Burton Agnes. And what of Willoughbridge Lodge, close to the Cheshire border, remote on its hilltop surveying the great plain to the north? It is another hunting lodge, of about the same date, built by the Gerards of Gerard's Bromley, but its history is unrecorded, its existence scarcely known.

Caverswall Castle is another 'progeny' house, perhaps designed by Robert (or John) Smythson, built for Matthew Cradock in 1615. And Ingestre is another great Jacobean house, built by the Chetwynds, which passed by marriage to the Shrewsburys. The interior was gutted by fire in the 19th century, but its façade is notable. There are grand timber houses of this date too, such as Broughton Hall (1637), lying close to the Shropshire borders, and home for centuries of the Broughtons and Delves-Broughtons.

But with Weston Hall, Lord Bradford's home, built only thirty-odd years later, we reach the first great Classical house built in Staffordshire. Of warm red brick, with stone centrepiece and balustrades, segment-crowned gables and sash windows, it is a far cry from the Tudor and Jacobean houses which we have been discussing. The house contains a great art collection, which deserves to be better known.

There are not many great 18th-century houses in Staffordshire. Chillington is one, a great house indeed, with a remarkable family history. The Giffards, perhaps the most noble untitled family in England, have held the property since 1178. The house was partly rebuilt by Smith of Warwick in the early 18th century, partly by Sir John Soane later in the century. There are important rooms of both periods, and a park landscaped by Capability Brown.

Another house which bridges the 18th century is Shugborough, home of the Ansons, Earls of Lichfield. In 1794 Samuel Wyatt added the grand Ionic portico, and refashioned the house built a century earlier, to which Athenian Stuart had already made additions. It contains some of the finest 18th-century interiors in England; the gardens and park some of the most impressive and evocative garden buildings and ornaments to be found anywhere.

And where are we to include Blithfield, home of the Bagots since the 14th century? It is in reality a medieval house, with a magnificent 17th-century staircase and some distinguished 18th-century rooms. But it was gloriously castellated and Gothicised in 1820—and in its quiet setting close to Abbots Bromley must be one of the most captivating houses in this lovable taste.

Of later 19th-century houses, Barry's Trentham is no more, and Alton Towers a mere shell. But Keele Hall is an impressive pile, built by Salvin for the Sneyd family in 1856. Mercifully it survives in its new incarnation as the University of Keele, founded in 1949. Sandon, home of the Earl of Harrowby, is a grand and little-known house in the Jacobean taste, built by William Burn in 1852. And Wightwick Manor, built for Theodore Mander by Edward Ould, is a house of exceptional quality and charm, a Pre-Raphaelite dream, decorated by Kempe, and filled with Morris materials and wallpapers.

And besides all these there is a host of other houses. There is a tenacity of ownership, a

◁ **Weston-under-Lizard**

Wootton Lodge

Broughton Hall

The *porte-cochère*, **Trentham**

Entrance to the new stables, **Ingestre** ▷

continuity of tradition, to be found in Staffordshire, where Okeovers still hold Okeover, Wolseleys Wolseley, Congreves Congreve; where Whitmore has remained in the same family for seven hundred years, and Statfold for five. Roots in this unknown county go deep.

Gardens

As for parks and gardens, Staffordshire is rich in its four great landscape parks created by Capability Brown: Ingestre in 1756, Trentham in 1760, Weston in 1766, Chillington in 1770. Each has its collection of temples and park buildings. Special mention must be made of that supreme work by James Paine: the Temple of Diana at Weston. The romantic grounds of Enville were inspired by the poet Shenstone, and the Gothick Summer House or 'Museum' there was designed by Sanderson Miller. Allusion has already been made to the garden and park at Shugborough, where the Chinese House of 1747 must be one of the earliest examples of this delightful taste; where Athenian Stuart built the Tower of the Winds, the Arch of Hadrian, and the Lanthorn of Diogenes. In the 19th century the Earl of Shrewsbury created the romantic gardens at Alton Towers, and James Bateman planted his own exotic garden at Biddulph Grange. At Sandon Hall is a great landscape garden with amphitheatre, and the top of Barry's Trentham tower resurrected as a temple. At Trentham Nesfield worked, and part of his elaborate parterre is still maintained. Alfred Parsons and T. H. Mawson laid out the garden at Wightwick. And in recent years at Eld's Wood at Willoughbridge a 200-year-old gravel pit has been converted into a unique woodland garden, with daffodils, azaleas and rhododendrons.

Canals and Railways

Staffordshire is an unknown county, yet it has always been the centre of things. Important roads have always crossed its frontiers—from the Roman Watling Street to the new M5 and M6 motorways which have been constructed across its face in recent years. In the 18th century the great canal system came into being, and in 1766 Josiah Wedgwood cut the first sod of the Trent and Mersey Canal, which connected Staffordshire with Liverpool in the north-west and Hull in the north-east. It was the work of James Brindley. At Great Haywood it joined the Staffs and Worcs Canal, to connect the county with Bristol, via the Severn. In 1790 a further link was formed with London, via the Coventry Canal which joined the Trent and Mersey at Fradley; from Coventry the Oxford Canal linked these waterways with the Thames. In the early 19th century the Shropshire Union Canal was formed, to link Ellesmere Port with the Staffs and Worcs at Autherley. In recent years there has been a great revival of these inland waterways, and the canals in Staffordshire are alive today with the long boats of their holiday-making clientele.

The first railway to cross the county was the Grand Junction built under an Act of Parliament of 1834 and opened in 1837, to connect Birmingham with Liverpool and Manchester. The following year this was extended to join the Birmingham–London line. In 1847 the Trent Valley line was established, to join the Grand Trunk line at Stafford, and reach London via Rugby.

The following year the North Staffordshire Railway was opened. This ran from Colwich to Macclesfield via Stoke; it also included the beautiful Churnet Valley line from Uttoxeter to Macclesfield, and other branches in the Potteries. Later it established

Chillington, **Brewood** *(top)*, **Statford** and **Swynnerton** ▷

Two bridges by James Paine: **Weston-under-Lizard** *(above)* and Chillington Park, **Brewood**

the Manifold Valley Light Railway, which ran from Waterhouses (where it connected with Leek) to Hulme End in the Peak.

There were endless squabbles in early days: the G.J.R. became the L. & N.W.R., and tried to absorb the N.S.R., and, when thwarted, tried to starve it into submission, by arranging the timing of its trains at the junctions at Macclesfield and Colwich so as to cause the maximum inconvenience to its passengers. But the 'Knotty'—as it became known from the emblem of the Staffordshire knot on its rolling stock—remained independent until 1923, and built beautiful stations, such as those at Stoke (its headquarters), Sandon and Alton.

Alton Towers ▷

Another bitter rivalry developed in the Black Country, where the G. W. R. built its own line, which resulted in two parallel and independent railways between Birmingham and Wolverhampton, and the 'High Level' and 'Low Level' stations there. Another intruder was the G. N. R., which built a line designed to carry traffic from eastern England to Shrewsbury and North Wales. This started from Grantham, passed through Nottingham and Derby to Uttoxeter, and so to Stafford and Shrewsbury—partly on its own, partly with running powers on other lines. The overgrown track between Uttoxeter and Stafford is a sad reminder of this and other early ventures.

Staffordshire Celebrities

This unknown county has produced a galaxy of distinguished sons and daughters. Allusion has already been made to its two great admirals: Lord Anson (1697–1762) born at Shugborough Hall, and John Jervis, Lord St Vincent (1735–1823) born at Meaford Hall, Stone. Its greatest soldier is Henry William Paget, Marquis of Anglesey (1768–1854), born at Beaudesert. To English literature it has contributed the great names of Izaak Walton (1593–1688) born at Stafford; Charles Cotton (1630–87) born at Beresford Hall; Samuel Johnson (1709–84) born at Lichfield; George Eliot (Mary Ann Evans, 1819–96) was not actually born in Staffordshire, but was brought up at Ellastone, where her father and uncle lived, and which she describes in *Adam Bede*; Mrs Craik (Dinah Mulock, 1826–87) was born at Hartshill; Jerome K. Jerome (1859–1927) was born at Walsall; Sir Henry Newbolt (1862–1938)

Shropshire Union Canal

Near Norbury   **At Norbury** Junction ▷

was born at Bilston; and Arnold Bennett (1867–1931) was born at Hanley.

To the world of art and architecture it has contributed Josiah Wedgwood (1730–95), potter, born at Burslem; Peter de Wint, (1784–1849), landscape painter, born at Stone; Samuel Wyatt (1737–1807) and James Wyatt (1746–1813) born at Weeford, and Jeffry Wyatville (1766–1840) born at Burton, architects.

Thomas Guy (1645–1724), founder of Guy's Hospital, was born at Southwark, but brought up and educated at Tamworth, his mother's native place, and was later M.P. for the borough. Sir Robert Peel (1788–1850), Prime Minister, was also M.P. for Tamworth, and is buried at Drayton Bassett, where he lived.

Gilbert Sheldon (1598–1677), Archbishop of Canterbury, was born at Stanton; and Elias Ashmole (1617–92), antiquary, was born at Lichfield. Both were notable benefactors of Oxford University, where the Sheldonian Theatre and the Ashmolean Museum gloriously adorn the Broad with Staffordshire distinction.

In the opening chapter of *The Old Wives' Tale* Arnold Bennett describes the situation of Constance and Sophia Baines:

They were [he writes] established almost precisely on the fifty-third parallel of latitude. A little way to the north of them, in the creases of a hill famous for its religious orgies, rose the river Trent, the calm and characteristic stream of middle England. Somewhat further northwards, in the near neighbourhood of the highest public-

house in the realm, rose two lesser rivers, the Dane and the Dove, which, quarrelling in early infancy, turned their backs on each other, and, the one by favour of the Weaver and the other by favour of the Trent, watered between them the whole width of England, and poured themselves respectively into the Irish Sea and the German Ocean. What a county of modest, unnoticed rivers! What a natural, simple county, content to fix its boundaries by these tortuous island brooks, with their comfortable names—Trent, Mease, Dove, Tern, Dane, Mees, Stour, Tame, and even hasty Severn! Not that the Severn is suitable to the county! In the county excess is deprecated. The county is happy in not exciting remark. It is content that Shropshire should possess that swollen bump, the Wrekin, and that the exaggerated wildness of the Peak should lie over its border. It does not desire to be a pancake like Cheshire. It has everything that England has, including thirty miles of Watling Street; and England can show nothing more beautiful and nothing uglier than the works of nature and the works of man to be seen within the limits of the county. It is England in little, lost in the midst of England, unsung by searchers after the extreme; perhaps occasionally sore at this neglect, but how proud in the instinctive cognizance of its representative features and traits!

So Staffordshire remains, mysterious and unrecognised among English counties. On one side its face is blackened and forbidding, on the other smiling and green. Its churches and houses and gardens are here to be enjoyed, its moorlands to be walked, its canals to be navigated, its unknown lanes explored. Mysterious may it remain: yet it is a county which deserves to be loved and honoured more.

Gazetteer

The number following the place name refers to the square on the map at the end of the book where the place is to be found.

Abbots Bromley [8] A small and ancient market town, which decayed graciously during the 19c—now little more than a village on the W edge of Needwood Forest. The roads from Lichfield and Uttoxeter and Burton lead into the little market place, in the centre of which is a 17c hexagonal timber Market Cross. Around and in the adjoining streets stand the Goat's Head Inn, and several half-timbered houses, the Bagot Alms-house (1705), and the late 18c Crofts House with its blind top storey and unusual iron railings.

The church has a splendid Classical W tower, built in 1688. The church itself is medieval, but much rebuilt by Street in 1852. Spacious interior, with much furnishing and adornment by Street; E window by Burlison and Grylls, 15c brass to John Draycote, priest, and a few 18c monuments. At the E end of the N aisle are the reindeer horns used at the Horn Dance, an ancient Abbots Bromley festival held annually on the Monday after the first Sunday after 4th September; it is of pre-Norman origin, and associated with the rights of the townsfolk in Needwood Forest. Dressed in gay medieval costume six men carry the horns, and another a hobby horse, and they perform the dance accompanied by a boy with a crossbow, a jester and a musician.

The school of SS Mary and Anne is a Woodard Girls' School—one of the oldest girls' public schools in the country. It was not actually founded by Woodard (who disapproved of girls' schools), but by Provost Lowe (first Provost of Denstone, q.v.) as St Anne's School (1874); six years later St Mary's was founded as a less expensive sister school: they became one school, of SS Mary and Anne, in 1921. Woodard himself became reconciled to the education of girls, and admitted the schools to the Corporation in his lifetime.

The chapel rises sheer above the village street; designed by R. H. Carpenter and built in brick, although on a smaller scale than his chapels at Lancing or Denstone or Ardingly, it has some of the same quality. As a building it has height, majesty, atmosphere; the eye is

Abbots Bromley

Alstonfield: Cotton pew and pulpit

immediately lifted upwards by the windows high in the walls, and eastwards to the altar by the brilliance of the marble reredos and the painted vaulting of the apse.

Behind the chapel—from the street unseen and unsuspected—rise considerable and impressive ranges of school buildings round small garden quadrangles: the original nucleus, an 18c house to which Carpenter added his first school-block, leads on and up to the Perham Hall and the new Assembly Hall, built in recent years 'that our daughters may be as the polished corners of the Temple'.

The place is redolent of the Woodard aura. And across the road ('NOTICE Be Careful! Beware of Motors!' reads a charming notice by the school gate) stand the buildings of St Mary's: in typical Woodard fashion these command a magnificent prospect across Rugeley to the heights of Cannock Chase.

Acton Trussell [11] Alarming suburban growth in the village: a whole crop of bijou residences has sprung up. But the lane leads on to the church, standing isolated to the S. Dec aisleless nave and chancel,

with W tower: the upper stage and short spire are dated 1566. Clayton & Bell glass. One good 18c monument. Between the church and the village stands the Moat House, an attractive combination of 16c timber and 18c brick. The M6 roars by, close to the village.

Adbaston [7] A remote village, close to the Shropshire border: a church, a plain early 19c red-brick rectory, and the Hall, now a square cream-washed stuccoed farmhouse looking like a pleasant little G.W.R. hotel, but in reality a much older house. The church has a Perp W tower with battlements and eight pinnacles; most of the building is of this date, though earlier fragments point to an earlier core. The interior is spruce and well-furnished. There is an incised slab to Reginald de Adbaston (1440), a Royal Arms of George III, and a Whitworth hatchment.

Batchacre Hall is a tall brick house a mile or so to the S beyond the Shropshire Union Canal, up a stony track, remote from everywhere. With its sash windows, and Gothick features in the first and upper storeys of the projecting porch, it appears to be 18c; but the stone basement with mullioned windows, and the extruding clutch of 16c chimneys on the S side point to an earlier date. This unknown house was in the 18c the home of the eccentric bachelor politician, Richard Whitworth, and inside are two panelled rooms, each with an 18c chimneypiece, each with an oil painting in the overmantel of Batchacre at that time. One shows the house much as it appears now—but crowned with a cupola; the other the surrounding countryside as Richard Whitworth created it. To the S of the house is an extensive lake with an island in the middle, and on the island a little fort with guns; there is an obelisk in the background, and a ship sails on the lake. The lake has dried up, and a hump in the ground represents the island. Fort and obelisk have disappeared. All that survives is a small look-out tower close to the farm buildings, and—now lost in deepest woodland—the late 16c pillared porch from Gerard's Bromley Hall (*see* Ashley) which Richard Whitworth moved and re-erected here. Whitworth had no heir, and soon after Batchacre became a farmhouse. Cows and crops took over.

Alrewas [12] (pronounced to rhyme with walrus.) The name means 'alderwash' or 'alder swamp', and the village stands in

the flat country close to the Trent. The A36 from Lichfield to Burton roars past, but the village itself lies on the quieter A513 to King's Bromley. The Trent and Mersey Canal makes its way through the village too. There are a number of black and white, and thatched cottages, and to the N of the church is an old cotton mill.

The church is exceptionally wide, and, with its N and S aisles as lofty as the nave, is light and spacious within. Two Norman doorways suggest the early origins of the church, but most of what we see is EE or Perp. Tall arcades in the nave (the N one is an excellent rebuilding of 1891); EE chancel with Perp clerestory. Perp W tower. 15c wall painting in chancel. 17c pulpit. Reredos by Basil Champneys (1892), and E window by Henry Holiday. In the SE chapel are 18c tablets to the Turton family, of Orgreave Hall, the late-17c house with projecting wings, approached by wide double avenues of lime trees, a mile or so to the W of the village.

Alstonfield (or Alstonefield) [6] Splendid scenery in Dovedale, and a comely village with stone houses and a tree-shaded village green. Charles Cotton lived at Beresford Hall, on the Staffordshire side of Beresford Dale, and Izaak Walton and he here fished the river Dove. Beresford Hall was pulled down about 1860, but the fishing lodge, built by Cotton in 1674, survives in an enchanted spot by the river.

The church is large and mostly of the Dec and Perp periods—but the chancel arch is Norman, and there are fragments of Saxon sculptured crosses in the porch. The furnishings, however, are the great thing: a wealth of 17c box pews, a magnificent two-decker pulpit of 1637, and the Cotton pew, with canopy, painted grey-green, at the E end of the N aisle.

Alstonfield Hall (dated 1587) is a small manor house to the N of the

pp48 & 49 Alton Towers ▷

church; the Georgian rectory stands close to the churchyard entrance.

Alton [5] The scenery of the Churnet Valley is remarkable in itself. The river runs through country steep, craggy, romantic, enclosed and secret. Only at one or two points does it open out at all, and then only to give a grander prospect of its steep and rocky heights. But it is still more remarkable to stand on its northern side at Farley, and catch sight through the trees of the long pinnacled, turreted, embattled silhouette of Alton Towers.

Alton had come to the Talbots, Earls of Shrewsbury, by marriage in the 15c, but the family had never lived there. Wingfield in Derbyshire, Worksop in Nottinghamshire, these had been their homes in Tudor and Stuart times, and these were succeeded by the great house built for them by Thomas Archer at Heythrop in Oxfordshire early in the 18c. At Alton there was merely a small lodge built for the agent overlooking a deep valley: it was this spot that the 15th Earl and his wife visited, and soon became enamoured of, early in the 19c. In 1814 he began to lay out the gardens; before he died (in 1827) he had added to the lodge in the Gothic manner. His nephew and successor completed this great folly palace—which after the burning of Heythrop in 1831 became the principal Shrewsbury seat.

So the heroes of Alton are the 15th Earl who laid out the gardens, and the 16th Earl who completed the house, and became Pugin's friend and patron here and at Cheadle. On his death in 1852 he was succeeded by an invalid nephew who died four years later. And that was the end of the Catholic Shrewsburys. The title passed to a remote cousin, an Anglican, Earl Talbot, the owner of Ingestre

Alton Towers

Alton Castle

(q.v.). A great sale took place at Alton, of all the best things in the house; Ingestre became the principal Shrewsbury seat, and finally in 1924 Alton was sold to a company that was formed to save the amazing gardens and open them to the public. Great success has attended the venture. The gardens are immaculately maintained; there is boating on the lake, a scenic railway, a model railway; there are donkey rides, pony rides, cable cars and endless amusements for the children. People flock here to enjoy themselves, and so help to preserve the private elysium of a shy romantic nobleman.

Quite apart from the amusements, there is much to see. The house itself is now little more than a roofless shell, for apart from military occupation in the war, it has not been lived in for fifty years. It is one of the grandest of 19c Gothic palaces. James Wyatt worked here, so did Robert Abraham, Thomas Allison, Thomas Fradgley, A. W. N. Pugin. It is difficult to disentangle their respective shares. Pugin was the chief decorator: he was responsible for the chapel (which now houses the model railway) and the Great Hall, which is still roofed, and whose broken heraldic glass (by Willement) may still be seen from the outside, high up in the great oriel window. The entrance tower led into a long armoury (now used as a shop), on and into a great gallery (now rebuilt and used as a restaurant), through an Octagon Hall, based on the Chapter House at Wells, and so to the state apartments which lay on either side of the Great Hall.

From the terrace there is a wide view across a lake to the stables. Below, and to the right, are the gardens. Here at the entrance is a monument—a replica of the monument to Lysicrates—to the 15th Earl: 'He made the desert smile.' Turning left along the N bank, it is possible to pass a whole succession of garden buildings approached by terrace walks. Here are Robert Abraham's conservatories, a fragment of 'Stonehenge', a stone rotunda, the Corkscrew Fountain and the Gothic Prospect Tower (sometimes called Chinese, which it isn't). Below, on a lower terrace, is

Alton Towers chapel roof

a stone loggia; opposite, on the farther bank, the Harper's Cottage. A stream waters the bottom of the valley, and may be crossed by a little bridge. Finally, the climax of the walk, at the farthest, deepest, greenest end is the pagoda, a great jet of water issuing from its top. Everywhere the valley and terraces are generously planted: behind the cultivated areas are wild and wooded walks with lakes and streams. It was a wonderful garden—its survival no less wonderful.

Leave this remarkable silhouette behind you, descend the hill and make your way to Alton village. Past the delicious Italianate pink lodge, past the more serious Tudor lodge, past the pretty little villa-like

railway station (the railway is departed, and the station now cared for by John Smith's Landmark Trust), past the Talbot Inn in its delightful secluded hollow—and a sight still more wonderful and improbable is before you and above you: on a crag above the precipitous valley stands an enchanted Rhineland castle, a solid stone fortress, with towers and gables and little copper spires, a sharp apsidal chapel crowned with coloured tiles; dungeons, no doubt, moats and battlements. What is this?

It is Alton Castle; close to the remains of the medieval castle, the 16th Earl and Pugin constructed this fairy fortress between 1847 and 1852. It was to be a house, an occasional residence perhaps. As

you climb up into the village it disappears from sight: the village street with old cottages and houses seems more down to earth—and leads on to the village church, all perched on the steep side of the valley. This contains a Norman arcade, but is mostly a rebuilding of 1830 in Churchwarden Gothic, with a 14c W tower. Off the street a lane leads to the castle.

But first comes St John's Hospital, built by Pugin and the 16th Earl between 1842 and 1846. It was to be a home for retired Roman priests, with a warden, a village hall, a village school, a church—a 'hospitium' in the old sense. Its quiet open quadrangle, with church on one side, school on the other, is now occupied as a convent

Spode House, **Armitage**

by the Sisters of Mercy: the church serves as the local R.C. parish church.

Across the ravine stands the castle, with medieval fragments in front, Pugin's fairy fortress behind, approached by a narrow bridge. This now houses a R.C. prep school. The chapel is tiny: a wider, squarer nave or antechapel leads into the narrow soaring vaulted apse of exquisite beauty. Richly coloured glass, richly coloured hangings, a few stalls, an altar, a sanctuary lamp and tabernacle—that is all. But it is a Holy of Holies.

The church itself has, alas, lost its Pugin screen, and the sanctuary its Pugin tiles; but alabaster reredos and Willement glass glow with colour. Here are buried on either side of the altar beneath brasses (perhaps by Hardman) the last two Catholic Earls of Shrewsbury—the 16th, the founder, and the 17th, his nephew, the young invalid who died in Portugal in 1856. It is the end of a chapter.

Amblecote [17] The large industrial village, close to Stourbridge, grew up in the early 19c, its fortunes established on glass-making and the valuable beds of fireclay in the district. The church has a bizarre charm—built in 1842 of yellow firebrick, with W tower, long lancet windows, wide aisleless nave, and short chancel. Melancholy monuments evoke those gas-lit days: one commemorates the first incumbent, the Revd John Crier, 'who died suddenly after preaching in this church' (1866); another is to Anna Amery (1844), with a cherub extinguishing the torch by her sarcophagus. Melancholy churchyard, too, packed tight with big 19c tombs. Amblecote is full of atmosphere.

Amington [15] Surburban village E of Tamworth: rows of villas line the roads; behind the villas the canal; behind the canal the railway. Small church of 1864 by G. E. Street—only nave, chancel and bellcote, but all Street's churches have something to say. Burne-Jones E window.

Armitage [11] Close to the Trent, close to the Trent and Mersey Canal, close to the railway, and on two main roads; above all, close to the Rugeley Power Station. Armitage is a spreading, suburbanised and industrialised village. It is the home of Armitage Ware, and the factory where this sanitary earthenware is made lies close to the A513. The church stands on its own at the end of a lane, above the river. The tower is early 17c, and the church itself is Norman of 1844, complete and thorough in every hard detail, and dark with Victorian glass—but in its way not unattractive. There is a picture inside of the original Norman church which preceded it. The font is genuine Norman, and, with its entertaining paired figures looking out beneath arcades, a splendid piece.

Along the road to Rugeley stands Hawkesyard Priory. Originally the Gothick stuccoed house, built by Nathaniel Lister in 1760, was known as Armitage Park. In 1839 it was bought by Mrs Spode, widow of Josiah Spode III the potter (see Stoke-on-Trent), who came to live here with her son Josiah Spode IV—the Spode Pottery having now passed into the hands of the Copeland family. Josiah IV was of an antiquarian mind, and renamed the house Hawkesyard after the medieval house which once stood here. He had no children, and on the death of his wife in 1868 his niece Helen Gulson came to live with him. It is an interesting story how both uncle and niece were drawn to the Church of Rome, and were received into that Church in 1885. They had friends among the Dominicans, and it was to the

52

Detail of **Armitage** font ▷

Dominican Order that Josiah left Hawkesyard on his death in 1893.

Here the Dominicans built the great Priory above the 18c house; the architect was Edward Goldie. The chapel is like a large Perp college chapel at Oxford, with towering stone reredos filled with the statues of saints; on the N side is a vaulted Founder's Chantry, where Josiah and his niece are buried. In the chapel is the great organ case from Eton College Chapel, adorned with the arms of William III, of Eton, and of King's, carved by William Bird, one of Wren's carvers, c. 1700. This had been discovered in a builder's yard, after Eton had replaced it with a great Victorian organ, and was installed in his house here by Josiah, who was a keen musician.

On the completion of the new Priory the 18c house was first used as a school; then, renamed Spode House in honour of the founder, it was opened by the Order for retreats and conferences. Pinnacled and battlemented it sits in its undulating park, the Priory Church erect above, the Trent and Mersey Canal placid below.

Ashley [7] There are many signposts to Ashley along the main road from Market Drayton to Newcastle (A53): the scattered village is tucked away in its woods and lanes, its church one of those delicious surprises that one associates with Staffordshire. Outside it appears a somewhat pedestrian building of 1860, with an earlier tower. The interior is anything but pedestrian, and unmistakably by Bodley. There is a very short nave of only two bays; the longer chancel, protected by elaborate rood screen, leads to a sanctuary brilliant with lavish gilded reredos screen, reminiscent of Elvaston or Laughton. Marble floors; splendid organ gallery; admirable furnishings—and everywhere brass candelabra. In fact the interior was not completed until 1910, by Cecil Hare,

Bodley's partner and successor, through the munificence of the Meynells of Hoar Cross. But this is not all. The church contains a remarkable collection of enormous monuments. In the S aisle a great alabaster Renaissance tomb to Sir Gilbert Gerard (1608) with recumbent figures; in the S chapel six magnifical monuments to Kinnersleys, by Chantrey (1820), Ternouth (1823), Noble (1859) and Hollins (1865); in the chancel a Nollekens to Hugo Meynell (1801), and other Meynell memorials. Yet despite all this marble, these families never lived at Ashley. The Gerards lived at Gerard's Bromley, two miles SE. After their time Bromley was bought by the Meynells, who soon afterwards bought Hoar Cross, and made that their home. The Kinnersleys had property here, but were wealthy bankers and iron founders of Newcastle, and lived at Clough Hall, to the N of Newcastle.

The little R.C. church was built in 1828, though the mission had been founded by the Gerards, an off-shoot of the old mass centre established at Gerard's Bromley. Gerard's Bromley is approached by a farm-track off the lane to Charnes. Dr Plot enthuses about the great house that once stood here. Now a noble pair of 17c gatepiers leads only into an enormous farmyard, enclosed by great barns. The last (7th) Lord Gerard was a Jesuit priest: the place was sold in his lifetime to the Meynells, who pulled the house down. But inside one of the barns is an elaborate plaster frieze of a hunt; the porch was re-erected in the wood at Batchacre Hall (*see* Adbaston); the stone farmhouse, perhaps a back wing of the Gerards' house, looks down the lonely hillside to the lake below.

Aston-by-Stone [8] Between the A51 and A34, but an undiscovered hamlet, approached by a hump bridge across the Trent and Mersey Canal. Gothic church of 1846, by

James Trubshaw, with spiky spire of 1870. Beautifully decorated interior, the E end brilliant with elaborate reredos, mosaics, and glass by Gibbs.

Close by stands the Hall, the only Staffordshire house, apart from Swynnerton, to have been in Catholic hands since the reign of Elizabeth I. Moated site, but the house enveloped in a Victorian rebuilding. It is now a guest house, and home, for retired priests. There is a little R.C. church bordering the drive, with low tower and spire, built in 1844. Until the 19c it was the property of the recusant family of Simeon, baronets, of Britwell Salome, Oxfordshire.

Little Aston [15] An expensive suburb of Sutton Coldfield. The leafy glades of the park are now occupied by a great crop of luxury villas, each with its double garage, each with its trim garden lush with rhododendrons and azaleas. The Hall survives on its own, a Victorian Italianate mansion, now used as offices; in fact it is an 18c house by James Wyatt, enlarged and encased in stone in 1857 (by E. J. Payne of Birmingham) for the Hon. Edward Parker-Jervis, younger son of the 2nd Viscount St Vincent, for whom Street built the church. This is a gorgeous affair of red sandstone, with broach spire and all the Street trimmings de luxe, both outside and in.

Audley [4] Great spreading colliery village in bleak country close to the Cheshire border, with grim streets of Victorian cottages and modern villas, and views across the industrial landscape to the moorlands N of Newcastle. The great Audley family took their name and title from this place: their castle was a few miles away at Heighley (*see* Madeley).

Imposing church of red sandstone: long nave, long chancel, W tower, all of the Dec period. Great E window filled with colourful glass

◁ The Gerard tomb, **Ashley**

by Wailes. Lofty chancel. Elaborate tiled sanctuary, with notable monuments: brass to Sir Thomas de Audley (1385); 14c tomb in a recess to Sir John Delves, one of the squires to Lord Audley at the Battle of Poitiers; Jacobean figure of Edward Vernon, vicar of Audley, and founder of the Grammar School. Finely carved sedilia. One tablet by Westmacott in chancel. Gilbert Scott restored the church in 1846, and added the nave clerestory. Almost embedded in the nave pews is a marble-topped tomb, with carved incised cartouche and inscription to John Cradock, 1721; at the W end of the nave are a few solid 17c pews.

On the high moorland to the E stands the Wedgwood monument, a great obelisk erected to John Wedgwood in 1839.

Bagnall [5] East of Norton-in-the-Moors the suburban growth of Stoke dies out: Bagnall is a hilltop village, with little church of 1834 in the Churchwarden Perp style, with small W tower and short Victorian chancel. Opposite, the Stafford Arms is a long, low, irregular 17c stone house.

Balterley [4] The attractive little brick church by the roadside is neither marked on the map nor mentioned in Kelly's *Directory*. It was built in 1901, by the Fletcher-Twemlow family of Betley Court, and designed by Austin and Paley.

Further to the E, and visible from the road, is Hall o' th' Wood, a very fine black and white house of the late 16c, characteristic of Cheshire whose borderland marches with the parish.

Barlaston [8] The village, with wide green, Hall and church, is well placed on a wooded ridge overlooking the valley of the Trent, S of the Potteries. Just before the Second World War Wedgwoods moved their factory from Etruria, and it was rebuilt here, in its new, land-scaped, park setting. With the estate they bought the Hall, and the subsequent history of this notable house has not been happy.

Barlaston Hall was built about 1756 for Thomas Mills, an attorney of Leek. It is of arresting design, exceedingly tall (three storeys high on the entrance side, four facing the garden), and built of brick on a rusticated stone base. The plan is rectangular, with a wide pedimented centre brought forward to form the entrance on the E front, and a great wide central bow on the W. On the N and S fronts there is a canted bay, with enormous Venetian window above, set in an arched recess. With its stone dressings and lozenge-shaped window panes it is a particularly pleasing house, of a type associated with Sir Robert Taylor. But its architect is not known; some of the features, such as the doorcase and stone window surrounds, so magnificently weighty, do not suggest the elegant Sir Robert. Perhaps it is a Taylor design, freely interpreted by its builder; that builder could be Charles Trubshaw, some of whose work does resemble Barlaston. One rococo chimneypiece, however, is certainly by Sir Robert. The house has unfortunately been empty for many years, and its future is uncertain. It stands in a setting of splendid trees, with grand views towards Swynnerton to the W.

The church was rebuilt by Lynam in 1886, to replace an 18c building by Trubshaw. Medieval tower. Interesting monuments to the Wedgwood family.

Great Barr [14] In one of Repton's *Red Books* is a water-colour of incomparable charm. It represents a house with a long Gothick front, a low corner tower at each end, traceried sash windows and crenellated parapet; a green sward descends to a long lake in front, and the park all around climbs up to a prominent hill behind. What can this idyllic scene be? It is Great Barr Hall. To anybody who explores Great Barr today the transformation is unbelievable. The place is now little but a suburb of Birmingham, cut in half by the A34 and M6, with the M6 and M5 intersection a mile or so away, and enormous housing estates all around. Even Barr Beacon seems to have shrunk. In fact Great Barr Hall still survives, much altered in the 1840s, and with a High Victorian chapel added to its front. It is now the administrative offices of St Margaret's Hospital, whose vast buildings dominate the scene behind. To the W, on the edge of the park is the Victorian church (by W. D. Griffin). The Scott Arms on the main road keeps alive the name of the Scotts, baronets, who owned Great Barr from 1618 to 1911, and created this once-romantic scene.

Barton under Needwood [12] A neat and attractive village, with spruce cottages and several early 19c houses. Along the lane to Dunstall is the Hall, a good 18c brick house.

The church is of special interest as having been built, in very late Perp Gothic, in 1533, the benefaction of a distinguished native of Barton, Dr John Taylor. Taylor, the son of a small tailor, was one of triplets—a fact then thought so singular that they were shown as a curiosity to Henry VII. The king was so pleased that he paid for their education; and John, the eldest, attended Henry VIII at the Field of the Cloth of Gold, was Archdeacon of Derby and Buckingham, and became Master of the Rolls. Apart from the aisles which were enlarged in 1864 the whole church is of a piece. Apsidal chancel with contemporary glass. Substantial W tower. Above the nave arcade are the gilded arms of John Taylor (three babes' heads), and an inscription: 'I. T. horum trium genellorum natu maximus: decretorum doctor et sacrorum canonum professor: Derbie et Bukkygham nec-

Barlaston Hall *(top)* and Hall o' the' Wood, Balterley ▷

non et magister rotulorum illustrissimi regis Henrici viii anno regni sui 20'. Mural monument (1691) to Joseph Sanders who married a More of Linley, Salop; Gothic tablet (1836) to Robert Hardy Wyatt.

The village itself is on a minor road: half a mile away to the E the river Trent, the Trent and Mersey Canal, the Midland Railway, and the dual carriageway of the A38 pursue their ways.

Bednall [11] Small village under the NW slope of Cannock Chase. Victorian church (by Henry Ward of Stafford), with heavy NW spire, and interior dark with 19c glass.

opposite & below
Biddulph Grange gardens

Betley [4] Main-road village, close to the Cheshire frontier. Plenty of good houses to see along the road. Betley Court, with its iron gates, is early-18c. The unusual baroque centrepiece is crowned with urns and the cartouche of the Fletcher family. The house is at present used as a rehabilitation centre, and the family now live at Doddlespool Hall (early Victorian Tudor) at the far end of the village. Betley Old Hall is timbered. Very red Victorian Nonconformist chapel. Behind the street stands the church, which is of interest because (apart from the tower and aisle walls) it is a timber building. Heavy timber piers in the nave carry a timber clerestory and heavy timbered roof; richly embellished chancel roof. 16c screen to N chapel. 18c monuments and

hatchments to Fletchers and Fletcher-Twemlows in nave: early 17c monument in chancel to Ralph Egerton, whose son built the chancel. 17c charity boards at W end with beautiful lettering.

Biddulph [5] Motoring N towards the Cheshire border, the great industrial sprawl N of Tunstall peters out; by the time that Biddulph church is reached, the towny streets are left behind and the high moorland country comes in sight. Apart from its Perp NW tower Biddulph church appears outwardly early 19c. Inside, the original EE arcade survives; it is round this that Thomas Trubshaw in 1833 added his spacious aisles and clerestory, and his elegant stone-panelled chancel. Interesting 16c Flemish glass in W window; fragments of

ancient glass in other windows. Tomb of Sir William Bowyer of Knypersley (1640). Agreeable early 19c furnishings. But the whole church is dominated by the spectacular tomb of William and Mary Heath by Matthew Noble (1872) in the S chapel, which was specially added to house the monument.

A short distance further N is Biddulph Grange, now an orthopaedic hospital, but famed for the legendary gardens formed here in the mid-19c by James Bateman (1811–97). James Bateman was the son of John Bateman of Knypersley, who had made a fortune building steam engines in Manchester. James as a young man was an enthusiastic grower of orchids: as an undergraduate at Magdalen he once overstayed his leave in search of rare plants, and was punished by being made to write out half the psalter. But he afterwards (1864) laid out the University Parks at Oxford. In 1842 he bought an old farmhouse at Biddulph, surrounded by swampy ground on the bleak hillside, and on this unpromising site he laid out in the next twenty-five years some of the most remarkable gardens in England, which thanks to the enterprise and devotion of the hospital have been wonderfully maintained for the past fifty years. In 1869 Mrs Bateman's health failed, and they were obliged to retire to Worthing: Biddulph Grange was bought by Robert Heath, who in 1897 rebuilt the centre of the house after a fire. The S front presents a tall and imposing late Victorian Baroque façade to the gardens.

The Chinese Garden is approached by two mysterious paths through pitch-dark tunnels: a lake is hemmed in by great rocks and boulders, and overhanging the 'Chinese Waters' is a Chinese Temple, embowered in bamboos and Japanese maples. China is encircled by a great hedge, the 'Great Wall of China', and within this magic world gaily painted

bridges cross and re-cross the streams. One emerges only to enter another world: Egypt. Here a temple of yews, clipped to resemble obelisks and pyramids and guarded by a pair of stone sphinxes, marks the approach to another world of fantasy. One of the greatest curiosities is the Obelisk Walk, whose gradients are so treated as to give the impression that what is really a path is an obelisk ahead; the 'obelisk' melts away like a mirage. Everywhere are magnificent specimen trees, and a great collection of old rhododendrons, some of them the first to be imported into this country.

Not far away, on a rough and unfriendly hillside, stand the ruins of Biddulph Old Hall, built by Francis Biddulph in 1588, and destroyed in the time of his grandson, a devoted Royalist, in the Civil

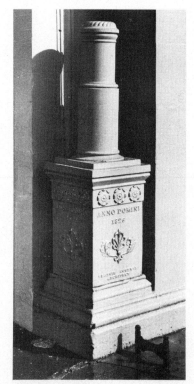

Architect's signature in cast iron, **Bilston** church

War. Fragments of the main façade remain, with protruding porch leading into central courtyard. One ogee-capped turret survives and, behind, a portion of the house is still lived in. A large farm, stone walls, and stunted hillside trees guard this romantic ruin from public view and access.

Biddulph Moor [5] Bleak moorland, defaced by rows of ugly houses. Small 'Norman' church of 1863 (by Ward and Ford), given by James Bateman of Biddulph Grange. Biddulph Moor was until recently a strange and remote place; the story goes that fifty years ago it was inhabited by a family called Bailey, dark-eyed and gipsyish, not trusted by their neighbours who regarded them as foreigners, and in some way different from themselves, so that they intermarried very little except among their clan. The supposition is that they were the descendants of the Saracen slaves brought back from the Crusades by the knightly Biddulphs, who engaged them upon the carvings in the church which they were building in Stafford (St Chad's, q.v.), and then settled them as bailiffs on the moor.

Bilston [14] has an air. It is unquestionably one of the best of the Black Country towns. There is a friendly Victorian-Lombardic Town Hall with low tower; and a cluster of 18 and early19c houses, inns and shops around. The tall Grecian tower of Francis Goodwin's parish church, with its low dome and great gilded weather vane, sails above its humbler neighbours. The scale of Bilston is simple, unpretentious, dignified.

The town has a distinguished industrial history. During the 19c it grew on iron, and japanned and enamelled goods. William White wrote (in 1834) of the local industries that 'the hissing of the blast furnaces, the clanking of the forge hammers, the dusty appearance of the workmen, and the various operations upon unwieldy masses of red-hot iron, combine to excite an idea of terror in those who are unaccustomed to such noisy scenes'. There is a delightful homeliness about Bilston.

The parish church was built in 1826: square, stately W front, and on each side of the W door two little cast-iron bollards inscribed 'Anno Domini 1826: Francis Goodwin Architect'. Distinguished galleried interior with shallow plaster vault, and elegant Ionic columns throughout. Read the endearing inscriptions on the marble monuments to the town's worthies: one commemorates a Mrs Pearce 'descended from three children of Edward I'; another urned tablet records one who practised as 'an attorney in this town with the greatest honour and integrity': another 'an old and much esteemed inhabitant of this town'. Bilston breathes the air of civic dignity.

There is another church to note: St Mary's in Oxford Street. Built in 1827, also by Goodwin, it is like a toy Perp chapel, with decorative pinnacled exterior, E apse and octagonal W tower. It is an adornment to the long main road from Wednesbury. Sir Henry Newbolt was born in the vicarage here in 1862.

Bishop's Wood [10] Hamlet close to Boscobel, on the very frontier of Salop. The tapering spire of the church (1851 by G. T. Robinson) is a pleasing landmark in this undulating, romantic countryside.

Blithfield [11] In one of the best parts of rural Staffordshire: the ancient trees and woodlands give a remarkable sense of antiquity and remoteness. At Admaston a Gothick lodge leads into Blithfield Park, for six hundred years the home of the Bagot family.

At the time of the Domesday survey the Bagots were established at Bagot's Bromley, a mile or two to the N: a marriage in the early 14c induced them to move their home to Blithfield, and apart from a break of a few years in the present century it has been the home of the Bagots ever since. The drive crosses the slope of the hill—and facing you is the full extent of Blithfield Hall: the house, turreted and pinnacled on the left, battlemented walls and gateway linking it to the stable block with its clock tower and playful array of battlements on the right. Blithfield was done up in romantic Gothick dress in the early 19c, but is in reality an ancient house.

Behind its stucco the entrance front is Elizabethan, and the porch tower with its plaster lierne vault leads into a little courtyard, with Great Hall opposite, like the quad of a small Oxford college. Here is a happy blend of Gothick windows and sash, of buttresses, flower pots, urns and lily pond, of domestic and collegiate. A doorway leads into the hall, the medieval hall, though twice transformed, first in the 18c into a classical dining room, then (and how gloriously!) into Gothick in 1822. No medieval hall was ever so resplendent. It has something in common with Ivory Talbot's Hall at Lacock, and is perhaps inspired by the Divinity School at Oxford. An elaborate lierne vault with bosses and pendants, all in plaster, rich canopies crowning full-length niches, pinnacled surrounds to doors and chimneypiece—these are the work of Francis Bernasconi. In the 18c a new range was added to the N side of the hall, and a richly carved staircase of the Restoration period leads up to an early-18c oak-panelled study, the panels divided by fluted pilasters supporting a triglyph frieze. The library nearby was originally the Great Chamber, and has a wide-barrel ceiling and 17c panelling; the dining room beyond is hung with an 18c Chinese paper.

A Gothick cloister on the ground floor, and a Gothick gallery above, connect the small rooms on the opposite side of the courtyard— some of them delightfully named; a little sitting room is called Paradise, a bedroom above Quality Cockloft.

The church is approached across the rose garden behind the house, past Athenian Stuart's orangery, which was built by Samuel Wyatt, then a local builder not yet fledged as London architect. The church is 13 and 14c; nave with EE arcades and later clerestories; long chancel with high-pitched roof. Much old woodwork, including Perp screen and grand set of bench ends. Medieval grisaille and heraldic glass. Many monuments to the Bagots—of special note the tombs in the sanctuary with incised slabs to Sir Lewis (1534), his son Thomas (1541) and grandson Sir Richard (1597), the last with effigies.

It was Sir Richard's grandson who was created a baronet in 1627, and his son who was the Royalist commander in the Civil War. The sixth baronet was created a peer in 1780, and it was his son, the 2nd baron, who Gothicised the house in 1820. As an antiquary he no doubt had a hand in the designs, probably aided by John Buckler, whose water-colour drawings of the house survive, though no designs or accounts for the work seem to exist.

At the end of the last war the 5th Lord Bagot sold the house, then in a dilapidated state, and part of the estate, to the South Staffordshire Water Board for the creation of the new Blithfield Reservoir. But shortly afterwards his cousin and successor, the 6th baron, with his wife, bought back the house and park, and were able to re-purchase some of the contents. Lady Bagot has described how, on succeeding to the title, she and her husband first went to Blithfield to sort out what remained in the house, with no idea of going to live there—and were so moved by the beauty and romance of the place that they decided to re-purchase and restore it.

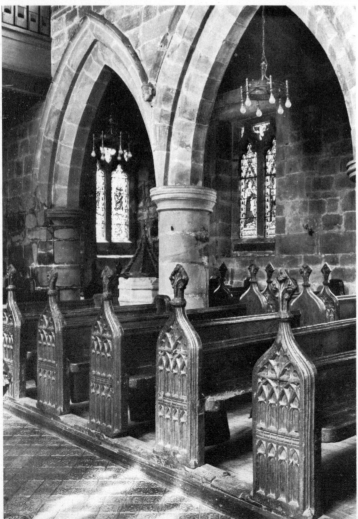

above **Blymhill**

left **Blithfield**

The story of its reclamation is one of triumph over almost impossible odds. Since her husband's death, Lady Bagot has continued to make her home here, and carry on the work of restoration. The house is regularly open to the public, and the reservoir, opened in 1952, now appears as a landscaped lake, and enhances the view. On its farther side, in Bagot's Park, a monument of 1811 marks the site of the original manor house of the Bagots. The historic herd of wild goats may still be seen at Blithfield, descendants of the special breed presented by Richard II to the Bagot of the day in acknowledgment of the excellent hunting that he had enjoyed in his park.

Blore [6] An isolated spot in the high country W of Dovedale. The old home of the Bassetts, long extinct, was the 16c Hall, now a farmhouse. A pretty 19c rectory stands S of the church. The church

Blore *(top)* ▷
and **Bradeley**

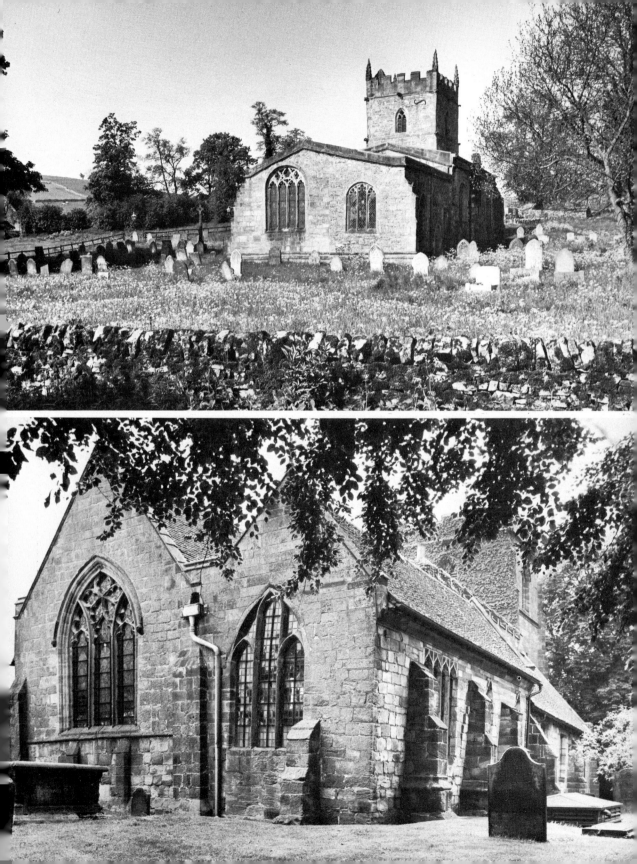

Bramshall

is a rewarding building, chiefly Perp in date, containing a wealth of old screens, stalls, pulpit, pews and panelling. There is a little old glass in the chancel (St Anne teaching the Virgin to read), and a brass in the N aisle to William Bassett (1498). The NE chapel, up a few steps, is entirely occupied by the great tomb of William Bassett (1601) and his family; it is rather like a small bedroom, with the whole floor-space taken up by an enormous bed, the recumbent figures lying between elaborate screens, which are like the head and foot of a bed.

Blurton [8] Suburban growth between Trentham and Longton. The little church is that rare thing, Gothic survival of 1626; but it has been enlarged (by Lynam, 1867), and some of its character lost.

Blymhill [10] (Pronounced Blimmil) A neat village on the Bradford estate, close to the Shropshire border. The church is of inter-est, having been largely rebuilt by Street in 1856–9, replacing a Georgian building of 1719. Medieval tower. Nave with dormer windows of some originality. A huge and magnificent animal gargoyle crouches on a buttress on the S side, ready to pounce. The Dec chancel survives from the original church, but with the many fittings and furnishings by Street, and the glass by Wailes and Hardman, the whole atmosphere of the interior is 19c— and 19c at its best. Village school by Street.

Bobbington [13] Small and seemingly remote on the Shropshire frontier. Flying from Halfpenny Green Aerodrome, in this parish, Prince William of Gloucester was killed in August 1972. On the approaches to the village are several good houses: Bobbington Hall is early 17c brick, with stepped gables; Blakelands is early 18c, with forecourt garden enclosed by brick walls—and with magnificent farm buildings; Leaton Hall is early 19c stucco, with Doric portico. Outwardly the church appears 19c, on account of a rather meagre Victorian tower; but the interior has a Norman arcade of four bays. Ancient yew tree in the churchyard. Victorian vicarage.

Bradeley (or Bradley) [11] (but pronounced Bradeley) is in the pleasant country SW of Stafford. The church is the great attraction. The exterior with W tower is chiefly Perp, but the nave flooded with light from the great Perp S windows has a lofty EE N arcade, with clustered shafts of considerable beauty and elegance. Rood screen and other excellent furnishings by W. D. Caroe, who restored the church in 1908. Behind the riddel posts is a medieval stone reredos. A few fragments of medieval glass; one or two 18c tablets; and 17c alabaster tomb, with kneeling figures, to Thomas Browne and his wife—'the oraculous Browne' as the inscription describes him. Norman tub font.

Speedwell Castle, **Brewood**

A mile to the NE, is Littywood. Here on a deeply impressive, ancient, moated site—perhaps Anglo-Saxon—stands a spreading, low, brick farmhouse. But the mellow brick only conceals a medieval timber-framed manor house: beneath plaster and later additions the Great Hall, Screens Passage and other features of the 15c house can be detected.

Bradley-in-the-Moors [8] A delectable spot in high country above the Churnet valley: there are views of Alton Castle from the road to this little hamlet. A few cottages, and concealed in trees close to a farmyard an 18c church with W tower, nave and chancel—untouched, unspoiled. Hanoverian Royal Arms.

Bramshall [8] Pretty country SE of Uttoxeter. The church was rebuilt in 1835, by the local architect Thomas Fradgley. It is a plain, lofty, hall-like chapel, without aisles or chancel, but with a W tower. One window contains fragments of medieval glass, including a kneeling figure marked 'Alice Tame, Lady Verney'—an ancestress of the 16th Lord Willoughby de Broke, the builder of the church.

Branston [12] Suburbanised village close to the Burton by-pass: small brick church of 1864, attributed to Street. On the high ground to the S is Sinai Park, in the Middle Ages the summer retreat of the Abbots of Burton. Here on the exposed hilltop stands a crumbling early 16c E-shaped house of stone and timber, now used for housing pigs. In the 18c William Wyatt, steward to the Pagets (Earls of Uxbridge—*see* Longdon) lived here. He was uncle to James and Samuel, uncle to Joseph, architect of Burton (*see also* Weeford).

Brereton [11] Now a suburb of Rugeley, with much new building along the main road to Lichfield. One or two 18c houses survive, such

as Brereton House, and the Cedars Hotel. The richly-decorative E end of the Victorian church looks on to the main road: the nave of 1837 is by Thomas Trubshaw, but the chancel of 1877 is by Gilbert Scott. It is his additions which make the church. Wide, vista-ed, devotional interior, with decorative painting by Heywood Sumner of 1897.

Brewood [11] (pronounced 'Brood') is a little town close to the Salop frontier, in romantic Charles II country. There are narrow streets of pleasant houses, presided over by the church with its tall Perp spire. This is a dignified building, with long nave and chancel, the nave 14c with an extra S aisle added by Street; the chancel EE, with lancets. Four 16c and 17c alabaster tombs to the Giffards of Chillington: the first to Sir John Giffard (d. 1556), Henry VIII's standard bearer; next, his son, Sir Thomas (1560); then Sir John (1613), and Walter (1652)—both of whom suffered persecution as Roman Catholics. Ledger stones to succeeding generations, and other monuments. Of special interest is the tablet, erected recently, to Colonel Carless, who accompanied Charles II in the Oak at Boscobel (and who lived at Broom Hall, a house now rebuilt N of the village): 'He not only assisted Charles I of ever blessed memory, but was also the chief preserver of his son King Charles II in the Royal Oak at Boscobel.' He is buried here.

There is a R.C. church by Pugin (1843), and several houses worth mentioning, such as the Chantry, West Gate and Dean Street House, all 18c houses close to the parish church. But Speedwell Castle in the Market Place, with its luscious Gothick front of 1750, with ogee-shaped traceried windows, is a special delight. It is, of course, not a castle at all, but a tall double-fronted town house, which was built on the proceeds of a successful bet on a horse called Speedwell.

Blackladies (two miles W) is a 16c house, built on the site of a Benedictine nunnery, with an attractive front of brick gables and dormers.

Chillington is about two miles to the SW. A long avenue from Giffard's Cross (where the 16c Sir John Giffard shot with his cross-bow a wild panther which had escaped from its cage) accompanies the lane to the edge of the park, and here the house stands, grandly exposed on gently rising ground. This long E front, with its pedimented portico, is the work of Sir John Soane (1786), and has raised pavilions at either end—that at the S end concealing the higher S front which had been built by William Smith of Warwick, sixty years before. The house incorporates a 16c house, and Soane's greatest room, the Saloon, occupies the courtyard of this Tudor house. The house is open to the public on certain days: grand early-18c staircase, and other good panelled rooms with stucco work, in the Smith wing; the drawing Room and Dining Room in the Soane E front. The park was landscaped by Capability Brown, and contains a large lake, a bridge by Paine, an Ionic temple close to the lake, a Gothick temple, and other delights. Just outside the park is the White House: on the park side it presents a pedimented classical façade, an eye-catcher from the lake; to the outside world it is a farmhouse. The Giffards have lived at Chillington since 1178.

The lane to the NW of the house leads to Boscobel. The Royal Oak and Boscobel House are over the hedge in Shropshire. Deep woods, as depicted in the famous picture now at Hampton Court, once clothed this border country, and here Charles II spent three days (4–7 September) before going on to Moseley 'by the advice of Mr Giffard' (Charles's own words). The King and Colonel Carless spent 6 September in the oak tree. In those days Boscobel was Giffard property: the name is derived from the

Broughton Hall

Italian Bosco Bello—the house seated in the fair woods.

A mile to the E stands Somerford Hall, in its own park: a mid-18c stuccoed house, of seven bays and three storeys, with lower attendant wings. Although now divided into flats, the house still belongs to the Moncktons, who came to Somerford in the 18c, and subsequently acquired Stretton (q.v.), where they live today. Across the park, and facing the Hall, is Somerford Grange, an amusing tall Gothick house, with bay windows and battlemented top—built as an eye-catcher for the big house. It is perhaps by the same architect as

Speedwell Castle, or the equally tall Gothick house at Coleshill (Warwickshire), and is a thoroughly practical folly, with charming rooms, and grand views all round from the top windows.

Brierley Hill [17] The quintessence of the Black Country. The town lies along the spine of its hill, with wide views to N and S, across factories and canals and railway sidings, and patches of derelict land and scrubby little woods, and terrace after terrace of Victorian houses—to Dudley, with the castle on its hilltop, to Netherton with its prominent church, to the W

suburbs of Birmingham, to the Clent Hills and distant countryside beyond the smoke and vapours. Brierley Hill grew up in the 18c, in the ancient parish of Kingswinford, as a settlement of squatters exploiting the industrial resources of a stretch of wild open commonland: coal pits, furnaces, forges and brick kilns appeared. The parish church was built in 1765; a red-brick Georgian box, and apart from the tower, rebuilt in 1900, it is of almost domestic appearance, with its low pediments and double row of windows. But the skyscraper blocks of flats just below have robbed it of its former dominating presence on the

Burton-upon-Trent

Chetwynd, Clerk to the Privy Council, was created a baronet in 1795.

Broughton [7] The long, empty road from Eccleshall climbs slowly through beautiful country, and brings you to Broughton: a 17c Gothic survival church stands solitary on the left, the tall square black and white Hall opposite. Broughton was the home of the Delves-Broughtons from the 13c to the 20c; in the 18c they came in for Doddington in Cheshire (the Delves property), which thereupon became their principal home and where Samuel Wyatt built their great house in 1776. Broughton became their secondary residence, and was finally sold in 1914. The exterior is glorious (it is dated 1637), with high gables, overhanging upper storeys, and much decoration; yet serene and restrained with its modest front door. The house was greatly added to after the First World War, and is now a R.C. Franciscan priory. Inside there is a grand 17c staircase, and a long gallery on the top floor with original plaster decoration.

The church is of rare beauty, a complete near-Perp building of 1630. Like some Cotswold churches there is an E window over the chancel arch; many of the windows are filled with 17c heraldic glass, but the E window of the chancel has jewel-like glass of the 15c, with figures of early members of the Broughton family. Box pews and other contemporary furnishings. Brasses in chancel to Thomas Broughton, who built the church, and his wife and daughter. Font at W end, like a holy-water stoup. Many 17c and 18c monuments to the Broughton baronets and their families.

If the church is locked the key should be obtained at the vicarage at Wetwood, the hamlet half a mile back towards Eccleshall. This is a church which should not be missed.

hilltop. There are few other buildings of note: the Brierley Hill Market Hall is filled with cheerful stalls; Christ Church, Quarry Bank (to the SE) is a Gothic Commissioners' church of 1845; St John's, Brockmoor (to the NW) a neo-Norman church of 1844—both by Thomas Smith. The R.C. church in the High Street is by E. W. Pugin, with characteristic features.

Brocton [11] Small village under the NW slopes of Cannock Chase. Brocton Hall is a handsome stone house of 1801, with central bow containing the porch with Roman Doric pillars. The house is now a golf club: impressive circular entrance hall, and elegant staircase beyond. It was originally the home of a junior branch of the Chetwynd family (*see* Ingestre); Sir George

Brown Edge [5] Suburban growth E of Tunstall along the main road: to the N is moorland country, and pretty scenery round the Greenway reservoir. 'Norman' church of 1844 by James Trubshaw junior, with heavy NW spire (by Ward of Hanley) of 1854. Ornate interior: one distinguished Morris window of 1874. Below the church is an unexpected stable building, where Mr Williamson, a rich parishioner who paid for the spire, stabled his horses and carriage during service.

Brownhills [14] A growth along the A5 close to Cannock, with factories and submerged countryside: open commons and housing estates along the A452 to the S. Victorian church of 1851, by G. T. Robinson. To the N of the A5 is the large expanse of Chase-water reservoir.

Burntwood [11] Colliery village on SE slopes of Cannock Chase. Small Gothicky church by Joseph Potter of Lichfield (1819), with W tower and later N aisle.

Along the road to Lichfield is Edial (pronounced Eddyal) where Samuel Johnson opened his ill-fated school in 1736. 'Young gentlemen are boarded and taught the Latin and Greek languages by Samuel Johnson'—so the advertisement appeared in the *Gentleman's Magazine*. There were only three pupils, of whom one was David Garrick, who accompanied Johnson to London when the school closed the following year.

Overlooking Lichfield, with good views from the terrace, is the late Georgian house called Maple Hayes. Dr Erasmus Darwin laid out his Botanic Garden here, and later the house belonged to the Worthingtons, the brewers. It is now a boarding house for Lichfield School.

Burston [8] Small village between Sandon and Stone. The medieval chapel, long ruinous, was rebuilt in 1859. Here the Trent, the Trent

Horninglow Street, **Burton-upon-Trent**

and Mersey Canal, the main railway line to Stoke, and the A51 run parallel, within a narrow half-mile.

Burton-upon-Trent [12] From the by-pass Burton looks splendid: it is a compact town, set between gently rising hills to E and W, with the river running its straight course N and S. From the road there is a view across towers and churches and chimneys and breweries and streets and houses to the country beyond. The mammoth power station of Drakelowe is on the far side of the river, in Derbyshire.

Burton-upon-Trent ▷
p70 Maltings
p71 top Marstons' Brewery
bottom Maltings interior

The practice of brewing seems to have been started here in the Middle Ages by the monks of Burton Abbey, the great and powerful foundation which stood by the banks of the river. The excellence of the ale is due to the water from the local wells, which contains a particular element of gypsum. On the dissolution of the abbey a number of small breweries sprang up, and many local inns brewed their own beer on their own premises. When the Trent was made navigable at the beginning of the 18c, Burton beer (which had long been drunk in London) began to be exported to the Baltic and to Russia: Catharine the Great is said to have been 'immoderately fond' of Burton Ale. Later, on the construction of the Trent and Mersey Canal, the beer could be sent to Liverpool, and thence to India; and the light 'India Pale Ale' was brewed for this market. By the end of the 19c there were no fewer than forty breweries in Burton. The most famous were Bass, Ratcliff and Gretton; Worthington & Co.; Ind Coope and Allsopp; Marston, Thompson and Evershed; and Truman, Hanbury and Buxton. Their breweries were all over the town, and the maltings all over the suburbs, and an elaborate network of railway lines between them crossed the streets in all directions. Now amalgamations and takeovers have reduced the breweries, and much re-organisation has taken place: Bass, Charrington (which includes both Bass and Worthington) has become one great group, Allied Breweries (which includes Ind Coope) another; Marstons' remains on its own, as does Everards', whose main office, however, is in Leicester. Ten years ago two things made an immediate impression on a visitor to Burton: the network of railway lines crossing the streets, and the all-pervading aroma of beer. The railway lines have gone: the aroma of beer remains.

The best way to see Burton is to start at the Trent Bridge. The present bridge, across the wide stretch of river and meadows, replaced the medieval bridge with its thirty-six arches in 1864. Along the W bank of the river is an attractive green stretch; Bridge Street becomes Horninglow Street, down which is a whole series of attractive 18c houses, and the Magistrates' Court, a fanciful and slightly frivolous little building with a baroque dome. But the first turning on the left is High Street, the very heart of the brewing industry. On the left-hand side is the large gabled house (incorporating 17c, 18c and 19c work) which was the Bass family's town house. Next door are the Bass Brewery Offices, still in use. Behind them stood the original Bass Brewery, where William Bass started brewing beer in 1777. A little farther on is the imposing 18c house which was the Worthington house: behind this the water tower remains, close to the river. William Worthington started brewing beer on this spot in 1744.

At the end of High Street is the Market Place. Here stands the parish church, rebuilt in 1719 by William and Francis Smith—handsome outside, with its balustrades and urns and solid W tower; distinguished inside with good fittings and woodwork, monuments to brewers, 19c stained glass and notable neo-Classical organ case (attributed to James Wyatt). The church is dedicated to St Modwen, the Irish lady who founded the first church here in the 10c. Early in the 11c the great Benedictine Abbey was founded here, of which so little remains.

Next to the church the Victorian Market Hall is worth noting; beyond this is the gabled Manor House, of 17c origins, which was used as the estate office for the Pagets, Earls of Uxbridge and Marquises of Anglesey, who obtained so much land here on the suppression of the monastery, and are still Lords of the Manor of Burton (*see also* Beaudesert). And behind the Manor, and close to the river, is the Abbey Club, a Victorian building which incorporates parts of the Abbey Infirmary.

Beyond the Abbey, parallel with the river, is the great slab of the Technical College. High Street continues as Lichfield Street: opposite the War Memorial are two good late Georgian houses with pedimented doorways (à la Wyatt); and where the street turns is the endearing Leopard Inn, with its early 19c front and cast-iron plaque commemorating the United Order of Smiths. Alas, this view down Lichfield Street is now ruined by the monstrous new Telephone Exchange, which rises, an enormous and aggressive lump, behind it. Shame upon our 'planners'! Lichfield Street becomes Branston Road, where All Saints, by Naylor and Sale (1903), is an art nouveau-inspired Gothic church, a building of some size and style: it was built by William Bass, brother of Michael Thomas Bass, whom we shall meet in the next paragraph.

Here it may be necessary to take to a car, and make the long journey to the Town Hall—down Station Street, a long street which leads off W from the High Street towards the railway. Beyond the station is the Town Hall, which stands in surprising isolation in a residential area. It is a magnifical Gothic building, standing in an oblong square, with the great church of St Paul at the far end. The Town Hall, begun in 1878 as the Liberal Club, and erected by Michael Thomas Bass, was completed in 1894 by his son Michael Arthur (1st Lord Burton), and presented to the town as its new Town Hall. The architect was Reginald Churchill. Lord Burton's statue stands in the middle of the square, and St Paul's (1874 by J. M. Teale and Lord Grimthorpe) is a church of great magnificence too—cruciform, with dominating central tower, and much

Butterton Grange, **Butterton (near Newcastle)** (Sir John Soane, 1816)

decoration and many fittings within by Bodley. It was built by Michael Thomas Bass.

Not very far away in Hunter Street is St Chad's, built by Bodley for Lord Burton (from King Edward's Place take Waterloo Street, which becomes Victoria Crescent: cross Horninglow Road into Hunter Street). This church was completed in 1910, after Bodley's death. The tall NW tower, capped by its low spire, leads by vaulted cloister into the church. Long nave, with elegant piers dividing spacious aisles, and barrel roof; chancel with distinguished Bodley fittings ascending to the grandeur of the sanctuary; Lady Chapel on N side with towering stone reredos—the interior impresses with its serene and simple splendour. The grouping of the E end outside is also remarkable: chancel extends beyond S aisle; N aisle beyond chancel, and attached to S aisle is what appears to be a tall octagonal chapter house, which is in reality a vestry, designed by

Cecil Hare, Bodley's partner who completed the building.

Horninglow Road continues on its way to *Horninglow*, now a suburb: St John's, a church of 1864 by Edwin Holmes, with characteristic Victorian features, turns out to have a beautiful and devout interior. From here it is but a short distance to *Stretton*. And Stretton Church, another 'brewery church' is a remarkable building by Micklethwaite and Somers Clarke (1895) for John Gretton (of Bass, Ratcliff and Gretton). The noble central tower with low pyramid roof is always an impressive landmark from the by-pass; the church itself will not disappoint, with its spacious, lofty clerestoried nave and chancel, E window by Sir William Richmond, and other furnishings (note specially the magnificent font).

Across the river there are two more Victorian churches: *Winshill*, by Edwin Holmes, was also built by the Gretton family (1869); *Stapenhill* (1880 by Evans and Jolly of

Nottingham) is a plain and sober affair, with a richly decorated tower.

Butterton (in the Peak) [5] Stone-built village in stone-wall country. Victorian church with tall spire (the church by Ewan Christian, 1871; the spire by Sugden, 1879). Interior a trifle bleak. Pitch pine 'lamda' pews. Gothic organ, earlier than the church. Old photographs of soldiers from the village who fought in First World War. The charm of the forgotten, the unsophisticated, and the remote.

Butterton (near Newcastle) [4] Well-wooded, undulating countryside S of Newcastle: the tiny village is approached by two lanes off the Stoke–Drayton road. One leads to the church, on the edge of the small park, an engaging 'Norman' building of 1844 by Thomas Hopper, with central tower and low pyramid spire. Box pews within, plaster vaulting, Victorian reredos with carved angels holding trumpets at least a foot long. Monuments to Milbourne-Swinnerton-Pilkington family. The other lane leads to the gates of the Hall. Stable buildings remain: the house built by L. W. Lloyd for Thomas Swinnerton in 1830 was demolished after the First World War. But in a corner of the park, close to the lane, stand some walling and a chimney-breast of the Tudor house. The Swinnertons of Butterton were a junior branch of the Swynnertons of Swynnerton (q.v.): the heiress of Thomas Swinnerton married in 1825 Sir William Pilkington, 8th Bt: their son became Sir William Milbourne Milbourne - Swinnerton - Pilkington. Near the main road to the E is Butterton Grange, a farmhouse

built for Thomas Swinnerton by Sir John Soane in 1816: with its low, overhanging eaves, long central chimney-block, recessed centre, giant pilasters, this square red-brick farmhouse is as interesting as it is unexpected. Swynnerton Old Park lies to the S.

Calton [6] Stone-built village in the splendid country W of Dovedale. Small early 19c church with bell turret. High Church furnishings within, including some magnificent continental altar rails.

Cannock [11] breathes the atmosphere of coal mines. Yet it is not an unattractive town, with its wide streets and open spaces. The parish

church is prominent in the centre, and of some size: medieval W tower, medieval nave—except for the two E bays, which, with the chancel, are of 1878. The Lady Chapel is a sympathetic addition of 1949. But it is a pity that the handsome 18c S doorway (with pediment and Roman Doric pilasters) has been replaced by a modern Perp porch (1957). It seems late in the day to go in for such anti-Georgian purism.

On the green, to the NW of the church, is an 18c house, with wide stuccoed front, with grand iron gates and screen (attributed to Bakewell); the house is now used as Council Offices.

Cannock Chase, the great wild

expanse of high moorland, stretches for miles to N and E. It was in origin a royal forest, but was purchased by Hugh de Nonant, Bishop of Lichfield, from Richard I at a time when he was raising money for the Crusades. The bishops in turn gave it up, much of the open ground has been enclosed, and the S half is scarred by coal mines. Yet much wild open heathland remains, with sudden and dramatic valleys, and reed-filled ponds. There are long straight roads of conifers and silver birches; and N of Cannock itself, on Pye Green, the great round concrete monster of the Post Office Tower (258 ft high). It is a magnificent landmark. Close to it is a beautifully laid-out German military cemetery.

Canwell [15] Close to the Warwickshire frontier. No village; only a park which has lost its great house—the home of the Lawley family, Lords Wenlock, who are buried in Hints church. James Wyatt added wings to an earlier house at the end of the 18c. But in the park is a church built by Temple Moore in 1911: W tower, with aisleless nave and chancel. The interior, simple, dignified and beautiful, with its vaulted roof, Dec windows, and good furnishings, is reminiscent of the chapel of Pusey House, Oxford. Stained glass by E. V. Milner and Geoffrey Webb.

Cauldon [5] Moorland village on the N of the Weaver Hills, below Cauldon Low. Grim, enormous quarries and works—and rows of Edwardian cottages for the workers. The village itself is tiny. Little 18c church, with tall 17c house behind, a few cottages, and the attractive Yew Tree Inn complete the scene. In the church, Royal Arms of George IV, 1820.

Caverswall [5] Suburbanised roads to the N lead to the outskirts of Longton: at Weston Coyney there was established until the

1930s the ancient Staffordshire family of Coyney, but endless roads of semi-detached villas have wiped out all but the memory of their domain.

But the village of Caverswall, with its little square, is still rural: the lane to the S leads to two churches, and the gateway to the castle. The parish church has a Perp tower and long nave with an arcade rebuilt in the early 17c. Long chancel with monuments to the Cradocks, and the Parkers of Park Hall, Longton, including the dominating monument by Chantrey (1818) to Countess St Vincent (wife of the admiral, and daughter of Lord Chief Baron Parker). Glass by Kempe and Holiday. On the other side of the castle entrance is the Roman church, by Blount, of 1863.

The castle was built, on the site of a medieval castle, by Matthew Cradock, *c*. 1614. It is one of the 'progeny' houses associated by Mr Mark Girouard with Robert (or perhaps John) Smythson, and bears a family resemblance to Wootton Lodge and Hardwick. Tall and elegant, the house rises from a balustraded garden wall above the moat: there are small polygonal towers at the four corners of the moat wall, and a toy gatehouse with bridge across the moat. The moat is now dry, and forms a lower grassy garden. Matthew Cradock of Stafford was the son of a Stuart *nouveau riche*, and the idea of a house on the lines of a medieval castle may have appealed to him. The castle passed through various hands, till in 1811 it was purchased by an order of Benedictine nuns, who had fled at the Revolution. It is now beautifully maintained as a R.C. guest-house.

Chapel Chorlton [7] High, leafy, lonely countryside, and a scattered village. The little church where three winding lanes meet is mostly by James Trubshaw (1826), but the tower is ancient. Central S door-

Cheadle R.C. church ▷
p80 The screen
p81 The sedilia

way, lunette E window, plaster ceiling, Jacobean pulpit. Norman font, Victorian carved reredos. The beautiful road to the W descends to Maer.

Chartley [8] The crumbling bastions of the castle are a romantic landmark on the hillside, close to the Uttoxeter–Stafford road. The castle was built in the early 13c by Ranulph Blundeville, Earl of Chester, and descended by marriage to the Ferrers family (John Ferrers becoming Lord Ferrers of Chartley), and again by marriage to the Devereux, Viscounts Hereford and Earls of Essex. Robert Devereux, Earl of Essex, Queen Elizabeth's favourite, entertained the Queen at Chartley Hall, the great half-timbered mansion which took the place of the castle, in 1575; and it was here that Mary Queen of Scots was imprisoned in 1586. But the Hall was burnt down in 1781, and the Shirleys, who had succeeded, again by marriage, and were created Earls Ferrers, rebuilt the house in 1847. It stands, beautifully sited, with its moat and evergreen plantations, up a long drive to the W of the castle; a lower, older wing survives at the back. In 1905 Chartley was sold, for the first time since the Conquest, to the Congreves of Congreve (*see* Penkridge), and it has changed hands once or twice since. It is worth climbing the hillside, across the park, to the great round towers of the curtain wall of the castle. Only earthworks of the keep survive.

Chartley Farmhouse, half a mile along the main road towards Uttoxeter, is a gabled half-timbered house of the early 17c.

Chasetown [11] A mining village on the S slopes of Cannock Chase,

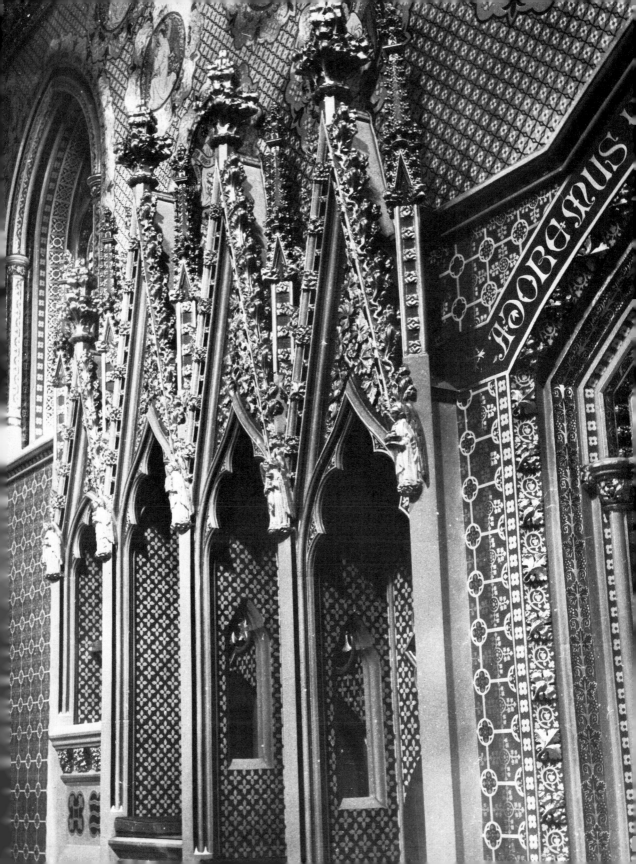

with long straight roads, miners' cottages, slag heaps, wasteland and all the usual accompaniments.

Remarkable church of 1865 (by Edward Adams). It is a Romanesque basilica in red, purple and black brick—with apsidal E end and Germanic details. It is a building of marked individuality. The architect was architect to the South Staffordshire Railway, and perhaps the building has some of the quality of a really fine railway station—yet devout, awe-inspiring and religious in feeling. Marble bust of John Robinson McLean, founder of the church and coalowner.

Cheadle [5] The little market town is set on a low hill, with hills around, and high moorland on every side. Wherever you go, the tall spire of Pugin's R.C. church pierces the sky. Where else in England does the R.C. church eclipse the parish church so completely? This is due to the influence and wealth of the 15th Earl of Shrewsbury, of near-by Alton Towers.

The High Street contains pleasant 18c and Victorian houses, and one three-gabled timbered Tudor house. Pugin's church stands just off the street: everywhere the spire floats above you, soaring and pinnacled. Lavish is an understatement: everything is decorated, from the ornate skyline of the church itself, to the great W doors decorated in ironwork with the Shrewsbury lions. The interior is ablaze with colour—screen, reredos, font cover, all by Pugin; tiles, metal work, glass (by Wailes), the walls brightly stencilled, every inch covered with crowns and crosses and flowers and trellises.

The parish church stands on higher ground on the other side of High Street. Kelly's *Directory* is usually a model of tact and good manners; but of this building Kelly actually forgets himself to remark 'a large edifice in a feeble Perpendicular style.' In fact it is quite a good church in Commissioners' style, of 1837, replacing the medieval building. The interior is wide, with short sanctuary; 17c altar rails; E window by Wailes. The side galleries have been removed.

Outside the town, to the E, stands Hales Hall, an exceptionally fine square brick house of 1712, built by a grand-daughter of Chief Justice Sir Matthew Hale. It is now owned by the County Council, and used for educational purposes.

Chebsey [8] Small village of farms and cottages in the rolling country between Stafford and Eccleshall. The church stands in a fine position overlooking the countryside. Perp tower, with extruding staircase; EE nave with a few Norman relics. Well-furnished interior. Kempe windows in chancel. Large Royal Arms, 1710. A modern tablet commemorates Commander Montague Wriothesley Noel, R.N., Financial Secretary to the Diocese, who died at sea in 1941—'descended from Robert and Celestia Noel, founders of Ranton Abbey in this neighbourhood, 1147'. (*See* Ranton.) In the churchyard is the shaft of an Anglo-Saxon cross.

Walton Hall, close to the main road, and visible from the churchyard, is an imposing early 19c stone classical house, now a school. At Shallowford, a mile to the E, is Izaak Walton's cottage, a small half-timbered house, close to the river Sow, where he spent much time in his later years. This is now a Walton museum, owned and administered by the Borough of Stafford. The peace of the spot is only disturbed by the busy railway line at the bottom of the garden.

Checkley [8] The small village lies just off the main road, the great church its glory. The prominent tower is Norman—with a plain Perp top; the nave is externally Perp, with embattled clerestory; but the finest feature is the long lofty chancel, with four great Dec windows, and still grander E window. Inside, first impressions are confirmed: noteworthy Transitional S arcade, EE N arcade, 17c timber roof and some 17c tracery in clerestory and aisle windows, Lady Chapel in S aisle enclosed by Comper screen—but the eye is drawn at once to the magnificent raised chancel. Through the jewelled 14c glass in the great Dec windows the light falls on this long spacious quire, with a single row of 16c stalls on either side, and High Altar with riddel posts by Comper. Memorials to Philips family in chapel—mill owners at Tean (q.v.) in the 18c, but a prominent family in the parish far earlier. There have been three Philips rectors, and the family still worship in the church.

Cheddleton [5] Grand moorland country S of Leek. The village stands off the main road, precipitously perched on the side of a hill. The Caldon Canal, the river Churnet, and the track of the old Churnet Valley Railway, are below. The church stands in a fine position on the edge of open country, with sweeping views to the wide hilly landscape to the N. Square Perp tower; nave and chancel under one long roof. But the interior with its Victorian decoration and Morris glass is the special interest of the church. Thomas Wardle, of the silk-dyeing firm whose factory was at Leek Brook, was a friend of William Morris and churchwarden here, and it was under his influence that George Gilbert Scott junior restored the church in the 1860s. Impressive devotional interior; wide EE nave with aisles, and Dec chancel, all under one roof; Dec sedilia and piscina. Notable set of Morris windows in chancel and aisles. Triptych, 15c Flemish work, with wings by Morris. 15c Flemish lectern. Painted decoration by Scott in sanctuary and on chancel roof. The lychgate and school in Dec style are attractive, and also by Scott.

The County Mental Hospital is a prominent Victorian–Elizabethan pile a mile to the N. Closer to the village is the 18c Flint Mill, recently restored and now open to the public. Flints were brought up by canal from Kent and Sussex and finely ground here for use in the potteries. A mile to the S is Ashcombe Park, an early-19c Grecian house by James Trubshaw, built for the Sneyd family. The Sneyds of Ashcombe, Basford, Belmont and other houses in this part of Staffordshire, are a junior branch of the great Sneyd family of Keele, and descend from a younger son of William Sneyd of Keele, M.P. for Newcastle-under-Lyme in 1685.

Church Eaton [10] A scattered village in the uneventful but pleasant countryside between Stafford and the Shropshire border: there is a cluster of houses with an inn and the Victorian village institute close to the church. This has a Transitional tower surmounted by a Perp spire. Long nave (with Tran-

sitional arcade) and chancel under one roof. There is much good glass by Kempe, but as a result the church is dark. The most remarkable thing, however, is the enormous Perp E window, occupying the entire E wall. According to legend, it was brought here from Old St Paul's. It is filled with excellent Kempe glass. 18 and early 19c monuments in NE chapel.

To the S are the engagingly named hamlets of High Onn and Little Onn. Little Onn Manor is a Victorian Gothic house of 1870. Near by are beautiful stretches of the Shropshire Union Canal—well-wooded, long, straight and silent.

Church Leigh [8] In the pretty countryside between Uttoxeter and Cheadle: a scattered village, with a large cruciform church, rebuilt in 1845 by the Bagot family (Thomas Johnson of Lichfield, architect). It is an astonishing building, with its commanding central tower, great aisled nave, transepts and vaulted

chancel: it is said to be built on the old foundations, and to incorporate part of the original church. The wealth of glass is astonishing too—some medieval, some by Wailes, Gibbs, and Burne-Jones. Alabaster tomb of Sir John Ashenhurst (1523).

Clifton Campville [12] The tall, tapering spire, with flying buttresses springing from lofty pinnacles, is a landmark across this flat eastern extremity of Staffordshire, which is here surrounded on three sides by Derbyshire, Leicestershire and Warwickshire, its gentle meadows watered by the river Mease. Clifton Campville is one of the great parish churches of England; yet who outside Staffordshire has ever heard of it? What book of architecture even breathes its name? It is distinguished not only for its architecture, but for its furnishings and its monuments.

It is worth walking round the outside first, to take in the noble scale of nave, chancel and S aisle,

The Caldon Canal, **Cheddleton**

The Flint Mill, **Cheddleton** ▷

Clifton Campville

oak screen divides nave from chapel, so its presence is not at first discerned. It has recently been refurnished, and a beautiful gilded crucifix adorns the medieval altar recess.

NE of the church stands the rectory (17–18c), still occupied by the rector. Opposite, the Manor Farm has a brick dovecote and a somewhat dilapidated gazebo. The village street, studded with 'bijou' villas, leads out to Clifton's final surprise. Along the road to No Man's Heath, approached by muddy farm track and surrounded by tractors and farm implements and machinery, stand two imposing early 18c brick pavilions—the wings, it would seem, of some great house no longer there. But the house never was there. Sir Charles Pye, the builder, apparently ran out of funds when the two pavilions were completed, and the family had to content themselves living in the pavilions, which they did for the next two hundred years. Grand they certainly are, with imposing doorways at the centre of the two main fronts. Now the windows are broken, shutters flap in the wind, and the rooms are used for storing grain. Ichabod, grand, melancholy Ichabod.

Haunton, a hamlet 1 mile W, is an unexpected R.C. enclave. The Georgian Hall is the Convent of St John of Bordeaux (with Chapel by Hansom, 1840), and there is a small R.C. Church of 1902 (by Edward Rigby), founded by the Pyes, a little shrine of charm.

Codsall [14] A towny, suburbanized village to the W of Wolverhampton, with railway station and shops for the commuters. The church is a rebuilding of 1846 (by Banks of Wolverhampton), but retains a Norman S doorway, and medieval tower. Tidy, towny, well-furnished interior, with Victorian glass by O'Connor. Tomb with recumbent effigy of Walter Wrottesley of Wrottesley (d. 1630) in the

to note the intriguing slim N transept, to enjoy the great Dec windows, to appreciate the commanding majesty of tower and spire. Go in by the N door. The first impression is one of spaciousness: the lofty base of the tower, pierced by tall windows, with its high arch into the nave, lantern-like floods this spacious nave with light. The nave is wide, the S aisle almost equally so. An early 16c screen leads into an equally spacious chancel, with 14c stalls and misericords. Another screen surrounds the S chapel, an extension being early 17c. Here is a notable alabaster monument to

Sir John Vernon (d. 1545) and his wife, with recumbent effigies and elaborate carved base. In the chancel are two standing monuments by Rysbrack, one to Sir Charles Pye, 2nd Bt (1721), the other to Sir Richard, 3rd Bt (1724), and Sir Robert, 4th and last Bt (1734). And there are monuments to Charles Watkins (1813) by Chantrey, and the Revd John Watkins (1833) by Behnes (S aisle). The tiny N transept is the final jewel of this great church. The ground floor is a chapel with vaulted roof; above is a priest's chamber with fireplace and garderobe. A solid, modern

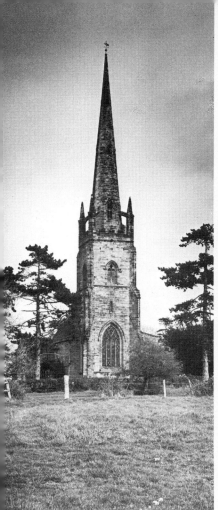

Clifton Campville

chancel. He was the grandfather of the 1st baronet.

At Kingswood Common, close to the Shropshire frontier, is a pretty little stone church of 1861; and in the garden of the house behind, a delightfully unexpected toucan.

Colton [11] Close to Rugeley; the long wall enclosed Bellamour Hall—now only a decayed park, the house destroyed before the Second World War. Colton House is a sad early-18c mansion close to the village street, with a decayed air—its stable yard and garden filled with modern villas. The church has a low EE tower with little lancet windows. The rest was mostly rebuilt by Street in 1850, and has many furnishings by him—pulpit, font, lectern, candelabra—and stained glass by Wailes.

Colwich [11] Two main roads, two important railway lines (which have a junction here), the river Trent, and the Trent and Mersey Canal all pass through the parish. Shugborough Park, protected by its long wall, is to the W of the village street, and another wall opposite protects St Mary's Abbey. This is a Benedictine Order of Contemplative Nuns, first established here in 1834, though founded in Paris in 1651. The house had been built as Mount Pavilion in 1824, by Viscount Tamworth, son of the 7th Earl Ferrers, but he died before it was completed. It is a severe Tudor Gothic building of blackened stone. The railway station is gabled Tudor of 1847.

The tower of the church is dated 1640, but looks a century earlier. Much of the church is a Victorian rebuilding (by Stevens, 1856), and is large and grand. The spacious chancel has an impressive set of

87

Victorian canopied stalls—worthy of a small cathedral. The N aisle retains its 18c plastered ceiling, and contains monuments of the Wolseleys of Wolseley, including Sir Robert Wolseley, 1st Bt (1646), and F. M. Viscount Wolseley. Monuments to the Ansons of Shugborough, including Admiral Anson, in chancel, and in the gallery on N side. E window by Wailes. Close to the S door is the tablet to Charles Trubshaw (d. 1772), the local architect and builder.

At Wolseley to the SE the Wolseley family have lived for 800 years. Their 19c house has been pulled down, but the Wolseleys are still established here. Wolseley Bridge (by Rennie 1800) spans the Trent here with three splendid arches; on the opposite side of the river Bishton Hall, a tall, pedimented, stuccoed 18c house, formerly the home of Sneyds and Sparrows, is now a R.C. prep school.

Coppenhall [11] Small village on the low hills S of Stafford. Ancient and interesting little EE church—really little more than a chapel—with original features. Victorian timbered bellcote.

Coseley [14] Another Black Country town: the sea of houses and factories borders the main Wolverhampton–Birmingham road. Parish church of 1830 (by Thomas Lee) with tall, pinnacled tower, and galleried interior.

Cotton [5] Driving along the B5417 in the lonely moorland N of Alton you will suddenly have a surprise: in a deep valley below are cricket fields and football pitches (unmistakably a school), and an ornate church with a tall broach spire. This is Cotton College, the R.C. public school. The chapel was built by Pugin in 1846, and the 18c Cotton Hall, which is the nucleus, was bought by the 15th Earl of Shrewsbury and given to Fr Faber and the Oratorians. They later moved back to Birmingham, and the school was founded here in 1868. The original school buildings are by Pugin; there are many later additions.

An even greater surprise is to find sheltering behind this Papist bastion a playful little Anglican church of 1795. This is an enchanting little brick Gothick building, with battlements and pinnacles, canted transepts, pointed windows, and a round window over the porch. Inside, plaster vaults rise from elegant marbled columns. Over the porch is a tablet inscribed:

LET future ages view this Sacred Place
And Praise the Almighty whose directing grace
With Heav'nly Zeal inspired the Founder's Mind
T' erect a Chapel to reform MANKIND.

The founder was Thomas Gilbert, of Cotton Hall.

Coven [14] Overgrown village, just off the Wolverhampton–Stafford road; there is one good timber-framed farmhouse (late 16c), and a Victorian church by E. Banks of Wolverhampton (1857), cruciform, bellcoted, prim.

Cradley Heath [17] (pronounced 'Cradley') Once a stretch of common heath land on the N bank of the Stour: in the 18c chain-makers and nail-makers settled here, making use of water power before the days of steam. Even now there are

Clifton Campville Hall

Colton *(top)* ▷

Croxall

Croxden

stretches of derelict heath behind the factories and endless terraces of Victorian cottages. The church is of Commissioners' type, familiar in this district, built in 1843; the apsidal chancel was added in 1874. Opposite the church is the United Counties' Bank (now Barclays), a powerful Victorian Gothic house. There are few other buildings of note, though the early industrial sites are of interest.

It was at Cradley Heath that the Staffordshire Bull Terrier was first reared; a cross between the old English Terrier and the Bulldog, the breed was not officially recognised for show purposes until 1935, but was long used as a pit dog in this district. It was here that the celebrated fights took place. One of the most famous progenitors of the breed was Champion Gentleman Jim, from whom so many pedigree Staffordshires descend; on his death in 1947 Cradley Heath went into deep mourning.

Cresswell [8] Suburban houses by the railway and the river Blythe, a large factory and water-works. But up Cresswell Old Lane (easy to miss) are old houses, and attached to one a R.C. church of 1815. It is a brick barn of a building, with all the simple charm of the first Roman churches built after the penal laws were revoked. Lancet windows; one filled with Pugin glass to the memory of the Dowager Lady Stourton, foundress of the church. The old Papist mission was first established here by the recusant family of Draycott of Draycott (q.v.).

Creswell (near Stafford) [8] The little church has been a ruin for centuries: fragments of the chancel survive in a field. The benefice is a sinecure attached to Seighford.

Croxall [12] Close to the Trent and the Derbyshire frontier: there is no village proper, but the Tudor brick Hall stands effectively in its wide

courtyards, surrounded by spreading meadows. In the foreground is a dovecote, crowned by a cupola. The house was partly rebuilt and enlarged after a fire in 1868. The church stands among trees on the high ground to the E, and is approached across a field. It is wide and aisleless, and dates from the 13 and 14c. It is mainly notable for its many incised slabs, chiefly to the Curzons of Croxall and the Hortons of Catton (across the frontier in Derbyshire); and for its monuments. Of special note are the tablet by Chantrey (1823) to Eusebius Horton, those by Reeves (of Bath) to Frances Levett (1835) and Margaret Prinsep (1837), and Denman's monument to Sir Robert Wilmot-Horton, Governor of Ceylon (1841).

Croxden [8] In a lush valley SW of Denstone, watered by a little stream, stand the remains of Croxden Abbey, a Cistercian house founded by Bertram de Verdun in 1176. In its remote setting here in unfrequented Staffordshire it must be among the least known of all ruined abbeys. A deep tree-hung lane leads off the minor road from Rocester to Tean: there are farm buildings and a handful of cottages comprising the tiny village—and the majestic ruins of W front and S transept are before you. The W front with its doorway of clustered columns below, and long sparsely-set single lancets above, is austerely splendid. Fragments of the nave connect with the S transept, of which the tall S wall is still standing, again pierced by long lancet windows, and this leads to the cloister court. Here the E wall is still standing, with three arches of clustered columns—the middle one the entrance to the chapter house. In the centre of the nave stands a great walnut tree, and the lane now cuts through the middle of the church—with the sparse fragments and foundations of the N transept and quire on the other side. The E end,

visible in the grass, was apsidal with a cluster of five apsidal chapels and ambulatory—the French *chevet* plan. There are other remains to the S, and to the SW stands an early 18c farmhouse.

The lane leads on to the little village church, rebuilt in 1884.

Croxton [7] In the well-wooded countryside between Eccleshall and Market Drayton. As the main road turns through the village there is a good view of the little Victorian church (1853), by Ewan Christian, with its apse and bellcote. It is worth a visit to see how a skilled Victorian architect set about designing a simple little church for a country village. The Vernon-Yonge Arms, round the corner, keeps alive the name of the family so long established at Charnes Hall, the late 17c house with its imposing 18c façade which lies a mile to the N, concealed in its leafy grounds.

Darlaston [14] It is often difficult to know where one Black Country town begins and the next one ends; Darlaston is such a place. It is in the confused townscape between Willenhall and Wednesbury, Bilston and Walsall. But it is in fact an ancient town, for all its amorphous growth of dingy red-brick terraces and forbidding factories, its pits of coal and ironstone. Nuts and bolts are made here, screws and fastenings and latches, coat hooks and hat hooks, pulleys, girders and bridges. There is nothing ancient to see. The parish church with its spire and galleried interior is 1872 Gothic by A. P. Brevitt, a local architect. All Saints is of 1952 by Lavender, Twentyman and Percy, to replace a church by Street destroyed in an air raid. It is a building of clean lines, and spacious pale interior.

Denstone [9] Denstone College was founded by Nathaniel Woodard in 1873. Woodard had an eye for magnificent sites for his schools: Lancing (1848) stands on a spur of

Croxden Abbey

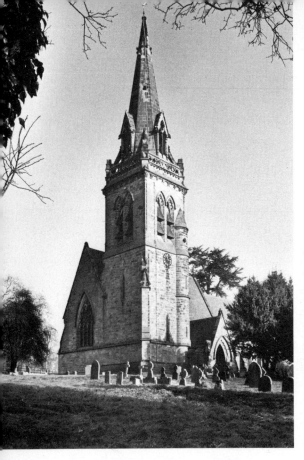

Dunstall (Henry Clutton, 1853)

Denstone (G. E. Street, 1862)

the South Downs, looking out to sea; Hurstpierpoint (1849) has a sweeping prospect of the South Downs from below; Ardingly (1858) a grand view over the wooded Sussex weald. Denstone, thanks to Sir Thomas Percival Heywood, of Doveleys, has a grand site above the village, with wide views over the wild North Staffordshire countryside, backed by the Weaver Hills.

The school is built on an H plan, and was designed by Slater and Carpenter (junior)—the firm that built the other Woodard schools. The buildings of pink stone are magnificently austere, even forbidding, with their Victorian Gothic details. All these schools by the Carpenters have features in common: like the Lower Quad at Lancing,

the front of Denstone with its long open arms embracing the view seems designed to strike awe in boy and master alike. The upper arms to the N comprise Hall and, of course, splendid lofty Chapel. If adornment of some of the school buildings had to be skimped, nothing was spared by Woodard for his chapels. Here at Denstone, as at Lancing or Hurstpierpoint, the eye of the worshipper is drawn, willy-nilly, to the altar. The Woodard schools are religious foundations.

Denstone church was founded by Sir Thomas Percival Heywood in 1860, and here the architect is G. E. Street. The interior is wide and spacious; with chancel loftier than the nave, with raised apsidal sanctuary and colourful glass by Clayton and Bell, the whole provides a

dignified and beautiful setting for Christian worship according to the ideals of the Oxford Movement. Richly detailed furnishings and features: reredos, pulpit, font, organ case, choir stalls—all are by Street. The exterior with its round tower capped with short tile-hung spire, and chancel roof so prominently higher than the nave, is equally strong and emphatic. Lychgate, churchyard cross, school and vicarage, all designed by Street, complete the picture.

Derrington [11] Villas, villas, villas: expensive villas, cheap villas, fancy villas, plain villas. Little else but a small church of 1847, with bellcote and attractively decorated interior. Commuter country close to Stafford.

Dilhorne [5] (pronounced Dillon) Gloomy disused coal shafts and slag heaps to the N of the village, and gloomy red brick Gothic gatehouse and lodges, leading to the site of the Hall, demolished in the 1930s, former home of the Bullers and Manningham-Bullers. It was a house of 1830. A former Lord Chancellor takes his title from this place. The church has a rare octagonal W tower (13–14c). The outside of the medieval nave appears late Georgian Gothick, with overhanging eaves and delicious rusticated Gothick doorways.

Dosthill [15] Many villas line the road from industrial Watling Street. A few older houses surround the church, which is of 1870, with a funny clumsy little broach spire. Close by stands the original church, with a few mutilated Norman features, now used as a parish hall.

Draycott-in-the-Moors [8] Main-road village on the A50. Some suburban development. The Draycott Arms keeps alive the name of the Royalist and recusant family who lived at Paynsley Hall (now a farmhouse, S of the main road): on the extinction of the family the property passed to the Stourtons (*see* Cresswell). The Dec church with sturdy tower stands above the main road; much rebuilt in 1848. The N chapel contains several 16 and 17c tombs to the Draycotts.

Drayton Bassett [15] Takes its name from the great family of Bassett (*see also* Blore). But its fame now is due to its having been the home of Sir Robert Peel. Drayton Manor was built for his father, the 1st Bt, a wealthy textile manufacturer, by Sir Robert Smirke. It replaced an older house, but in its turn was demolished about fifty years ago. The park is now occupied by a golf course, a small zoo, and a steak house with attendant lounge bars. There are a few fragments of outbuildings and garden ornaments.

With the exception of the Perp tower the church was rebuilt by the great Sir Robert in 1840. The only feature of interest is the large Gothic monument to Sir Robert: 'In memory of the Rt. Hon. Sir Robert Peel, Bt. to whom the people have raised monuments in many places. His children erect this in the place where his body has been buried. Born 1788. Died 1850'.

Close to the main road and crossing the canal is a little Gothic footbridge with tiny round towers.

Dudley Castle [14] The *Shell Guide to Staffordshire* treats of the historic county of Stafford; so Dudley is in Worcestershire, an enclave, an island surrounded on all sides by Staffordshire. So for Dudley see the *Shell Guide to Worcestershire* by James Lees-Milne. But Dudley Castle always has been in Staffordshire: mystery of mysteries. It stands today above its town, on its long wooded escarpment, detached, aloof, above the fumes, the factories, the railways and canals, the genuine medieval castle, in ruins. The buildings date back to the 11c, but there is little to see of this date. Most of what we see is 14c: gatehouse, barbican, keep, all in ruins. The castle passed from the de Somerys to the de Suttons, who became the Lords Dudley. In the 16c it passed into the hands of John Dudley, Duke of Northumberland, who descended from a junior branch of the de Suttons; but on his execution the castle reverted to the senior line. It was John Dudley, however, who built the state rooms, the Tudor mansion, as it were, within the old castle. The gabled shell of these buildings survives and forms the inner, upper court: indeed until a fire in 1750 Dudley Castle remained habitable. The male line of the de Suttons came to an end in 1621, and was succeeded by the Wards, who inherited the ancient barony, and became in time Earls of Dudley. Upon the destruction of the castle in the fire Himley Hall (q.v.) became the principal home of the family.

It is exciting to walk or drive up the road which encircles the castle hill—into the castle itself. What is not expected is to discover that the castle now houses a zoo, founded in the 1930s, complete with fanciful concrete buildings in a playful, amusing, 1930s architecture (by Tecton). These buildings do not conflict with the medieval: they are to be found around the castle mound. There are penguins and polar bears; seals splash about in the moat, and beyond the N gate a strange enclosure leads to the dinosaurs, headless and extinct animals standing among the trees!

On a winter's evening Dudley Castle is at its most fascinating: through the leafless trees around the castle mound the neon lights of the streets and factories throw up weird shadows through the gaping holes and windows: all around is the hum of industry, with the seals splashing and baying in the moat below.

Dunstall [12] In the lush countryside SW of Burton-on-Trent, this is a thoroughly pretty village, in a Victorian way. The Hall is a comfortable early-Victorian classical house, with plenty of evergreens in the gardens, and splendid stables. Holly trees line the approach to the church, a dominating building by Henry Clutton, with tall spire, marble-lined chancel—and reredos, pulpit and font encrusted and elaborate. A tablet records: 'In memory of Charles Arkwright, Esq. of Dunstall, founder of this church, and the schools connected with it. Fifth son of Sir Richard Arkwright of Willersley, Derbyshire'. The church was consecrated in 1853.

Dunston [11] The little village stands close to the main road from Stafford to Penkridge. Sturdy Victorian rock-faced church (1876, by

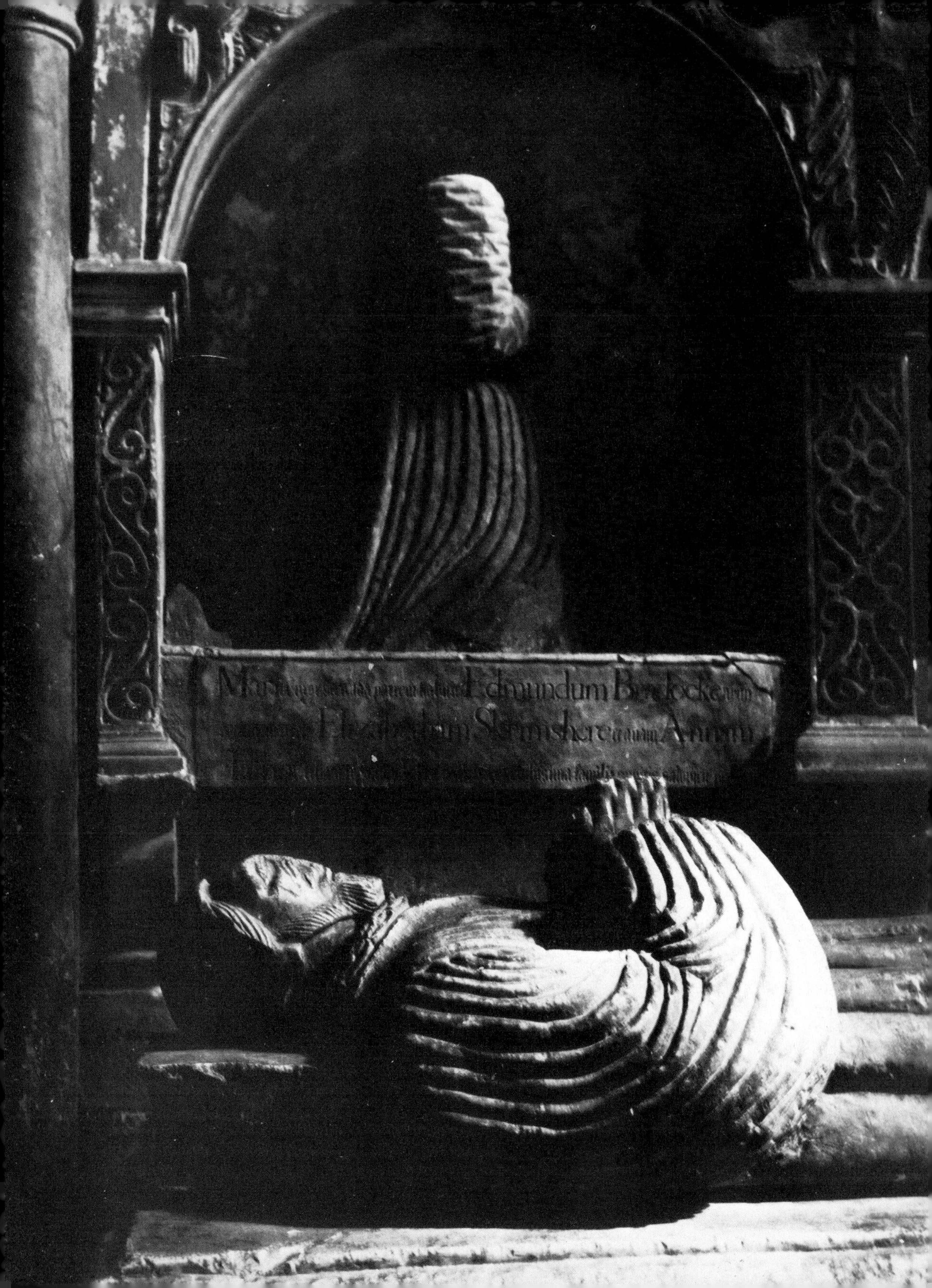

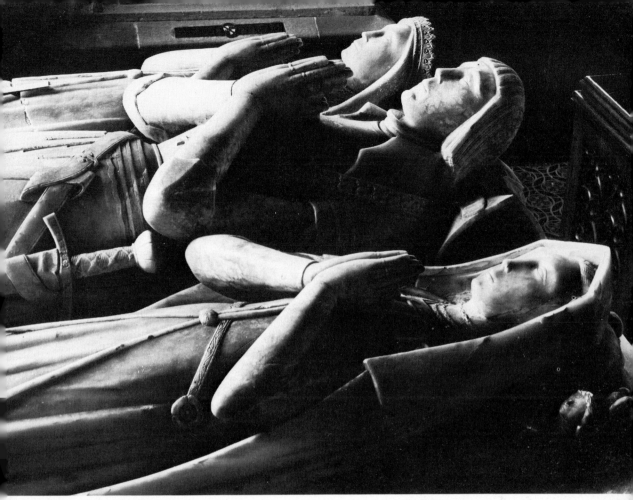

Sir William Smythe, **Elford**

the Wolverhampton architect W.D. Griffin). Elegant spire. An enormous marble tomb outside the church commemorates Frederick Charles Perry, who rebuilt the church.

Eccleshall [7] Little episcopal market town in the undulating and well-wooded country between Stafford and the Shropshire border. The main roads from Newcastle, Stone, Stafford, Newport and Market Drayton all meet here, and there is a wide and attractive High Street with cobbled verges, many Georgian houses, and the Crown and the Royal Oak with arcades built across the pavement. The cli-

max to the street is the imposing parish church at the W end, where the street turns into a country road, and climbs slowly through miles of wooded countryside on its way to Shropshire.

From the 13c to the 19c Eccleshall Castle was the principal residence of the Bishops of Lichfield. It was built by Bishop Walter de Langton in the late 13c and originally comprised four towers at the angles, with connecting ranges which would have included Great Hall and Chapel, together with domestic quarters, all surrounded by a moat. The castle was besieged and partially destroyed in the Civil War (1643) in the time of Bishop

Robert Wright, who actually died during the siege. In 1695 Bishop Lloyd restored the castle, retaining one angle tower, to which he attached the late-17c house with its long L-shaped façade. The place remained the bishops' residence until after the death of Bishop Lonsdale, when the Palace in Lichfield (built in 1687, but rarely occupied by the bishop) became the episcopal residence. The castle is now a private house.

The great church of Eccleshall was of course used by the bishops for many functions (such as ordinations), and this explains its size. The wide nave and aisles are 13c, as is the spacious chancel, though this was much restored in 1868 by Street, who rebuilt the E end with its five lancet windows. Lofty arcades in the nave, with round

Eccleshall

piers and stiff-leaf capitals. Much glass by Clayton and Bell (1870). Reredos by Champneys (1898). Elaborately carved Lady Chapel and organ case by Caroe (1931). The lower stage of the W tower is EE, but the handsome top with its elaborate parapet and pinnacles is Perp, as are the nave clerestory and the S porch. Several bishops are buried in the church. In the N aisle hangs a comic and fanciful (late 17c?) oil painting of the castle, which almost looks like an illustration from *Struwwelpeter*.

Ecton [6] Tiny hamlet in remote and deep valley close to Warslow: site of old copper and lead mines. The track of the old Manifold Valley Light Railway (*see* Sheen) is still visible, and half-way up the hill is an amusing castle-folly house, with copper spire.

Edingale [12] on its little bank, surveys a fertile valley through which wanders the little river Mease, marking the frontier of Staffordshire and Derbyshire. Old elm stumps on the diminutive village green, a long, brick farmhouse with timbered gable marked I.W. 1664, and the usual row of villas opposite the church—a brick building of 1881, by Charles Lynam, with small tower on its N side with oddly shaped crown.

Elford [12] An estate village, in an exceptionally pretty setting on the banks of the river Tame. Farmhouses, cottages, gardens, copses, a weir, a great bridge across the river, high walls, a long lime avenue up to the church—all contribute to the scene. By the churchyard entrance great wooden gates, now locked and overgrown, led into the Hall grounds, but the big brick 18c house, built for the 4th Earl of Berkshire, perhaps by Francis Smith of Warwick, has been pulled down.

The church was grandly rebuilt in the 19c, with the exception of the tower which is dated 1598; nave and chancel are by Salvin (1848), S aisle and chapel by Street (1869). The interior is glorious with Victorian decoration: roof and walls are brilliantly painted and gilded; angels carry corbels or coats of arms all richly blazoned; stained glass by Wailes and Ward and Hughes admits dark, lustrous light; ornate brass altar rails guard an elaborate sanctuary. The S chapel is a gallery of the tombs and monuments of the Lords of the Manor, which passed by marriage from the Ardernes to the Stanleys, then to the Stauntons, Smythes and Bowes, finally to the Howards and Pagets. The oldest is Sir Thomas Arderne (1391): the grandest Sir William Smythe with his two wives (1525). The most famous is the Stanley boy—John Stanley, killed by a tennis ball *c.* 1460. He holds the fatal ball in his left hand, his right points to his head: 'ubi dolor, ibi digitus' reads the inscription. It was real tennis, of course, not the modern game with its light fluffy ball. He was the last of the Stanleys, a younger branch of the Stanleys, Earls of Derby. William Staunton, who married his sister, is in the chancel, with his figure sunk in a stone surround. There are later monuments to the Howards: Craven Howard married the Bowes heiress, and Henry Bowes Howard, his son, built the early-18c house, and became eventually 4th Earl of Berkshire and 11th Earl of Suffolk, Elford at this time being held with Charlton in Wiltshire and Levens in Westmorland. The house was pulled down in 1964.

The W window in the S aisle is 16c Flemish glass, which like the windows of the apse in Lichfield Cathedral came from Herckenrode Abbey near Liège. It was brought to Elford in 1825.

Elkstone [5] A delectable spot in the High Peak: a narrow lane leads off the B5053 (Cheadle to Longnor), and climbs to Lower and Upper Elkstone. Stone walls, stone cottages, ash trees, lonely farms—and at Upper Elkstone a church of 1786, of rare charm. Domestic in appearance and plan, the exterior has round-headed sash windows and a small bellcote; the interior box pews and a gallery, two-decker pulpit with tester, Royal Arms (George III), Creed and Lord's Prayer above the altar, Commandment Boards and great fluffy bell-rope, all beautifully restored and loved.

Ellastone [6] The river Dove here divides Staffordshire from Derbyshire: an 18c bridge carries the road across to Norbury and the wooded country beyond. The great Weaver Hills stand above. The village is Hayslope of George Eliot's *Adam Bede*, and her father Robert Evans spent his early life here as a carpenter. Her uncle Samuel Evans's house is easily visible from the road that leads up to Wootton, with its trim garden, and wall adorned with odd stone ornaments. In the book Loamshire is Staffordshire and Stonyshire Derbyshire, Oakbourne is Ashbourne and Norbourne Norbury.

The church is largely late 16c in date (the tower is dated 1586), but the nave was rebuilt in 1830. Monuments to the Fleetwoods of Wootton (q.v.)—including tomb with effigies of Sir John Fleetwood, d. 1590—their successors the Davenports and Bromley Davenports, and the Granvilles of Calwich.

Calwich Abbey, close to the river to the E, was an Augustinian foundation. The 18c house built on its site was the home of Bernard Granville, friend of Handel and brother of Mrs Delany, and the regular resort of Jean-Jacques Rousseau when living at Wootton Hall. The house was pulled down before the war, but a small late-18c fishing temple survives.

The Old Hall is a good late 17c house in the middle of the village.

Ellenhall [7] Ellenhall is the perfect little Staffordshire village—unpretentious, away from main roads, its praises unsung. A few cottages, high hedges, a small church, and a Hall now a farmhouse. The church, up a sloping churchyard, has a Georgian brick tower, a Victorianised brick nave, and a medieval chancel with a small Norman window. 18c oak pews. 18c marble monument to a Cope (of the Bramshill family). The red-brick Hall has two 18c gables, with sash windows, and round sham windows in the gables; it is surrounded by farm buildings. The manor originally belonged to the Noels, one of whom founded Ranton Abbey near by—ancestors of the Earls of Gainsborough; it then went to the Harcourts of Stanton Harcourt.

But the house is now one of those splendid old red farmhouses which are such a feature of the county.

Endon [5] Suburban growth along the A53 from Burslem, but off the main road the village on its steep escarpment is intact. Several good houses and cottages, a ford, and a village well which is 'dressed' in May—like many wells in Derbyshire, but unique in Staffordshire. The W tower of the church is dated 1730 and is Gothic survival; the rest of the church is by J. Beardmore, of 1876. Dark interior: Morris E window of 1893.

Enville [16] Patriarchal village in glorious country close to the Shropshire border. A pink sandstone church, with an unexpected

Ellastone Old Hall

The Museum, **Enville** Hall

Lowe of Enville in the 15c; the Greys became in time Earls of Stamford and Warrington, and possessed of great estates in Cheshire and Leicestershire. After the death of the 7th Earl in 1883, the estates were divided, Enville being inherited by Sir Henry Foley Grey, whose grand-daughter is the present owner. Enville has thus been cherished by the family for over five centuries.

From the village street a glimpse of the Hall is visible up the lime avenue: long range of red-brick stables (18c), with central arch and cupola; behind that the pinnacled and embattled stuccoed house itself. The S front was done up in Strawberry Hill Gothick in the 18c, but the deeply recessed centre with its two little octangular towers clearly reveals its 16c origin—and an engraving in Dr Plot's *Natural History of Staffordshire* shows this front as it was in the 17c. The N front is plain 18c classical. There was a fire in 1904, and the interior was rebuilt then, and the *porte-cochère* added.

The gardens and grounds are the special glory: a wide lawn rises to the W of the house, adorned by a great pond with fountain and stone horses; beyond rises the park, thickly treed and ornamented with follies. William Shenstone, the poet and landscape gardener, creator of his own celebrated garden at the Leasowes, near Halesowen, laid out the grounds here in the middle of the 18c. There is a chapel in the woods, dedicated to his memory, with a cascade near by, a triple-arched Gothick gateway, recently restored, and, nearer the house, a lightly overgrown Gothick summer house called the Museum, and designed by Sanderson Miller. This is now roofless, but it is hoped to restore it. Facing the S front of the house is a lake; in all directions informal paths lead through the woods to the Sheep Walks, the higher wilder reaches of the park.

The garden itself contained one

Somerset-type tower, presides over spruce red-brick cottages, and the Cat Inn; the wooded slopes of the park of Enville Hall provide the backcloth to the W; deep woods protection on the E. The tower with its Somerset crown is the work of Gilbert Scott, who restored the church in 1872–5. Long Norman nave of four bays, wide aisles, Dec chancel with elaborate Victorian reredos and sanctuary. In the spandrels of the nave arcade are two curious carved Saxon figures, one of a bishop, one of an Eastern

priest with flabellum (or fly-switch!). On the N side of the chancel is a founder's recess, with the tomb of a 13c rector. 15c chancel stalls with misericords. Many monuments to the Greys in the S aisle, starting with the alabaster tomb of Thomas Grey (1559). Other monuments elsewhere in church to Amphletts of Four Ashes and Moseleys of the Meer.

Robert Grey, third son of Reginald Lord Grey of Ruthin, married the heiress of Humphrey

of the most spectacular and extravagant conservatories in all England. Crowned with two glass domes, a fairy-story palace in glass, it was erected in the mid-19c, and pulled down after the last war.

Round the periphery of the estate are several good houses: Brindley Hall was the home of James Brindley, the canal builder; Cox Green and Meere Hall are 16c brick; the Lyons early 19c. This is all remote Shropshire border country.

Essington [14] Suburbanised village N of Wolverhampton, close to the Hilton Park Colliery. Imposing brick church of 1932 (by Wood and Kendrick) with tall narrow S tower. The Wyrley and Essington Canal, which connected the Coventry Canal and the Birmingham Canal Navigations, is now disused.

Fairwell [11] A hamlet approached by deep lanes to the W of Lichfield: a couple of farms, and almost hidden by trees across the grass the 18c brick tower of the church. The 14c chancel survives, with some old stalls; the nave is of brick and, like the tower, was rebuilt in 1745. The Hall is a tall and imposing late-17c brick house with shell doorhead, long since sunk to farmhouse status.

Farley [5] In the dramatic country N of Alton. An early-19c Gothicky hall—and wonderful views of Alton Towers, and across the Churnet Valley.

Fazeley [15] A somewhat grimy manufacturing village on Watling Street. Here in the late 18c Sir Robert Peel, father of the Prime Minister, established one of his textile mills, and this, greatly enlarged, still stands, together with terraces of workers' houses along the road to Drayton Bassett. The church (1853, by Stevens of Derby) was built by the great Sir Robert, though completed after his death.

Flash [2] 'The highest village in England' proclaim the notices (1,518 ft above sea level): intimidating country in a blizzard. The main road from Leek to Buxton crosses Axe Edge, and close to the Travellers' Rest a lane leads to the church and village. The church is late Victorian Gothic (by W. R. Bryden of Buxton) with low W

Forton, folly

tower and elaborate stone pulpit, the gift of Lady Harpur-Crewe. Date-stones by the W door record 'Built A.D. 1744', 'Rebuilt A.D. 1901'. Derbyshire, Staffordshire and Cheshire meet at Axe Edge.

Forsbrook [8] Busy level-crossing on the line from Derby to Stoke, which here crosses the A50: built-up village, and large new school at Blythebridge; these are the out-

skirts of the Potteries. Forsbrook church is Victorian (1848) with a bellcote, built in the local dark stone.

Forton [10] The main road from Eccleshall to Newport passes the Monument (a conical 18c folly), and at the Swan Inn a lane turns off and descends into Forton. On the left is Forton Hall, a stone gabled house of Jacobean appearance, but dated 1665. Next comes the church with its graveyard sloping down the hill. A church of delightful contrasts: square W tower of the 13c, crowned by a Perp top with eight pinnacles and weather vane, and a Georgian nave and chancel with large round-headed windows and an *oeil-de-boeuf* over a doorway at either end. The E wall with Gothic window and buttress is medieval again. Inside, a Tuscan arcade divides Georgian nave from medieval N aisle. Some Georgian furnishings, and an alabaster tomb of 1633 to Sir Thomas Skrymsher and his wife.

The lane twists on, and leads to the wooded, mysterious park of Aqualate Hall, with its great lake called Aqualate Mere. Aqualate was a Jacobean house built by Edwin Skrymsher in the early 17c. At the end of the 18c it was bought by Sir George Boughey, 2nd Bt, who in 1803 employed John Nash to rebuild. The house he built was a large, romantic, spectacular, battlemented, pinnacled mansion, with buttresses and ogee domes—like a Gothic version of Brighton Pavilion. Its fantastic outline is familiar from pictures, but alas! it was destroyed by fire in 1910. A much more sober, smaller house was built in its place by W. D. Caroe in 1927, in restrained Tudor style, added to a surviving wing of the original house. It still belongs to descendants of the Boughey family. The park was landscaped by Repton; a castellated house called the Castle, and picturesque lodges provide further delights.

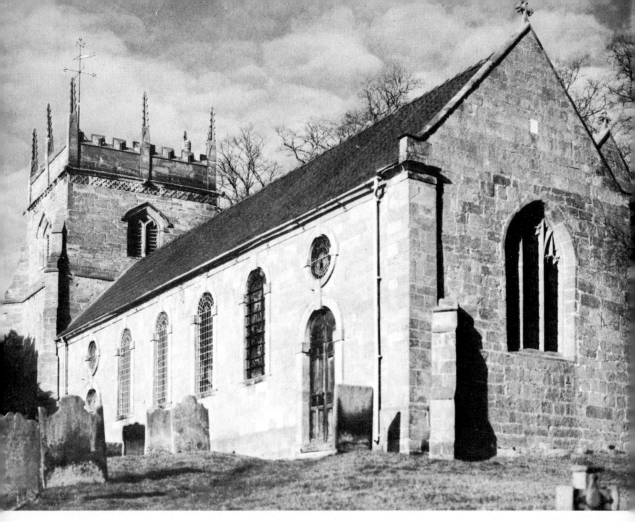

Forton

Foxt [5] Moorland hamlet above the Churnet Valley. Engaging small stone Gothic church of 1838, with simple interior, and prim little tower with machicolated top.

Fradswell [8] It is easy to miss the church, which is hidden in trees near the Hall, away from the village—not that there is much village. The church is in an exceptionally pretty setting, and has an 18c tower of purple brick, rock-faced Victorian nave, and 13c chancel. Well-furnished interior, dark with 19c glass (by Wailes and others). 17c monument to Jane daughter of the 4th Lord Cromwell, with Latin inscription ('Siste gradum, viator, siste, quid properas?'). Royal Arms of George I. The Hall next door is a neat early 19c house, with gardens sloping to a pool.

Freeford [12] A mile S of Lichfield, in its own private little world of home farm, dovecote, orchards, woods and parkland, stands Freeford Manor, for four hundred years the home of the Dyott family, who have been so closely associated with the history of the city. (*See* Lichfield.) It now appears a long low-spreading early 19c house, of late Georgian charm; but its core is 16c, and perhaps earlier.

Freehay [8] Scattered parish in the wooded moorland between Cheadle and Tean. The little church by Scott and Moffatt (of 1842) is undistinguished without, distinguished within. It is like a lofty college chapel, the eye led at once to the E end with its tall lancet windows filled with excellent glass by Wailes. In the sanctuary a brass commemorates Richard Rawle, Bishop of Trinidad, 'formerly Rector of Cheadle, and founder of this church'.

Fulford [8] Hill country S of Longton. Villas along the village street—but on a hillside to the N stand Fulford Hall, a tall early-18c farm-house, with gazebo at the end of its garden wall; and the church. This is a pretty little early-19c brick Gothick toy, with battlemented tower and Gothick windows.

Gailey [11] A roundabout where the Stafford–Wolverhampton road (A449) crosses the Watling Street (A5): little Victorian church by G. T. Robinson (1849), with later chancel (1874) by James Fowler of Louth. Half a mile to the E is Gailey Wharf on the Staffs and Worcs Canal; two miles or so to the W the Shropshire Union Canal crosses the Watling Street on a highly orna-mental cast-iron bridge, by Telford (1832).

Gayton [8] The church is at the end of a lane, and has an 18c tower of purple brick with a modern weather vane of St Peter with his fishing net. Much of the church is a 19c rebuilding by Habershon and Pite of London (as a brass plate in the chancel records). Norman chancel arch. Medieval tiles.

Gentleshaw [11] In the middle of Cannock Chase. An ill-assorted brick church, with low embattled W tower and humble little nave—then much taller transepts and chancel, the former of 1839, the lat-ter of 1903. Open heathland, close to Beaudesert Park. The Park Gate Inn leads on to Castle Ring, a great Iron Age hill fort, 800 ft above sea level, with striking views.

Glascote [15] Industrial suburb of Tamworth. Among the drab little houses, at the end of a side street (S) off the B3500, stands a church of unusual outline, with a tall central tower crowned by a saddleback roof. It is the work of Basil Champneys, and was built in 1880. Inside, vaulted chancel and two Burne-Jones windows. Views over open ground to the S, to fac-tories and the low hills of Warwick-shire beyond the Watling Street.

Gnosall

Gnosall [10] (pronounced Nozall or Nawzall.) A large village on the main road from Stafford to New-port, which here crosses the Shrop-shire Union Canal. The church is one of the best in the county. It is large and cruciform, and was originally collegiate, with dean and four canons. Externally it is all Perp, with large windows and clerestoried nave, and dominating pinnacled central tower. Inside, the earlier origins of the church are revealed. EE nave arcade. Great Norman pillars to the tower. Dec E window with flowing tracery. Perp SE chapel. But the greatest thing is the S transept, which reveals two bays of a Norman triforium on the W side, with carved string course below. An EE arch leads into the aisle of the nave—with one small arch of a Norman arcade at its side. The Victorian S porch by Lynam is original and highly decorative.

Audmore is a hamlet to the N. Audmore House is 17c brick with gables, with many features of this date within—and an elegant late Georgian staircase.

Upper and Lower Gornal [14] The road from Sedgley to Dudley passes through vintage early-19c industrial landscape. Close to the road at Upper Gornal stands a

Pell Wall, **Hales**: Lodge by Soane

church of the usual Commissioners' type, built in 1841, with turreted W front, lancet windows, fine proportions, but few architectural details—a workaday church, of necessity built on the cheap. At Lower Gornal is a more ambitious church, slightly earlier in origin, enlarged and embellished during the century with W tower and apsidal chancel. Attractive galleried interior. Every district of the Black Country has its own individual character: here, it is said, pure Chaucerian English is still spoken.

Gratwich [8] A remote hamlet deep in narrow lanes in the undulating country SW of Uttoxeter. The church is an endearing, humble little brick affair of 1775, with plain Gothic windows—and a rare early-17c brick chancel with Tudor features.

Grindon [6] Magnificent Peak country: the needle-like spire of the church is a landmark for miles across these lonely hills. The church

itself is of interest: built in 1848 by the Francis brothers, it is orderly and restrained in early 19c taste. The elegant arcades lead up to a clear, spacious chancel. Monument to the Revd Samuel Bradshaw, the founder.

Hales [7] The hamlet of Hales is on the hillside overlooking the valley of the Coal Brook towards the Shropshire border, and the Shropshire Union Canal. The late Georgian Hall is a little below the church, which was designed by Scott in 1856. The church was founded by a squarson, the Revd Alexander Buchanan, who lived at the Hall; it is of stone with a W tower, and a dark, well-furnished Victorian interior.

A short distance to the E are the remains of a Roman villa, and at Tyrley Locks there are gay scenes in summer, when the long boats climb five locks (a total rise of 33 ft). The bridge was built by Telford, and the road leads on to the public house called the Four Alls. Just out-

side Market Drayton is Pell Wall one of Sir John Soane's last country houses, built for his friend Purney Sillitoe in 1822. The exterior is in Soane's unmistakable style, with an incised band of key pattern between the ground and first floors on the garden side, and incised pilaster strips dividing the compartments of the entrance front; and an original roof line with unusual attic windows. At the end of the N drive stands an unbelievable little triangular lodge, also by Soane, with classical and Gothic motifs, surmounted by a hexagonal lantern with weather vane. It has recently been rescued and done up, with a small new house attached to its back.

Hammerwich [12] Not far from the terrible growth of Brownhills, but set on its little hill the village preserves its country air. From the churchyard there are views W and N across Cannock Chase with collieries in the distance, and a large farm with old outbuildings beneath you. Victorian church with broach spire, all of blackened stone. Old pictures of the former chapel hang inside.

Hanbury [9] The great tower of the church dominates the broad valley of the Dove to the N, and presides over Needwood Forest to the S. Only fragments of the Forest now survive: originally it comprised some 8,000 acres, and was the property of the Crown in right of the Duchy of Lancaster. It was enclosed by Act of Parliament in 1801. But the forest atmosphere survives in this beautiful, well-wooded countryside—and in many inscriptions in the church.

King Ethelred of Mercia founded a nunnery here in 680, and appointed his niece, the future St Werburgh, as Prioress. At her death she was buried here—but subsequently her body was moved to Chester, where her shrine still remains in the Cathedral. The

priory was sacked by the Danes in 875, and nothing survives.

The church is a building of some grandeur, medieval in origin, but much rebuilt in stages during the 19c. Indeed a High Victorian atmosphere pervades the interior 12c nave arcades. 17c roof. Chancel rebuilt in 1862—aglow with Victorian murals, tiles and glass. E window (by Ward and Hughes) in memory of Prince Consort. Alabaster reredos, pulpit and font; much well-polished brass. Interesting tombs: alabaster effigy of Sir John de Hanbury (d. 1303) at E end of S aisle—perhaps the oldest alabaster effigy in England; Sir Ralph Adderley (1595) and Sir Charles Egerton (1624), Axe Bearer of Needwood Forest, on either side of sanctuary. Best of all are the busts of two Puritan ladies above the vicar's stall: wearing broad, black hats and gowns with white ruffs, they survey the scene with eyes of prim disapproval. They are Mrs Agard (1628) and her daughter Mrs Woollocke (1657). And at the E end of the N aisle is Sir John Egerton (1662), the Royalist and Axe Bearer of the Forest. The tomb was erected by his sister here, instead of in the chancel, so that he might be 'away from the gaze of the Puritan ladies'. There is also a brass to a 15c priest in vestments.

At the W end of the nave are the monument to John Wilson (1839) by Hollins, sculptor of London and Birmingham; and the inscription recording the restoration of the clerestory in memory of George Edward Anson, Keeper of the Privy Purse to Queen Victoria, and Axe Bearer of the Forest—who died at the New Lodge in 1849. George III and William IV often stayed at New Lodge (a mile SW of the village), and Queen Victoria made a generous contribution to the building of the imposing village school.

Harlaston [12] The little river Mease turns and twists in the valley

Hanbury The Puritan Ladies and Sir John Egerton

Haselour Hall

to the N. The village street contains two or three good houses (including a half-timbered one), and leads to the church. This was rebuilt in brick in the last century, except for the stone W tower which survives from the medieval church: sturdy and stocky, it is surmounted by a timber belfry, which gives it the appearance of a church in Surrey or Sussex. Heavily timbered interior. Ornate early-18c marble tablet (Anne Lady Egerton) in the sanctuary.

Haselour [12] The first sight of Haselour Hall is unforgettable. Set in gentle pastoral country, watered by the river Mease, the house stands in a little oak-studded park, bounded by thorn hedges: a five-gabled black and white mansion,

with medieval chapel attached. A late-19c lodge by Sir Edwin Lutyens, a ha-ha, a wide-spreading lawn, a brick dovecote—and the house is upon you. Like its neighbour Elford, the property passed through the Ardernes, Stanleys, Stauntons, Smythes, and Huddlestones to the Brookes, who came into possession in 1557 and perhaps built the house we see today. Originally protected by a double moat with guard house, the place sank to a farm in the 18c, and the chapel became a cow shed. Rescued by Mr Thomas Neville in the early 19c, the restoration was completed later in the century by Mr A. H. de Trafford, whose family still live here. He built the northernmost gable, so tactfully that it is difficult to detect the new work, and

restored the chapel for Roman Catholic worship. A devout little church of the 13 and 14c, with narrow W spirelet, ancient timbered roof and low deep-set windows, the interior glows with rich Victorian stained glass, rood screen, and other objects of piety. It is a private chapel, and not open to the public. Beyond the Hall, along the road to Elford, is a Georgian farmhouse. There is nothing else of Haselour.

Hatherton [11] Turn off the A5 at the Four Crosses (part half-timbered, part 18c brick), past St Saviour's church (a small conventicle of 1864), and the winding lane soon leads to the little park of Hatherton Hall—one of those amusing Georgian Gothick stucco houses, with pinnacles and sash windows. It was built by the Walhouse family, who in the early 19c married the Littleton heiress (*see* Pillaton *and* Penkridge), and became the Lords Hatherton, moving their principal home to Teddesley. It has now passed into other hands.

Haughton [11] On the main road between Stafford and Newport, but surrounded by lush meadows. The Old Hall is a 16c timbered house by the roadside. The church was mostly rebuilt by Pearson in 1887, to replace a brick Georgian building. Four members of the Royds family have been rectors here: it was G. T. Royds who employed Pearson to rebuild the then despised Georgian church. 'Pastor fidelis' records the inscription to his memory 'hanc ecclesiam restauravit, ornavit, amavit.' The N wall is medieval, as is the narrow NE chantry, containing the incised slab to an early-16c rector. The tower with eight pinnacles and richly decorated frieze is also medieval.

Great and Little Haywood [11] The attractive street of these two contiguous villages borders the E boundary of Shugborough Park. The church at Great Haywood is by Thomas Trubshaw (1840), and has W bellcote, and interior elegant with Perp arcade. The Roman church is by Joseph Ireland, and was originally built at Tixall in 1828, and moved here when Tixall passed into Anglican hands in 1845. Solemn, devotional interior of Perp character.

Near the Clifford Arms (which recalls the last Catholic owners of Tixall) a narrow lane ('No Through Road') leads under the railway to the Essex Bridge and a garden gate to Shugborough. On each side is an elegant terrace of Georgian cottages, with a sturdier house at the end. The Essex Bridge was built towards the end of the 16c by the first Earl of Essex (of Chart-

Hednesford R.C. church (1927!)

ley) to transport his horses and hounds to Cannock Chase. It is long and narrow, little more than a footbridge; fourteen arches carry the path across the three channels of the Trent and the Sow (which join here) and the Trent and Mersey Canal. A beautiful reach of the river.

Hednesford [11] ('Hednes' pronounced as in 'Wednesday') Bustling little colliery town, with busy streets, and terraces of miners' houses. On the hilltop to the E is the Victorian parish church of 1866 (by T. A. Rushworth) in the usual blackened stone, and the usual kind of Gothic. But a little lower down, along the road at right angles, is the R.C. church (1927, by G. B. Cox of Birmingham), a remarkable and indeed enormous building in an unusual brand of French Gothic. Grand vista-ed interior with altars and shrines—and a grotto of Our Lady of Lourdes in the hillside outside the W door.

In the middle of the town, the Anglesey Hotel is a Tudor gabled building of 1831. It was originally built by Edmund Peel of Fazeley (q.v.), as a summer residence. He was uncle of the Prime Minister, and trained his race-horses on the excellent turf of the Hednesford Hills.

High Offley [7] Good countryside close to the Shropshire border. The church and cluster of inn and cottages stand on the hill and command the view. Much of the church is Norman or Transitional, but the upper stages of the tower are 17c: there is a date-stone of 1667. 17c Skrymsher monuments.

To the S the Shropshire Union Canal passes through the parish on an embankment with aqueducts: the Grub Street cutting is a particularly pretty stretch of canal scenery.

Hilderstone [8] In wooded and unspoiled country to the E of Stone.

The church of 1827, by Thomas Trubshaw, is a period piece of some charm. Built of stone, with a short spire and lancet windows, the interior has box pews and many other contemporary fittings; plain glass with bright orange border—but unfortunately the E window has been removed. 19c marble monuments to the Bourne family, who built the church and inhabited the Hall, a stuccoed Georgian house in a small park.

Hilton Park [14] Hilton Park is now the name of a service station on the M6 a few miles NE of Wolverhampton; Hilton Park itself, though assailed by colliery villages and suburbia, and deserted by its former owners, unexpectedly survives. The park is mostly ploughed up, and pot-holed drives lead up to the enclosure round the house itself, where a notice announcing 'ST JOSEPH'S GUEST HOUSE' greets the visitor. But the magnificent house still stands. It is of the early 18c, of brick with stone quoins and dressings, three storeys high; the long W front faces a lake and is crowned with urns, with a baroque centrepiece with decorative pediment, carved cartouche, garlands, scrolls and vases. Within are fine panelled rooms, and a good staircase. The precise date of the house, and the name of the architect are unknown, but the house was built by Henry Vernon in the early 18c. The Vernons acquired Hilton by marriage with the Swynnertons, who are buried in Shareshill church. On a derelict upland in the park stands an embattled folly called the Portobello Tower, built to commemorate Admiral Vernon's capture of Portobello in 1739.

Himley [14] An astonishing oasis, almost completely surrounded by the industrial growth of Wolverhampton, Dudley, Brierley Hill, Kingswinford and Wombourn. Its survival is due to the presence of the great house of the Earls of Dudley.

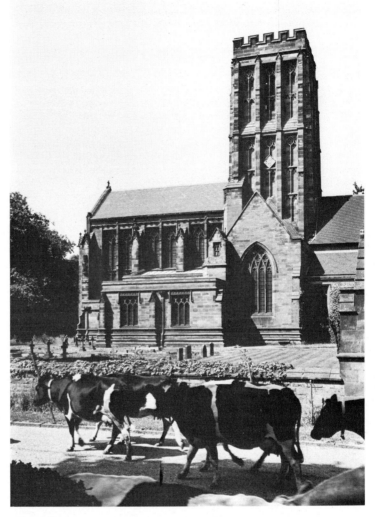

Hoar Cross

Low hills hung with beech woods provide the backcloth to the long austere S front of the house with its giant Ionic portico, built in 1824 by William Atkinson; the W front, with its tall pedimented centrepiece, is the original 18c house. It was after the fire at Dudley Castle in 1750 that Himley became the principal seat of the family; in 1934 pictures of Himley appeared in all the papers when it was chosen by the Duke of Kent and Princess Marina for their honeymoon. It is now used as a teachers' training college, but the house and beautiful park are well maintained.

Himley House Hotel, on the main road, is the Georgian dower house; the tall rectory next door is dated 1767. The plain little stuccoed church of 1764 contains the monument by Sir William Reid Dick to Rosemary, Viscountess Ednam, killed in an air crash in 1930: 'sunt lacrimae rerum'. Behind the church is the private Garden of Remembrance: approached by a high-walled orchard, this secret garden watered by a stream contains four grave-slabs to the family by Eric Gill, and a portico-ed loggia.

Half a mile away the Crooked House, or Glynne Arms, is a well-known curiosity: a 16c timbered house, of which one end has sunk several feet as a result of underground workings. And just off the road to Stourbridge, Holbeche House, an early-17c brick house (much done up in the 19c), was the home of the recusant Stephen Littleton. Here on 7 November 1605 the last stand of the Gunpowder Plotters took place: Fawkes had already been arrested, but Catesby, Digby, Winter, Littleton and the rest were captured here, and a few days later taken to London.

Hints [15] The curious name apparently derives from the Welsh word 'hynt' meaning a road, and the village is just off Watling Street. A lane dives off the A5, and descends into an abrupt and pretty valley, past a large brick farmhouse, to the church. The churchyard descends still further into the valley, where flows the `Bourne Brook. The church with its bellcote is not large, but it is an accomplished design by Oldrid Scott (1882): 18 and 19c monuments to the Lawleys of Canwell Hall (q.v.), and to the Floyers of Hints. Hints Hall was pulled down after the Second World War—a two-storey brick Georgian house, each bay divided by giant Corinthian pilasters, with low central pediment, and parapet adorned with urns. It was a handsome house.

Hixon [8] Large village, with an industrial estate close to the A51. Prominent church with N tower and broach spire, by Gilbert Scott, 1848.

Hoar Cross [12] Hoar Cross church stands on an unlikely by-road in Needwood Forest: the forest road E to W passes through Newborough, and the road N to S passes through Newchurch. Both by-pass Hoar Cross, and there is no proper village of Hoar Cross: such houses and cottages as there are are scattered, the by-roads are leafy— and suddenly the silhouette of a great church is before you, a silhouette solemn and severe, with tall, unpinnacled central tower, lofty clerestoried chancel, lower unclerestoried nave, and short transepts. Its presence at first seems unaccountable, but it will soon be seen that a great house adjoins it. Hoar Cross church is in origin the church of a great house, and the family who built it, that great church-building family, the Meynells.

The Meynells of Hoar Cross descend in origin from a younger son of a Meynell of Meynell Langley near Derby: in the middle of the 18c they bought land at Ashley (q.v.), and half a century later Hoar Cross. The 18c Hoar Cross belonged to the Talbots, Earls of Shrewsbury, so was in recusant hands; there was no parish church (*see* Woodlane). The church we see was begun in 1872, and dedicated in 1876; it was built by Mrs Meynell-Ingram in memory of her husband, Hugo Francis Meynell-Ingram, and the architect was Bodley. It is one of the most beautiful 19c churches in England, and Bodley's masterpiece. There is a sense in which Bodley put all of himself into Hoar Cross, as Comper put all of himself into St Mary's, Wellingborough; and indeed both churches are parallel and comparable in their sophisticated lavishness and taste.

The nave at first seems dark: it is lower, shorter, less ornate than other parts of the church; originally it comprised only two bays, and it will be seen that it serves as a prelude, an antechapel as it were, to the church itself. Stand or sit in the nave and look up, through the narrow arches of the crossing, through the rood screen, to the chancel and the High Altar beyond. This part of the church is bathed in light, and glows with colour.

In the nave note and enjoy the glass by Burlison and Grylls; the stations of the cross by the Antwerp carvers de Wint and Boeck; and the narthex by Cecil Hare, Bodley's partner and successor, added in 1906. As you move eastwards and enter the chancel, the great glow and glory of this part of the church will at once affect you: the stalls, the organ case, the glass (all by Burlison and Grylls), the marble floor with the arms of Meynells and Ingrams; the richly carved walls, the vaulted roof, the reredos, the crucifix and candlesticks, the height, the vistas to the chapels, the statues of the saints, the figures of the angels, the embroidery, the tomb of Hugo Meynell-Ingram—all is the work of the master hand. To the S is the Chantry Chapel, with the tomb of the foundress close to that of her husband; beyond that, All Saints' Chapel. On the N are the Lady Chapel and St Hugh's Chapel. And in addition to all the furnishings and works of art there is a great collection of vestments, ancient and modern.

But apart from the beauty, it is the piety of the building that will impress. It was built indeed to be the House of God, the Gate of Heaven. It is a church to pray in.

Hoar Cross Hall was rebuilt for the Meynells in 1862 by Henry Clutton: in a photograph or on a dark evening the garden front with its symmetrical Jacobean gables framed in clipped yew will seem attractive; in broad daylight the hard, bright, red brick will not. The Meynells gave the house up after the Second World War, and moved to a smaller house in an idyllic setting not far away.

Hollington [8] Fine position in high moorland, with views to N and S. The Hollington stone quarries are here, which have provided the familiar pink stone for so many Staffordshire buildings. Interesting

Hopwas church

and original church by G. E. Street
(1859) with round apse, and interior with many characteristic and
attractive Street features.

Hollinsclough [2] Northernmost
Staffordshire: the infant river Dove
flows close by and marks the Derbyshire frontier; groups of Peakland hills stand around. Stone-built
hamlet, with little church of 1840
attached to a house, handsome with
obelisk-crowned gables.

Hopton Heath [8] The Battle of
Hopton Heath took place on 19
March 1643: the Parliamentary

forces under Sir John Gell and Sir
William Brereton were defeated by
the Royalists, though the Royalist
commander, the Earl of Northampton, was killed. This was a fortnight after the capture of Lichfield
Close by the Parliamentary forces
(*see* Lichfield); the names of the
soldiers slain are to be found in the
parish registers of Sandon and
Weston-on-Trent. Attractive brick
church, converted from a barn in
1876.

Hopwas [15] On the Lichfield
road W of Tamworth. 18c bridge
across the river Tame. On rising

ground against the wooded hillside
of Hopwas Hays stands a striking
church by John Douglas, built in
1881. It is of red brick, but the
upper E gable is of black and white
timbering, and the central tower a
wide black and white saddleback,
its staircase lit by a gabled dormer
window. The wide roof of the nave
is lower than the chancel—and the
whole composition is an interesting
and unusual interplay between the
domestic and the ecclesiastical,
with the architect's ingenious use of
tiles and timber. Harmonious interior in white brick.

Horton [5] From Rudyard Lake
the road climbs to Horton, a compact village with notable houses
and a church with pinnacled Perp
tower. Close to the lane from Rushton is Dairy House Farm, a beautiful, slightly decayed gabled stone
house of 1635. At the bottom of the
hill leading up to the church is Horton Hall: with its recessed centre
and gabled wings inscribed R.E.
1647 and T.E. 1668, it was built by
the Edge family in fine ashlar; the
sash windows are 18c insertions. N
of the church is the early-18c
vicarage, with its elegant brick
façade.

The church is chiefly Perp, with
some mid-19c restoration by
Sugden (1864). Of special interest
are the monuments to the Wedgwoods of Harracles Hall—the
senior branch of this ancient Staffordshire family, whose name has
been immortalised by Josiah. The
family first came to Horton in the
14c: John Wedgwood (d. 1494)
married the heiress of Harracles;
his grandson John married a
Bowyer of Knypersley, and his
great-grandson an Egerton. It was
he who received a confirmation of
arms and the grant of crest in 1576.
From him stemmed the senior line
of Harracles. A younger grandson
of the John who married the
Bowyer settled at Biddulph; his
grandson is described as Master
Potter at Burslem in 1640 (*see*

Ilam font

venticle serves as the church, and there is a somewhat overbearing Gothic pumping station of 1876.

Ilam [6] There is always a tendency for books to write of Dovedale and the Peak as though they belonged exclusively to Derbyshire. But, as we know, 'the best parts of Derbyshire are in Staffordshire'— and Ilam is such a one. The river Dove here is the frontier, and the Izaak Walton Hotel stands on the Staffordshire side. Dovedale itself, Thorpe Cloud, the Bunsters, and the wooded valley behind Ilam Hall known as Paradise, form the setting for the village.

Ilam itself was bought in the early 19c by a wealthy manufacturer, Jesse Watts Russell. John Shaw rebuilt the Hall for him in 1821, in romantic Gothic battlemented style; the 'Eleanor' Cross in the centre of the village commemorates his wife (1840), and the school and many cottages *ornées* were built in the years following.

The church with its saddleback tower stands by the approach to the Hall. It is ancient, but was largely rebuilt by Gilbert Scott in 1855, and is dominated on the N side by the octagonal Watts Russell mausoleum, built in 1831. The chapel on the S side was rebuilt in 1618, and contains the shrine of St Bertelin (or Bertram) who was much venerated in Staffordshire in the Middle Ages. The interior is full of Scott furnishings: the reredos, the tiling, the screens of wrought iron made by Skidmore; there is a Norman tub font. In the S chapel stands the quatrefoil-decorated base of St Bertelin's shrine; nearby is the tomb (1626) of Robert Meverell of Throwley, the last of the Meverells, and his daughter and heiress who married the 4th Lord Cromwell. Opposite, in the vaulted octagonal Watts Russell Chapel, is the large monument by Chantrey to David Pike Watts, Jesse Watts Russell's father-in-law. He is seen reclining on his bed, surrounded by his

Burslem). He was followed by three generations of Burslem Master Potters, and the 7th son of Thomas of Burslem was the great Josiah, born in 1730.

The earliest Wedgwood monument is a brass of 1589 to the John who received the confirmation of arms in 1576. There are also handsome 18c marble tablets to John (d. 1724), and his son John (d. 1757).

Harracles Hall stands in a fine position up a long track off the Rudyard–Longsdon road. It is an early-18c brick house of two storeys, with wide central pediment adorned with garlands, and hipped roof. It is now a farmhouse.

Huntingdon [11] Mining village on Cannock Chase. A small con-

Ingestre

daughter and grandchildren. Here too is the bust to Jesse Watts Russell by Laurence Macdonald (1863). In the churchyard are two Saxon crosses.

Much of Ilam Hall was pulled down in the 1930s, and the remaining part converted into a Youth Hostel. The estate with its idyllic park and woodland, watered by the Manifold which here emerges from its subterranean course from Darfur Crags, was given to the National Trust by Sir Robert McDougall in 1934.

Up a lonely track which leads to Calton stand the ruins of Throwley Hall, the early-16c house of the Meverells, with farmhouse and old buildings attached. To the N of the village, in a solitary situation, stands Castern Hall, a tall early-18c house built by the Hurt family of Alderwasley (Derbyshire): remote and beautiful, it is once again a home of the family.

Ingestre [8] Ingestre today is a sad place to visit: Ichabod is written over it—or over most of it. The Lion

Gates are padlocked, and the drive behind them overgrown; the service road at the side is pot-holed, and the verges are unkempt; the new stables are desolate, the old stables divided into dwellings; the great domain has been sold piecemeal, and it looks it.

Ingestre was the seat of the Chetwynds, whose heiress married in 1763 John Talbot, son of Lord Chancellor Talbot and father of the 1st Earl Talbot. It was his grandson the 3rd Earl Talbot, who succeeded his distant cousin as 18th Earl of Shrewsbury in 1856 (*see* Alton). The place thereafter was the principal home of the Shrewsburys, until in 1960 it was sold. The Hall itself was bought by the county borough of West Bromwich, and opened for residential courses in the Arts; and this is well-maintained, albeit an institution.

The S front of the house is the mansion built by Sir Walter Chetwynd who died in 1638. It is of Jacobean brick, with stone dressings, many windows, bows, gables and a pillared porch crowned by a

cupola. There was a fire in 1882, which destroyed the interior; and some of the brickwork of the front is hard red Victorian. The N and the W fronts, which had been Georgianised, had been in 1808 rebuilt in Jacobethan by John Nash (an odd style for Nash). The whole house was reconstituted after the fire by the architect John Birch, and the rebuilding has given the house a somewhat mechanical Victorian hardness.

The old stables, next to the church, are late 17c; but the grand domed 19c stables on the approach road are opulent Victorian (by Birch), and almost grander than the house. They stand desolate, the ornate iron gates broken and padlocked.

The church is dated 1676. It may be by Wren—though definite proof is lacking. But Walter Chetwynd, the builder, was a friend of Wren; and the very fine quality of the work suggests no ordinary, no provincial hand. 'Deo Optimo Maximo' reads the inscription over the porch; and the whole church

proclaims this dedication. The nave is of four bays, and the arches are supported on clusters of four Roman Doric pillars. The clerestory is lit by circular windows. There is glorious plasterwork, sumptuous woodwork (screen, pulpit, panelling), and an array of monuments to Chetwynds and Talbots. The electric lighting, on delicate wrought-iron fittings, was installed in 1886—one of the earliest installations in any parish church. The church has been carefully restored in recent years, and is anything but Ichabod.

Ipstones [5] High moorland countryside, stone-walled, windswept. The village crowns the high ground: several good stone houses, and a church of 1790, with sturdy W tower, built by John Sneyd of Belmont Hall. Externally it appears a barnlike building in elementary Gothic: internally it surprises, for a chancel of 1902 has been added (by Gerald Horsley), and an all-encircling screen in Arts and Crafts style encloses it, and leads the eye to mysterious, beautifully furnished sanctuary. Above the screen the tympanum is painted with Christ in Majesty and the twelve apostles. A Norman tympanum from the earlier church is built into the S wall inside the church. In the sill of a S window is an early-19c Sneyd monument with urns and simple inscriptions; under the tower a remarkable Sneyd monument, in the form of a family tree in black and white marble.

From the centre of the village the road W (to Cheddleton) is one of the best in Staffordshire: a bleak moorland lane suddenly dips down into a wooded dell, watered by a

left **Ingestre**

Ingestre
Stable gates *(top),* and Royal Arms in the church ▷

stream and ponds. Here stands Belmont Hall, an 18c house, graceful in its rustic way: at the gate a curiosity, a cottage shaped like a church. John Sneyd (rebuilder of Ipstones church) quarrelled with the patron of the living, and started to build his own church here. The quarrel was patched up, and the chapel turned into a cottage. The lane leads on, out into wild moorland again, past Mosslee Hall, a stone Jacobean house of 1640, now a lonely farmhouse.

Keele [4] The tall spire of Keele church is a prominent landmark across the wooded countryside: closer at hand, across the motorway, the conglomeration of university buildings in the park provides an unexpected picture, hard to interpret. What can these buildings contain?

Keele Hall was from the end of the 16c till the middle of the 20c the seat of the Sneyd family; although untitled they were one of the oldest of the county families, at times among the richer, and certainly among the most cultivated. Almost to the end they were devoted to their home, their estate and their county. The family had held land at Bradwell in the parish of Wolstanton (*see* Newcastle) since 1400: they had close connections, too, with Cheshire. But in the 16c they began purchasing land in Staffordshire from the Audley family, and in 1580 Ralph Sneyd built the first Keele Hall. Royalists in the Civil War, they re-made their fortune in the 18c through their coal and iron interests, but took little part in national life. In the middle of the 19c Keele was rebuilt by another Ralph Sneyd, who employed Salvin to build the house we see today.

The house rises like a great fort close to steeply sloping ground. It is L-shaped, and built of red sandstone, with a balustraded tower rising over the main staircase in the corner of the entrance front, and two imposing façades to E and S on the garden side. It is in Salvin's Jacobean style, to accord with the old house, and there is a grand two-storeyed Great Hall just inside the entrance porch. The principal room on the S side is the Library, which at one time housed a valuable collection of books. The state rooms occupy the E side—Dining Room, Breakfast Room and Drawing Room opening out of one another in sumptuous succession, decorated in Renaissance taste and employing some 18c chimneypieces and columns.

Partly through mismanagement, partly through misfortune, the wealth of the family declined. For ten years at the beginning of this century Grand Duke Michael of Russia rented the house, where he was visited for a long weekend in 1901 by Edward VII. But after the First World War the house remained empty for several years. After occupation by the army during the Second World War, Colonel Ralph Sneyd sold the house (and 154 acres) in 1947 for the establishment of a new University College, which opened in 1949. In December of that year the last Ralph Sneyd of the senior line died; but there are still Sneyds in Staffordshire, descendants of the junior line of Belmont and Ashcombe (*see* Ipstones *and* Cheddleton). The new University College became the University of Keele in 1962.

The university use the Hall as Senior Common Room and for administration; the Clock House, part of the stable quadrangle built by Blore in the 1830s, is the Vice-Chancellor's residence. The new university buildings have been erected for the most part to the W of Keele Hall.

There is the large Library (1960) by Sir Howard Robertson, relieved by its cupola, but otherwise looking much like a long office block with great plate-glass windows. Opposite is the chapel, by George Pace (1964), which appears enormous, with two round towers at one end, crowned with little triangular spires. Inside, the main (interdenominational) chapel is like a great hangar; the round towers turn out to contain small chapels (one C. of E., one R.C.), devotional and intimate, with rooms for the clergy or for religious purposes upstairs. The Walter Moberly Hall next door is one of the earlier buildings, in a neo-Georgian idiom, by J. A. Pickavance (1954).

Building has been going on all the time, and the blocks which house the various departments, the Halls of Residence, and the houses for the dons are all around. The layout suffers from the hard tarmac drives and concrete-bordered paths which cut across the park like runways, from the suburban street lamps and the rather cramped conditions in which so many buildings seem to be huddled together—a sad contrast to the grand park, the spacious gardens.

The church is outside the park: it is a large and imposing Victorian building by John Lewis of Newcastle (1868), erected by Ralph Sneyd who rebuilt the Hall; it is perhaps a trifle stark and towny. Early-17c table-tomb with effigies to William Sneyd and his wife (1613), and many later monuments to the family.

Kidsgrove [4] Industrial, colliery landscape close to the Cheshire borders, and a drab little town with rows of Victorian villas and modern housing estates. But near the church a portion of the park of Clough Hall (demolished between the First and Second World Wars) makes a pretty, well-wooded oasis, and on the hill above the railway is a circular 18c folly tower. W of the church are the two entries to the Harecastle canal tunnels: the smaller (no longer used) is by James Brindley (1766 ff), the larger by Thomas Telford (1824 ff). The church with its brick W tower was built by the Kinnersleys of Clough:

the nave of 1837, reputedly designed by Mrs Kinnersley, the more correct chancel of 1853 by Gilbert Scott. Kinnersley monuments (see also Ashley), and Royal Arms of William IV, 1837.

King's Bromley [12] King's Bromley after the Mercian kings, as opposed to Abbot's Bromley after the abbots of Burton.

At the junction of main roads, in the triangle between Lichfield, Rugeley and Burton. A cul-de-sac leads to the gates of the vanished Manor House, which was the seat of the Lane family, the descendants of Colonel John Lane, who with his sister Jane was the preserver of King Charles II. The family removed from Bentley Hall (now swamped by Wolverhampton) at the end of the 18c. Now only the Victorian water tower survives of their Georgian house here.

The church has an eccentric plan, with an eccentric roof line. Flat-roofed clerestoried nave: higher gabled chancel. The lower parts of the nave are Norman. Handsome Gothick S porch: ogee-headed N doorway. Stone missal-stand in sanctuary (as found in a few churches in Derbyshire). 16c screen. 17c font and pulpit. The long N arm of the church is a vestry containing in a window fragments of 18c glass by Eginton. There are a few memorials to the Lanes; their principal monuments are in Wolverhampton church (See also Willenhall, Wolverhampton and Moseley Old Hall.)

Kingsley [5] Wide moorland views across the Churnet Valley. Stone village. Stone walls. Solid stone church, rebuilt by Thomas Trubshaw in 1820, except for the medieval tower.

Kingstone [8] An impressive but rather gloomy church by David Brandon (1861), with stumpy spire and apse, is finely placed overlooking the village. Mural monument to Sir Simon Degge (d. 1702), the antiquary and judge, removed from the old church. Well-wooded countryside between Abbots Bromley and Uttoxeter.

Kingswinford [17] There are fragments of the old village, once a royal manor, around the church—a tall 18c house with Gothic windows, a row of cottages, a public house. The church itself, the mother church of the many industrial parishes carved out of this enormous parish during the 18c and 19c, is medieval, and over the vestry door is a Norman tympanum of St Michael slaying the dragon. But the building was much enlarged and re-edified in the late 18c, and even closed for a time after the new parish church was built at Wordsley in 1829. Sturdy W tower; 16 and 17c Corbyn monuments; Breeches Bible (1605); 17c font with gilded canopy by Sir Ninian Comper; vicars' board by Sebastian Comper.

The rest of Kingswinford is overgrown and vandalised. At the crossroads an old row of black and white cottages, and an attractive Georgian house, were destroyed after the Second World War to create a new 'shopping precinct', and rows of new houses climb the hills. Summerhill is a brick mansion of 1756, with a grand façade crowned with urns, central Venetian window on the first floor, lunette window above. The house is now an hotel, and the garden in front one enormous tarmac car park; but the elegant staircase survives within, together with many features of the Adam period. There are other houses surviving from the days when the early industrialists built themselves fine Georgian houses here, but the gardens are built over; and Bradley Hall, a 16c timber-framed house, was actually uprooted after the last war, and re-erected at Stratford-upon-Avon.

Kinver [16] should be approached from the N. The road from Enville is through wooded heathland, and the High Street of the village (or, rather, ancient borough) is long and winding, adorned with a number of 17 and 18c houses. Above the village is the wooded and rocky escarpment of Kinver Edge, and perched above the High Street in magnificent isolation stands the church. Kinver Edge belongs to the National Trust, and has become a resort for visitors from the Black Country. Half-way up the hill the rock has been hewn out to form a house known as Holy Austin Rock—perhaps a medieval hermitage. On the farther side several 'rock cottages' exist, and old photographs are to be found of their rooms furnished and inhabited.

It is a long climb to the church, but the view from the churchyard is very fine. And the church itself, with its nave and spacious aisles, E chapels, monuments, and embattled W tower, is also of great interest. Most of the building is 14 or 15c: the N aisle was handsomely rebuilt by Thomas Smith in 1856. There are plans to reduce this aisle, which would spoil the spacious symmetry of the interior, and the bold impact of the exterior: it is much to be hoped that this scheme will not be implemented. Norman rood staircase (a great rarity); 14c font; piscina and sedilia in S aisle; 17c pulpit. The S chapel contains the altar tomb of Sir Edward Grey (of Enville), his two wives, seven sons and ten daughters—almost perfect brasses; the N chapel the mutilated figure of John Hampton of Stourton Castle, and monuments to the Foleys of Prestwood (see Stewponey).

The parish is intersected by the Stour river and the Staffs and Worcs Canal, with its old locks, wharves and warehouses.

Knightley [7] A hamlet to the N of Gnosall, with a slightly comic little white-brick church by

Thomas Trubshaw, of 1840. The Knightley family, of Fawsley, Northants, sprang from here.

Knypersley [5] Angry industrial countryside between Tunstall and Biddulph. The church, with its unmistakable Victorian silhouette and characteristic blackened features, was built in 1848 for James Bateman of Biddulph (q.v.) by R. C. Hussey. Bateman's father had lived at Knypersley Hall, and James kept on the walled gardens here to grow plants for his great gardens at Biddulph. Only outbuildings of the house survive, encroached on by suburban villas: the back garden, however, is—suitably enough—now used as a 'garden centre'.

Lapley [11] An unspoiled village, a mile or so N of Watling Street, with several good houses and a church with an immense central tower. There was a Benedictine priory founded here in the 11c. but apart from a few fragments built into farm buildings near by only the church survives—and that has been shorn of its transepts. It is, all the same, an awe-inspiring building. The orientation of nave and chancel varies markedly, and the chancel seen from the nave through the great dark space under the central tower appears distant and mysterious. The structure of the building is Norman, but there are later windows, and the upper part of the tower is Perp, with ornamented parapet and eight pinnacles. Under the tower are some handsome pieces of continental furniture.

Down a lane to the S is Park House, an amusing castellated building with gatehouse and turrets.

Leek [5] stands in magnificent country. In character it is a decidedly north-country town: its mills, its chimneys, its houses of blackened stone, its steep streets and cobbles, its surrounding moorland, its in-

dustrial atmosphere—yet homely, domestic scale, all combine to remind one of the small textile towns of the West Riding or rural Lancashire. The town took to silk, hosiery and dyeing in the 18c, and grew prosperous. But it is not a large town, and it is possible to walk round and enjoy its streets and its buildings on foot.

All the roads—from Macclesfield, from Buxton, from Ashbourne, from Cheadle, from Stoke—meet in the Market Place, cobbled and blackened, with the Red Lion and a number of other houses making a good ensemble, presided over by the late 18c house called Foxlowe on the N side. The road E is Stockwell Street, and a few yards down is Greystones, a late 17c stone house, behind which is the Nicholson Institute. This is an admirable foundation, established in 1884 by Joshua Nicholson (of Brough, Nicholson and Hall, the silk firm) as Public Library, Lecture Hall, Art Gallery and School of Art, and designed by a Leek architect, William Sugden, in a friendly Caroline style in red brick, with a tall tower. Sir Arthur Nicholson (of the same firm) gave the clock tower in Derby Street near by, designed by Thomas Worthington, as a war memorial.

The road W from the Market Place passes the parish church. The nave and tower (with pinnacled Perp top) are Dec, with unusual rose windows to N and S, decorative early-16c nave with carved bosses, and S porch of 1670. The chancel was rebuilt by Street in 1865; reredos and sanctuary, pulpit and stalls—all vintage Street, and very good. Victorian glass, including Morris glass in Lady Chapel. Several frontals and other embroidery the work of the Leek School of Embroidery, founded by Lady Wardle in the 1870s. The W part of the nave is occupied by an enormous 18c gallery, which rises tier upon tier like the dress circle in a theatre. 16c brass to John Ashen-

hurst and his family; memorial to William Trafford of Swynthamley (see Rushton Spencer) who foiled the Roundhead soldiers, and died in 1697; and several 18c monuments. There are also remarkable fragments of Saxon crosses in the churchyard—one a tall cylindrical Preaching Cross over 10 ft high. At the E end of the church is the early-18c vicarage, where the Young Pretender spent a night on his way to Derby in 1745. W of the church, Mill Street leads down to the large silk mill of Wardle and Davenport of c. 1860.

St Edward Street leads off to the left (S of the church) and here is the finest street in the town, with many good 18c (and later) houses. At the end of the street, in Broad Street, are the almshouses, founded by Elizabeth Ash in 1676, a pretty group, stuccoed in the last century, with the names of the beneficiary parishes inscribed in nice lettering.

All about are other mills, and in Queen Street is a large church of 1847 by the Francis Brothers—St Luke's—with tall, distinguished W tower, and interesting Victorian fittings: reredos by J. D. Sedding, screen attributed to Norman Shaw, E window of S aisle designed by Shaw and made by Heaton, Butler and Bayne. Brick villas of 1897 opposite the N side of the church.

In Compton is the impressive R.C. church (by A. Vicars, 1886); and, beyond, All Saints—the distinguished church by Norman Shaw, built in 1885–7. The exterior makes an immediate impact with its squat central tower; the interior is broad and exceptionally spacious, and on entering by the N porch the eye is carried at once across a wide, light, lofty vista to the sanctuary, commanding and colourful with great E window by Morris and reredos by Lethaby—the whole chancel a fitting prelude with handsome stalls, and murals by Gerald Horsley. Many windows by Morris, and much needlework

Lichfield

by the Leek School of Embroidery. Pulpit, Lady Chapel, font—all in keeping; but the clutter of the nave altar and inharmonious N door seem unnecessary and ill-mannered in an otherwise perfect interior. No one can get far away from sight of the High Altar in this church, anyway.

A mile NW of the town is Dieulacres Abbey ('May God give it increase!' as the Countess of Chester remarked to her husband, the founder, in 1214), a Cistercian house moved to this valley from Poulton in Cheshire. Only fragments remain, built into the farm buildings: the timber-framed farmhouse is early 17c, and was built by the Rudyards, who acquired the property soon after the Dissolution.

Lichfield [12] The three spires of Lichfield Cathedral are unique in England. They stand out prominently, and beckon the traveller approaching the city, from whatever direction he may come. Across the flat lands of the Trent Valley, soon after Burton the silhouette of the spires comes in sight. From the high ground of Cannock Chase the city seems to lie far away, hazy per-

haps; but the spires are distinct. Across the gently rising ground S of the city, the tops of the tapering spires rise above the low hills and spreading suburbs; descending into St John Street their full glory is comprehended, dominating, serene.

The importance of Lichfield is that it is the mother church of the Midlands—not just of Staffordshire. Ever since the time of St Chad, who died in 672, this has been a holy place. In 700 the first cathedral was built—the cathedral of all Mercia—and the body of the saint buried here. Lichfield became a place of pilgrimage, and for a brief time in the 9c an archbishopric.

The best way to see Lichfield is to turn off Ryknield Street, past the Trent Valley Station (Main Line), and stop at St Michael's church. St Michael's has a tall Perp spire, and its core is EE, but it was much rebuilt in 1842 by the local architect Thomas Johnson; Samuel Johnson's parents and brother are buried here. However, the great thing is to stand here in the sloping churchyard, and enjoy the view of the cathedral and the town. This is the third cathedral to occupy the

site: first came the little shrine church of 700; then between 1135 and 1140 Bishop Roger de Clinton built a larger, Norman cathedral, with nave, short choir and apse. A century later the present cathedral was rising; about 1330 the great apse at the E end was built, and the cathedral we now see completed. At the E end of Stowe Pool stands another church, St Chad's. This is not quite visible from St Michael's, but must be mentioned here. For it was there that St Chad had his hermitage—Stowe means 'hermitage' or 'holy place'—and St Chad's well is there. It is at St Chad's that the history of Lichfield begins.

Drive on into the city: it will perhaps be possible to leave a car near the City Station, and then proceed on foot. Walk N up St John Street. On the left stands St John's Hospital, with its eight chimney breasts facing the street; founded by Roger de Clinton, it was refounded by Bishop Smyth (who also founded Brasenose College) in 1495. Inside the gateway is a quiet little quadrangle, the W side by Louis de Soissons (1966), the N side the chapel, with its devout, beautiful interior. The services here may be attended by the public. St John

The Bishop's Palace, **Lichfield**

Street becomes Bird Street, and Bird Street Beacon Street, and up this long thoroughfare the delights of Lichfield as a Georgian town may be savoured. Among 18c houses must be mentioned the George Hotel, with its magnificent ballroom on the first floor, the Swan Hotel opposite, and West Gate House and the Angel Croft Hotel, both with good iron gates and railings. Opposite stand Erasmus Darwin's house with its Venetian windows, and the street front of the principal house in Vicar's Close, which can be admired again from the other side.

But before ascending so far, turn right at the Minster Pool and walk along the S bank, enjoying the view of the long S side of the cathedral above the garden fronts of the houses in the Close. Crossing Dam Street it is possible to continue the walk along Stowe Pool to St Chad's. St Chad's is a charming medieval church, with an 18c Gothic clerestory to the nave, and simple plaster vaulted roof. To the E stands Stowe House, and behind

Charles II: originally on the west front now against south transept

that Stowe Hill, grand 18c brick mansions, the latter somewhat submerged by recent bungalows. In the cottage garden to the W is St Chad's Well. Returning, the gorgeous view of the E end of the cathedral is a special treat. Back in Beacon Street, notice the Victorian public library, before climbing the gentle slope to the Close.

The approach to the cathedral is perfect. On the right of the narrow street is the long stone front of Newton's College (1800 by Joseph Potter senior), the centre bays rusticated at the base, and pedimented; on the left a medley of brick and stone and timbered houses, with steep steps and railings to their front doors; ahead the W front of the cathedral.

The W front is the cathedral's most spectacular architectural feature. This great façade, built in rich red sandstone, is adorned with a wealth of statues and arcading, of trefoils, quatrefoils, cinquefoils; at the centre a geometrical window, at the base three sumptuously carved porches. The W towers themselves

Entrance to The Close

Guildhall

p120 West front
p121 Lady Chapel & Choir *(top)*▷
Choir & Chapter House *(bottom)*

l to r Boswell, Johnson and Johnson's house

Across Minster Pool

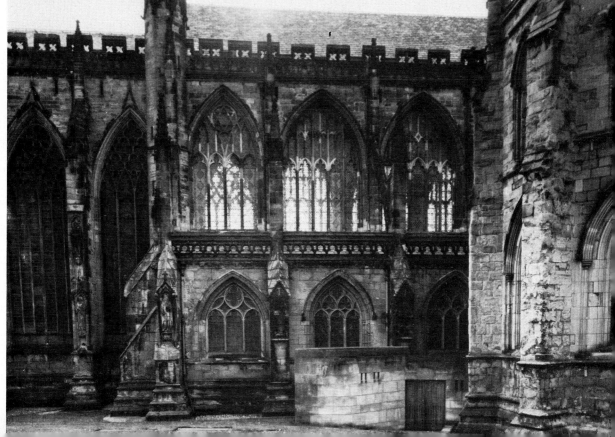

form part of the façade, and carry on the scheme albeit less elaborately, round the N and S sides. The spires themselves rise in a great cluster of pinnacles and crockets, to be capped by elegant gilded 18c weather vanes. The W front was completed c. 1300.

The beauty of the interior consists in its delicate feminine grace; the nave was built in the second half of the 13c, when the simplicity of the EE style blossomed in the richly cultivated perfection of the Dec. The clustered columns are adorned with foliated capitals, the spandrels of the arches decorated with cinquefoils divided by the long shaft of the vault; the triforium is richly ornamented with stiff-leaf capitals and dogtooth, and the clerestory lighted by unusual windows of spherical-triangular shape, filled with geometrical tracery. Stand at the W end and enjoy the remarkable vista to the great windows of the E apse, and the even rhythm of the nave and chancel vaulting: this is Dec architecture at its most exquisite, and Gilbert Scott and his son Oldrid knew what they were doing when they undertook the restoration of the cathedral, which began in 1857.

The crossing is adorned by the magnificent Victorian pulpit of brass and iron, with its double staircase; and even more by the chancel screen. Both were designed by Gilbert Scott, and executed by Skidmore (1859). The screen is a High Victorian masterpiece, delicate, transparent, ornamental, and now that it has been cleaned it has come fully into its own. Alas for Salisbury! Alas for Hereford! Since they have destroyed their Skidmore screens, this at Lichfield will be increasingly admired.

The S transept was built about 1230, though the great window is a Perp insertion. Here are massed the colours of the Staffordshire regiments, and St Michael's is the regimental chapel; both here and in the N transept is a delightful collection

of 18c marble tablets, all recently cleaned and regilded to great effect. They reflect the taste and elegance of 18c Lichfield, when the cathedral dignitaries and local gentry enjoyed each other's company in the perfect setting of Close and city.

The three W bays of the chancel represent the earliest portion of the present cathedral (c. 1200), though they were later skilfully blended into the five later bays of presbytery and retrochoir. The chancel with its Gilbert Scott reredos, Gilbert Scott stalls, Gilbert Scott screen, comfortable and opulent, seems the Victorian setting *par excellence*. The arcades are low, the clerestory windows lofty, and some of them 17c Perp insertions of Bishop Hacket's restoration after the Civil War. There is no triforium proper: below the windows is a galleried walk with embattled parapet, the splays of the windows patterned with a beautiful relief of quatrefoils.

The Lady Chapel was begun about 1320, and its costs defrayed by funds left by Bishop Walter de Langton. It is the great glory of Lichfield. Nine great windows of trefoil tracery fill the entire upper space above the panelled and canopied arcading of the lower wall; and there is an impressive late-19c Oberammergau triptych altarpiece. Seven of these nine windows are filled with 16c Flemish glass from Herekenrode Abbey near Liège. They were bought by Sir Brooke Boothby of Ashbourne at the sale of the dissolved abbey: even on the dullest day the splendour and glow of the glass fills the E end of the cathedral with colour. The glass in the two W windows of the apse is also Flemish, of later date, but their exact provenance is unknown.

On the N side of the chancel a vestibule leads to the Chapter House (c. 1240). There is richly carved arcading in the vestibule; the Chapter House is octagonal, and the vaulted roof springs from a central clustered column. There is

a further vaulted chamber over the Chapter House, which serves as the Library. On the S side of the chancel is the Consistory Court (c. 1220), with the Chapel of St Chad's Head above it.

In addition to the monuments already mentioned, there are others which should be specially noted. First, the busts of Samuel Johnson and David Garrick in the S transept: both are of 1793, and both by Westmacott. Garrick, whose death 'eclipsed the gaiety of nations', was Johnson's first pupil at Edial. Hard by is the Egyptian-style cenotaph of black and white marble to the 80th Regiment of Foot, by Hollins (1846—'dum jacent clamant'.) In the N chancel aisle are the kneeling figure of Bishop Ryder (1836) by Chantrey, the bronze bust of Bishop Woods (1953) by Epstein, and the recumbent figure of Bishop Lonsdale (1867) by G. F. Watts. In the S chancel aisle is Chantrey's celebrated monument of the sleeping children (1814)—the two daughters of Canon Robinson; close to them the recumbent effigy of Bishop Hacket (1670) who was responsible for the restoration of the cathedral after the Civil War. In the small chantry off the S side of the Lady Chapel is the tomb of Bishop Selwyn (1878); the effigy is by Nicholls, the tiles by de Morgan. In the S aisle of the nave is the monument to Dean Addison, Joseph Addison's father; close to the NW door the tablet to Lady Mary Wortley Montagu, by Scheemakers.

There is much decent Victorian glass in the cathedral—by Kempe (N and S choir aisle, and Chapel of St Chad's Head), by Clayton and Bell (W window), by Burlison and Grylls (N and S nave aisles) and Ward and Hughes (S nave aisle).

It is a pleasure to wander round the Close, not only to gaze upon the exterior of the cathedral, but also to admire the houses in the Close. In the SW corner are two houses with Gothick features; tucked behind the NW corner is Vicars' Close, a small

William Morris glass at **Madeley**: figures by Madox Brown, Morris and Burne-Jones

was finally captured by the Round-heads, and terrible damage inflicted on the cathedral. The central spire fell, to be rebuilt by Bishop Hacket; it was the damage in the Civil War that led to the inevitable restoration in the 18c by Wyatt, and in the 19c by Scott.

Dam Street is an unspoiled Georgian street, and leads into the Market Place. Here stands St Mary's church (rebuilt by James Fowler of Louth, 1868, the spire by Street, 1852). In its shadow, at the corner of Market Street, is Johnson's birthplace, an imposing plastered house (of late-17 or very early-18c date), with recessed ground floor, and steps beneath Tuscan pillars to the front door. Here Michael Johnson the bookseller came in 1707, the year after his marriage; and here Samuel was born in 1709. The large downstairs room was the bookshop; the house is now an admirable Johnson Museum. Opposite the front door stands the monument to the doctor (by R. C. Lucas, 1838): a few yards away is the bronze figure of Boswell (by Percy Fitzgerald, 1908).

The Market Place leads into Bore Street. Here is an early-16c timber house (the Tudor Café); next to it Donegal House, a distinguished early-18c town house, once the town house of the Donegals (of Fisherwick), now part of the Guildhall. The Gothic Hall of 1846 adjoins. A short step leads back into St John Street, and so back to the City Station.

There is not a great deal to see on the W side of the main thoroughfare. The R.C. church of Holy Cross is at the upper end of St John Street, and is early-19c Gothic. In Friary, incorporated in the Friary School (1921–8) is a fragment of the medieval Friary; and at the W end of the street is the Clock Tower, built by Joseph Potter junior in 1863, in the Norman style! In Lemansley (NW) is Christ Church, a church of 1847 by Thomas Johnson. The chief object of interest here

quadrangle of timber-framed houses, with the mid-18c house, whose outside front looks on to Beacon Street. The Deanery is an elegant brick house of 1704, of two storeys with central pediment and sash windows; next door the splendid Bishop's Palace. Built in 1687, and designed by Edward Pierce, one of Wren's masons, it is the perfect 17c house, built of stone, with hipped roof, and cartouche and garlands in the pediment. At the E end of the cathedral stands solitary 18c Selwyn House, with its grand view over Stowe Pool. The house at the SE corner is built on to the medieval wall which once sur-

rounded the Close and was destroyed after the siege of the Civil War.

Here a gate leads into Dam Street and back into the centre of the town. It was here that Lord Brooke, the Parliamentarian general, was standing on 2 March (St Chad's Day), 1643, at the height of the siege, when he was shot dead by a bullet fired by 'dumb Dyott' (the son or nephew of Sir Richard Dyott, the Royalist commander) who had posted himself on the central tower of the cathedral. A tablet on Brooke House records the spot: Dyott's gun remains in the possession of his family. Lichfield is the tomb of Samuel Lipscomb Seckam, the creator of Park Town, Oxford. Seckham afterwards lived at Whittington Hall (q.v.). The tomb is easily missed: it is outside the N transept, in a recess in the E wall. He was one of the founders of the church.

Longdon [11] There are agreeable houses prettily set around the green, to the W of the main road from Lichfield to Rugeley: the church is on the high road and the rest of the village to the E. The church has a Norman nave (with curious 19c roof), Norman S door, and Norman chancel arch, Victorian N transept, Perp S chantry chapel built by John Stoneywell, abbot of Pershore and native of Longdon. Monument by Edward Stanton to Thomas Orme of Hanch Hall (1716); fragments of medieval glass.

Hanch Hall, a mile to the E, has a grand early-18c S front with pediment, facing the meadow; from the road only the large Victorian additions are visible. The lane from Longdon Green passes Lysways Hall, an 18c house now cut in two by the demolition of its centre.

A lane to the SW leads up to Beaudesert, in a high position on Cannock Chase. Here medieval bishops of Lichfield had a palace, but in 1546 the place was acquired by Sir William Paget, Secretary of State to Henry VIII, afterwards 1st Lord Paget of Beaudesert (d. 1568). A great Tudor mansion was built on to the episcopal manor house; his successors became Earls of Uxbridge and Marquises of Anglesey, of whom the most celebrated was the 1st Marquis who lost a leg at Waterloo: ('Good God, Paget, your leg's blown off,' said the Duke of Wellington. 'I'm damned if it isn't,' Paget replied.) Beaudesert was abandoned for Plas Newydd in Anglesey in 1932, and the great house demolished. The upper park and walled gardens became a camping ground for the Scouts, but

Marchington

down an overgrown drive it is possible to discover on the exposed hillside facing Longdon the site of the great house, and a fragment of the medieval Great Hall of the bishops. On the lane, at the foot of the hill, stands the Grand Lodge, an early-19c turreted red-brick building, now converted into a house.

Longnor [3] A miniature market town in farthermost, northernmost Staffordshire. A square with small Market Hall of 1873, two or three inns, the Crewe and Harpur Arms with its attractive 18c façade, and stone-built streets and alleys leading off into nothing—except to

views, and the gorgeous Peakland countryside all round. Up such an alley is the Georgian church (1780), Classical—but the W tower pinnacled and Gothick. The interior is disappointing, as the upper windows have been sealed off by a shapeless later ceiling, and the galleries removed. Venetian E window. Norman font.

Longsdon [5] The road from Leek climbs to the SW through suburban houses and gardens: looking back there are splendid views across the town with its church towers and chimneys, to the wild moorland country beyond. Longsdon church is a distinguished building of 1903 by Gerald Horsley: imposing W tower crowned by low broach spire, light airy interior, Comper E window. Spacious layout, with hall and vicarage in the church garden.

Madeley [4] The main-line train to Scotland rushes through the village: it is now electrified, but in the days of steam this was one of the speed tracks on the way N. Here in the summer of 1937 the new streamlined L.M.S. 'Coronation Scot' just managed, on its first run, to beat the record put up by the L.N.E.R. 'Coronation' on the East Coast route—but not without a good deal of the lunch being scattered across the dining car.

Three hundred years earlier Madeley was the home of John Offley, friend of Izaak Walton: it is to him that the *Compleat Angler* is dedicated. His black and white manor house, engraved by Dr Plot, has disappeared, but the Old Hall in the village street is a good timbered house of 1647, bearing the cryptic inscription 'Walk knave: what lookest at?'

Large church. EE nave, Perp transepts, Victorian chancel—'this chancel was rebuilt by Hungerford Lord Crewe 1872' reads the inscription in the tiled floor. The Crewes, who held the manor until this century, were descendants of the Offleys. The interior is dark with Victorian glass—by Clayton and Bell, Kempe and Morris; the Morris window (W window of S aisle) is of real beauty. Egerton tomb (N transept) 1522, and Egerton brasses and 18c monuments in S transept. Hidden in the vestry is the imposing marble pedestal monument surmounted by an urn to John Offley (1658). 17c W gallery.

To the NW beyond the village pond is a sprawl of council houses to serve the local colliery. On a wooded outcrop of the rocky hills to the N stand the scanty ruins of Heighley Castle, largely over-

grown. Held by the Audley family (*see* Audley *and* Mucklestone) in the Middle Ages, and later by the Gerards, it was demolished after the Civil War.

At *Wrinehill*, on the road to Betley, is a tall early-18c brick house called the Summer House. The grand façade has pilasters and a mutilated pediment. It was an occasional *pied-à-terre* of the Egertons, for whom James Wyatt built the grand Heaton Hall, Lancashire—now owned by the Corporation of Manchester.

Maer [7] The beautiful valley, with park and lake, leads to the tall, gabled Jacobean Hall behind its high wall, with the church perched above on the opposite side of the road; to a high, pedimented, 18c gateway to the Hall stables, and so to the little village. The sequence is dramatic.

The Hall was built by the Bowyer family, passed into the hands of Josiah Wedgwood II, and then to the Harrisons, a Liverpool shipping family—who built great 19c additions. These have recently been pulled down.

The little church has an early-17c Gothic tower; the rest is medieval, Victorianised. Raised chancel. Tomb in sanctuary of Sir John Bowyer (1604). Two modern windows by Shrigley and Hunt.

Marchington [9] On the N fringe of Needwood Forest: hilly, wooded country to the S. Village of deep lanes, some good small houses, and Marchington Hall, a distinguished late-17c brick house. The façade is of two lofty gables, joined by stone balustrading, with stone mullioned windows and central doorway.

The church is of 1742, by Richard Trubshaw. The exterior is wholly delightful: warm red brick, W tower with octagonal top crowned by a small dome. Unfortunately, in 1892, the interior was robbed of its gallery and contemporary ceiling, the box pews

and three-decker cut down, and a Gothic chancel added. Dignified altar, however, in Arts and Crafts manner. Tomb, with incised figures, of Walter Vernon and his wife, of Houndhill, 1592.

Marchington Woodlands [9] Dramatic and beautiful country, where the high lands of Needwood descend to the valley of the Dove: the hill from Bagot's Park is here 1 in 5. The church is on higher ground opposite, and looks across to the Victorian Smallwood Manor, now the prep school for Denstone. The church is singular and ornate: tall spire with pinnacles and strange flying buttresses; richly decorated interior with elaborate arcades into N and S chancel chapels. The architect was A. D. Gough of London.

Marston [8] A hamlet between the Trent and the A34 S of Stone. Endearing, modest little church of 1794, with stone nave and red-brick chancel, and few architectural details.

Mayfield [6] The first village in Staffordshire across the Hanging Bridge from Ashbourne. The Mills on the river Dove here, with terraces of Victorian workers' houses, make this part of the village towny: further to the S is the church in rural setting. Tower dated 1515, with inscription and French motto. Norman nave. Dec chancel (with Gothick crenellation). 17c benches and pulpit. To the W at Middle Mayfield stands the late-Georgian Hall. Grand stables with domed stone cupola, which bears a distinct family likeness to Mapleton church, across the Dove in Derbyshire. The Old Hall nearby is a gabled house of the early 17c.

Meerbrook [2] The spectacular road from Buxton to Leek passes the Roaches, those dark millstone-grit rocks which rise to 1,500 ft, fantastic in outline and forbidding in

The Roaches (Meerbrook)▷

appearance. A lane to the W follows the path of the Churnet to Tittesworth reservoir and the little village of Meerbrook. Views across reservoir. Norman Shaw church (1869), with squat central tower, and interior distinguished for its ironwork and woodwork, and those touches of originality which one associates with Norman Shaw. Even the beautifully fitted vestry, with its low side window, displays sensible domestic details typical of Shaw. The lane leads on to Swythamley and the Cheshire border.

Milwich [8] The B road from Uttoxeter to Stone runs through the village, but this is deep, undulating, mysterious countryside, with the Milwich brook watering the valley. There is a slightly decayed black and white gabled Hall, now a farm, half hidden in a dell; and the church on higher ground down a rustic track. This has a Perp tower with richly decorated parapet, and the rest is in purple brick of 1792 with plain Gothic features. Victorian Gothic vicarage next door.

Moddershall [8] Well-wooded moorland country between Longton and Stone. Up a lane past the pond and opposite the Boar Inn stands a little church of considerable originality—built in 1903 by the Wedgwood family in the Arts and Crafts manner. The fittings are all contemporary and excellent—such as the lead tub font—and altogether it is a little building of some charm. The architect seems unknown.

Moreton [10] Scattered village on the Shropshire border. The little Norman church of 1837 by Thomas Trubshaw looks down the hillside to the brook that divides the counties.

Moseley Old Hall [14] An unattractive casing of Victorian brick disguises a timber-framed manor house built in 1600 by Henry Pitt of Bushbury (near by)—whose daughter married Thomas Whitgreave. It was his son, another Thomas Whitgreave, who with his mother sheltered Charles II here for two days and a night after the Battle of Worcester in September 1651. The story is well known, and the details, as dictated to Samuel Pepys, have been described by the King himself. The house, therefore, is one of great romance, and a place of pilgrimage.

Thomas Whitgreave was a Roman Catholic, and his chaplain was Fr Huddleston. It was from these upper windows that he and his pupils—three boys who lived in the house, two being nephews of Whitgreave—kept watch. It was in the window over the porch that Charles sat, and watched soldiers from his defeated army pass by.

The interior of the house is remarkably unchanged—sympathetically restored when it passed into the hands of the National Trust after the Second World War. The Hall is heavily timbered: a spacious staircase of *c.* 1630 leads up to the King's Room, and Mr Whitgreave's study. The former contains the bed in which the King slept, marvellously preserved in the house till 1935, when it was sold. It was later returned to the house by Sir Geoffrey and Lady Mander of Wightwick. To the right of the fireplace here is the entrance to the hiding-place, cleverly concealed under a trap-door in the floor. At the top of the house is the Oratory where the King spent some time the following evening, before setting out with Jane Lane on his long journey that eventually took him to Brighton and to France.

Sir Arthur Bryant, in his *Life of Charles II*, has written how at the end of his life, as he lay dying, the King's mind went back 'across the starlit meadows towards Moseley, where in a plain upper chamber two candles burnt before an ancient and secret altar'. It was Fr Huddleston who at this moment came to administer to him the last rites of the Church.

To the S of the house the National Trust has laid out in the garden a parterre and arbour of great charm. And, even encased in brick, the silhouette of the gables and the ancient chimneys is an unforgettable sight to the departing traveller.

Mow Cop [4] The great rocky hill, nearly 1,100 ft high, stands on the very frontier of the county: here the wild moorland of Staffordshire descends to the green pastureland of Cheshire. There is a straggling village, with a barnlike Gothic church of 1841, just in Staffordshire: across the border is a ruined castle folly, built in 1754 by the Wilbraham family of Rode Hall as an eye-catcher. Mow Cop (pronounced to rhyme with 'cow') is the birthplace of Primitive Methodism. Here in 1807 Hugh Bourne, a carpenter of Stoke, held a great camp meeting, from which stemmed the Primitive Methodists, with a membership of 100,000, and 5,000 chapels. They were reunited with the Methodists in 1932. Mow Cop is now the property of the National Trust; sometimes the hilltop is embowered in thick cloud: at others there is an astonishing view across the Cheshire Plain.

Mucklestone [7] The most westerly parish in the county: Shropshire embraces it to the N and to the W. The Battle of Blore Heath, the second battle of the Wars of the Roses, took place a mile or two to the S on 23 September 1459. Queen Margaret, wife of Henry VI, watched the defeat of the Lancastrian forces under Lord Audley—according to tradition—from the church tower. Lord Audley of Heighley Castle, a few miles to the N, was slain, and is commemorated by Audley's Cross, a medieval cross on an 18c base, which stands in a field close by the A53, near the Hempmill Brook.

Mucklestone church is the rebuilding by Charles Lynam (1883) of an 18c building, of which old photographs hang in the church. Medieval tower. Correct, well-furnished interior, with much Kempe glass. 18c and later monuments to the Chetwode family of Oakley in the NE chapel.

Oakley Hall, on the banks of the river Tern, which divides the counties, is a house of 1710, built for Sir John Chetwode, 1st Bt. It has a long ornamental E façade of brick, with stone centrepiece and stone dressings, urns, quoins, balustrade, Corinthian pilasters and highly decorated pediment adorned with carved swags and garlands. It was the home of the Chetwode baronets (also of Chetwode, Bucks); the 7th baronet became Field Marshal Lord Chetwode. In recent years it has changed hands once or twice.

Not far from the gates of Oakley, on the B5415 and against a great wood, stands an entertaining folly: a large brick barn, with an 18c tower like a church. Alas, it is in poor repair.

Newborough [9] Crossroads village in Needwood Forest. The church was rebuilt by Oldrid Scott, and consecrated in 1901. Lofty nave and chancel. But the memorable feature is the tall, slender, octagonal tower, which with its tapering spire rises needle-like 120 ft above this pleasant valley.

Newcastle-under-Lyme [4] The first thing to remember about Newcastle is that it is not one of the Potteries: it is much older as a borough (incorporated in 1180—when the Pottery towns were only villages), and returned two members to Parliament as early as 1335. Little is to be seen of the New Castle (the old castle was at Chesterton, former

Newborough

Roman fort, and now a suburb), except for the mound in Queen Elizabeth Garden, and the fragment of wall in John of Gaunt's Road. The 'Lyme' of the town's name is the great forest of Lyme, which in medieval times covered much of Cheshire and NW Staffordshire.

Even though the country is entirely built up between here and Stoke, it will at once be appreciated that Newcastle has an individuality and character all its own. Drive up the London Road into the town, and walk up the High Street: you will at once feel that you are in a country town, with its red-brick Guildhall prominent in the middle of the street—as at Reigate or Amersham. This was erected in 1713, and its ground floor was originally open: it was extended in 1860 at the N end, and the portico and clock tower added at the S. There are many decent Georgian façades above the shop fronts: notice the former Castle Hotel, and the timbered houses (nos. 14–16). Turn left into Church Street, and the great 13c tower of the parish church looms ahead. The present church is a rebuilding (1873–6) by Sir Gilbert Scott: stately, correct and a little lifeless. Inside, dark Victorian glass, but a pelican lectern of 1733, and an 18c font and cover. The present building replaced a brick church of 1730, which in turn replaced the medieval one. Behind the church is a Unitarian Chapel of 1717, and from the high ground here there is a wide view of the modern town, with its factories and suburbs and near-by collieries.

Return to the High Street, and walk up Ironmarket (the name is a reminder that the town was a centre of iron-making in the Middle Ages): here again are decent Georgian façades above the shops. Nelson Place contains a pleasing Regency terrace; Queen Street (half left) leads to St George's (of 1828, a Commissioners' church) with its tall Perp

tower. Opposite is a good Georgian house (no. 6), with a handsome doorway. The street leads into the road called Brampton, where there are some attractive Regency and early Victorian villas in big gardens. To the S (in Victoria Road) is St Paul's, a large church of 1905 by Richard Scrivener, with its graceful spire on an octagonal base rising from a lofty tower.

Back in London Road, and you will find the R.C. church, a remarkable building of 1833 designed by its parish priest, the Revd James Egan. The splendid Gothic façade borders the street: reminiscent of a medieval Gothic church in Italy, tier upon tier of little Gothic arches rise in multi-coloured brick to an embattled flat parapet, the corners of nave and aisles punctuated by square pinnacles, with three large ogee-topped windows filled with cast-iron tracery painted dark green. It is a rich, colourful exterior—leading to a rich, luminous interior.

One more church should be mentioned: on the A53 N of the town is the large brick church of St Michael, built in 1938 by Austin and Paley, in the latest phase of 1930s Gothic, a handsome and stately building, one of the last works of that distinguished partnership.

At *Basford* to the E is a smaller church of 1914, by Austin and Paley, in their distinctive and scholarly Gothic—with a sympathetic W end added in 1969.

Chesterton to the N is an old village engulfed in dreary Victorian houses and terraces. The church is of 1852, by Ward of Hanley, with S spire and conventional Victorian details. The name suggests a Roman station: it is supposed to be Mediolanum, and the fort occupied a flat-topped hill, on which a castle was built after the Conquest, the predecessor of the New Castle.

Knutton to the NW is curiously named, and apparently means 'Canute's Town', the property of

King Canute. The village grew on iron and coal in the 19c. The church is a Gothic building of 1872 (by T. Lewis and Son), of simple blackened outline: it has even lost its bellcote.

Wolstanton to the NE is in a commanding position overlooking Stoke, an old village overtaken by industry. Approaching from Newcastle there is a wide green with a few older houses; Moreton House, dated 1743, is a good brick building. At Bradwell to the N is a fragment of the original home of the Sneyd family.

The church was rebuilt in 1860 by the local architects Ward and Son; the chancel by Salvin, fresh from his work at Keele. The chief interest of the church is the Sneyd monuments—most notably the canopied altar tomb of Sir William (1571), with recumbent effigies of himself and his wife. There are other 17 and 18c tablets. (*See also* Keele.)

Newchapel [5] High moorland: rows of drab houses lead to the church in an exposed position with wide views across the half-industrial countryside N of Stoke. This is a red-brick Victorian building (1878 by Lewis and Son of Newcastle) with bellcote. In the SE corner of the large churchyard is the grave of James Brindley (d. 1772) with long inscription recording his principal works.

Newchurch [12] Close to the main road (A515) in the middle of Needwood Forest, where it intersects with the minor road from Hoar Cross to Burton, stands an early-19c brick church. Christ Church-on-Needwood was built in 1809, at the time of the enclosure of the forest, for the use of the disafforested parishioners. It has a W tower, and is a simple barnlike structure of some charm, with short chancel or sanctuary. Royal Arms of George III in plaster over W door. Hatchments. Monuments to

Newtown

the Bass family. One stained glass window on the S side shows Byrkley Lodge, the Victorian Bass mansion in the parish, demolished since the Second World War. Forest scenery. No village.

Newtown [2] Lonely village in the High Peak. Solid barnlike church of 1837, with Classical windows, Gothick pinnacles and battlemented bellcote, in fine position overlooking moorland. Little Methodist chapel of 1821; Georgian façade, sundial and text: 'A LIFE IN FLIGHT'S SOON OUT OF SIGHT'.

Norbury [10] Well-wooded, undulating country close to Shrop-

shire. Small village of farms and cottages, dominated by the Georgian Gothick brick tower of the church, which is surrounded by a little park. The church itself, with wide, aisleless nave and long chancel, is an exceptionally fine 14c Dec building. Sanctuary with sedilia and piscina. Jacobean altar rails. Early-17c pulpit. 18c font. Many monuments, including late-14c brass to Lady Hawys Botiller; the effigy of a cross-legged knight, Ralph Botiller; and large marble wall monument to Sir Charles Skrymsher (1708). A floor slab to Rupert Skrymsher records the fact that his father was Adjutant General to Prince Rupert.

A mile SE is Norbury Junction—not a railway station, but the junction between the Shrewsbury and the Liverpool and Birmingham sections of the Shropshire Union Canal.

Norton Canes [11] (or Norton-under-Cannock) The tower of the church is a prominent landmark to travellers along the A5. The village stands on rising ground, and there are views over local collieries, and across to the white tower blocks of Walsall. The church was built in 1832 by Thomas Johnson, and rebuilt after a fire in 1888: blackened stone, and very red tiled roof. Tablets to the Fowke and Hussey

131

families of Little Wyrley, including marble monument by B. T. Evans of Longton, with mourning figure, to Phineas Hussey, 1833.

A mile or two to the S stands Little Wyrley Hall, a house with a Tudor core, encased in brick and enlarged in the 17c. The house is L-shaped, with shapely gables and dormers which give it its special charm. From Elizabethan times it has belonged to the Fowke and Hussey families and their descendants. Little Wyrley has long been an oasis among surrounding collieries: now the coal workings are becoming extinct, and the old slag heaps covered with grass. The house has survived all.

Norton-in-the-Moors [5] Blackened, overgrown village to the E of Tunstall. The church looks down from its hilltop upon the desolate scene below, where bulldozers are flattening out the old pits and slag heaps between here and Tunstall. Brick church of 1737, by Richard Trubshaw, with W tower and interior of square piers, low arches and flat plaster ceilings. In 1914, J. H. Beckett made a successful addition of chancel and transepts to the original nave, continuing the rhythm of low arches and flat plaster vaults, creating thereby an impressive vista-ed interior. The Adderley family take their title from here (*see* Hanbury): Sir Charles Adderley, Victorian Cabinet Minister and statesman, was for many years M.P. for North Staffordshire.

Oakamoor [5] A village in the spectacular scenery of the Churnet Valley. The Churnet Valley Railway ran here on its way from Leek to Uttoxeter: an endearing little station building survives. There are 19c villas, and copper works established by the Patten and Bolton families in the 18c. The church, 'a neat chapel of ease', was built by J. W. Pritchett of York in 1832—like a Perp chapel, with W tower.

On the other side of the valley is a Free Church—the Bolton Memorial Church—built in 1878; architect, Edward Clarke of London.

Oaken [13] Wolverhampton suddenly ends here: there are green fields and thick plantations, and several good houses like Greenhills, with its restrained mid-Victorian Tudor gables, its walled garden and its peacocks. On the main road to Shifnal are the gates to Wrottesley, from 1164 to 1963 the home of the Wrottesley family. Like Wolseley of Wolseley, and Okeover of Okeover (q.v.) here was a family who took their name from the land on which they dwelt: the manor passed in direct male succession for twenty-three generations. The family played a leading part in early Staffordshire history; Sir Hugh Wrottesley fought in the Black Prince's retinue at Crécy, Sir Walter was appointed Governor of Calais by Warwick the Kingmaker. The family were Royalist in the Civil War, and obtained a baronetcy in 1642, and a barony in 1838. It is therefore melancholy to record that on the death of the 4th Lord Wrottesley in 1963 the whole estate was sold. Wrottesley Hall, a three-storeyed brick mansion of 1696, with projecting wings and central pediment, was gutted by fire in 1897. The walls survived, and the house was rebuilt in the 1920s as a two-storeyed central block, with pediment—with the projecting wings of only one storey; a sensible and indeed attractive solution to the problem of an over-large house in the 20c. The house stands on higher ground in its park, commanding a wide view over this pleasant Staffordshire–Shropshire border country. The great cartouche of the Wrottesley arms in the pediment, with its luxuriant garlands, keeps the name alive.

Okeover [6] Close to the Derbyshire frontier: the river Dove here divides the counties, and on the Staffordshire side the old oaks of Okeover Park climb the gentle hills. Here is the ancient demesne of the Okeover family, who enjoyed the remarkable distinction of holding this property in direct male descent for over 800 years. On the death in 1955 of Mr Haughton Ealdred Okeover, the last representative in the male line, *The Times* accorded him a leading article entitled 'A fallen tree': 'More than an announcement of five austere lines ... is required to take sorrowful leave of one of the dozen or so oldest families in England. Okeover of Okeover is one of that tiny group, of which Tichbourne and Wrottesley are younger members, who have held from the 12th century till today the land from which they took their name, and have never lacked a male heir till now.' Fortunately, since that leader was written, Mr Okeover's nephew, Sir Ian Walker-Okeover, has succeeded to the property, so the family blood and name continue. Moreover in the last twenty years the house has seen a tremendous revival.

An engraving in Plot's *History of Staffordshire* (1686) shows the old timbered, moated house. In 1745 Leak Okeover began rebuilding the house, but his grand schemes were never completed. The E range and an imposing stable block were built; parts of the rest of this 18c house were subsequently demolished, and Victorian additions made hugger-mugger. But now, thanks to Mr Marshall Sisson, remodelling and rebuilding have taken place, and the house stands much as Leak Okeover intended it. There is excellent 18c plasterwork within, and a staircase by Bakewell. Ornate gates, with piers crowned by obelisks, lead across the park from the road; and there are two 18c garden buildings, the Temple of Pomona, and the Necessary House (or lavatory).

The church is hard by the E

132

front, a small aisleless Dec building, with Perp tower, restored by Scott in 1856. Brasses and monuments to the family, including marble tablet to Leak Okeover and his wife by Joseph Wilton (1765). Some medieval glass in the chancel; Victorian glass in the nave by Warrington.

Onecote [5]

Small Peakland village, surrounded by stone walls and wind-swept trees. Georgian church (1753) with tower. Well-furnished interior, with contemporary pulpit and pews. Venetian E window. Modern plain glass, with Victorian panels inserted: heads of patriarchs and prophets (including, oddly, Plutarch!). Enormous Commandments board at W end, with painted figures of Moses, Aaron and Joshua: 'J. Woolf pinxit. W. Brown sculpsit. 1755'.

The river Hamps comes down close to the village from the high moorland—on its way to Waterfall and Waterhouses; a high and lonely stretch of country is oddly named Lousybank.

Oulton [8]

St Mary's Abbey is a Benedictine convent of nuns, originally founded in Ghent in the 17c for young English ladies of Catholic families, but transferred to England in 1794. The core of the buildings is an early-19c brick house, but the chapel is of 1854 by E. W. Pugin, and has a lofty clerestory. The parish church is Victorian (of 1874) with bellcote. Oulton is close to Stone, and there is some suburban development.

Patshull [13]

The large and gloomy house stands in its park a few miles to the W of Wolverhampton, and is now a hospital. In fact it is of interesting architectural ancestry, having been built by James Gibbs for Sir John Astley, 2nd Bt, c. 1750. The approach is of some magnificence: a wide forecourt with pedimented gateways and an archway crowned with a cupola leads into another courtyard, and to the house itself. Walls and gatepiers and low wings build up in a dramatic, almost Vanbrughian, manner. But the house with its plate-glass windows seems forbidding: it was altered and enlarged by Burn for the 5th Earl of Dartmouth in the 1880s. The ground falls away on the S side, and there are terraces and stairways to the Victorianised gardens.

The church stands near by, embowered in trees, close to the lake. It was also built by James Gibbs for Sir John Astley (1743), but enlarged by the addition of a N aisle in 1874. Monuments to Sir John Astley (1532), and Sir Richard, the 1st Bt (1687). Two late-18c monuments to Lord Pigot (1795) and Sir Robert Pigot (1796)—Lord Pigot bought the place on the proceeds of the Pigot diamond; it was subsequently purchased by the 4th Earl of Dartmouth in the mid. 19c, and there are later monuments to that family. Against the N wall of the churchyard is an intriguing stone figure, perhaps of the Duke of Monmouth, which came from Sandwell Park, the former Dartmouth seat, now submerged by West Bromwich (q.v.).

Pattingham [13]

Pattingham and Patshull form what is almost a peninsula of Staffordshire, surrounded by Shropshire on three sides. The tall spire of Pattingham church is a handsome landmark: imposing villas set in spacious grounds border the road that leads from Tettenhall, but the village is still a village. The church is unusual in plan, and although much restored by Gilbert Scott in 1871 is of considerable architectural interest. The N arcade is Norman, the S is EE; EE chancel with lancets. The large tower was built into the W end of the nave in the 14c, so the interior is one of unexpected vistas, with Kempe glass, and reredos by Oldrid Scott. The spire was originally added by Gilbert Scott, but twenty years later his son Oldrid added the tall pinnacles and flying buttresses: a great success.

There are several good Georgian houses, the best being the vicarage, NE of the church.

Pelsall [14]

Large, spreading, suburbanised village to the N of Walsall: great wide greens give the place character. Red-brick church of Commissioners' type (1843), with later chancel and pinnacled tower. Victorian monuments; elaborate stone reredos (Ten Commandments) re-erected on nave wall.

Penkridge [11]

lies between the roar of the M6 motorway and the clatter of the main line railway to Stafford—yet remains an uneventful little town, surrounded by green meadows watered by the river Penk and the Staffs and Worcs Canal. The place is dominated by an unusually fine parish church, built of local red sandstone, which was until the Reformation one of six collegiate churches in Staffordshire, with a Dean and four Canons. Perp exterior, with W tower and S porch with parvise above. Lofty interior, with long clerestoried chancel, and clerestoried nave. EE arcades. Dec E window. Old woodwork incorporated in choir stalls and screens. Chancel screen of wrought iron, dated 1778, of Dutch workmanship.

In the S chancel aisle is a 15c alabaster slab to William and Katharine Winnesbury, whose daughter married Richard Littleton and is commemorated with her husband by a slab under an arch in the S nave aisle. The Staffordshire Littletons descend from a common ancestor with the Lytteltons of Worcestershire. Sir Thomas Littleton the judge, and author of Littleton's *Tenures*, was the son of a Devon squire, Thomas Westcote, but assumed the name and arms of his mother, Elizabeth Littleton of

The Littleton monument, **Penkridge**

There are various later monuments to the family, who lived originally at Pillaton (q.v.), two miles to the SE, and afterwards at Teddesley, two miles to the NE, where William Baker built a large brick mansion for them in the 18c. This was demolished after the Second World War: the Snetzler organ (1769) from the house is now in St Andrew-by-the-Wardrobe, in the City of London.

There are a number of good houses in the little town, such as the Old Deanery, to the N of the church, partly stone, partly timber, dating from the late 16c; and the White Hart, with its gabled, timbered front in the main street; there are Georgian houses too. Pride of place goes to the Littleton Arms, at the corner of the street leading to the church.

Two miles to the SW (across Cuttlestone Bridge, which spans the Penk) is the hamlet of *Congreve*—the cradle of the Congreve family. Here, on gently rising ground, stands a modest and attractive 17 or early-18c brick manor house, on the site of something older and grander. In the 14c the family acquired Stretton (q.v.) by marriage, where they built the distinguished early-18c house. The Congreves, a gifted family which produced William the playwright, and eminent soldiers, including, in this century, two V.C.s, sold Stretton in the 18c, but did not sell Congreve; subsequently they held Chartley, and the two V.C.s are commemorated at Stowe-by-Chartley (q.v.). Sir Geoffrey Congreve of Congreve, who was created a Baronet in honour of his father and brother, was killed after winning the D.S.O. in the Second World War, and is commemorated in Penkridge church.

Pensnett [14] Scarred industrial landscape between Dudley and Kingswinford; in a green and wooded oasis to the N of the main road stands an unexpectedly inter-

Frankley, Worcestershire—a very early case of a change of name—and was the father of Richard Littleton who married the Winnesbury heiress and brought the family here. There are two splendid late-16c tombs to Littletons in the chancel, and a very grand two-storeyed monument at the end of the N chancel aisle to two Sir Edwards:

Reader, 'twas thought enough
  upon ye tombe
Of that great captain th' enemy
  of Rome
To write no more but HERE LIES
  HANNIBAL.
Let this suffice thee then instead
  of all
Here lie two knights ye father and
  ye sonne
Sir Edward and Sir Edward
  Littleton.

The Commandments board, **Onecote** ▷

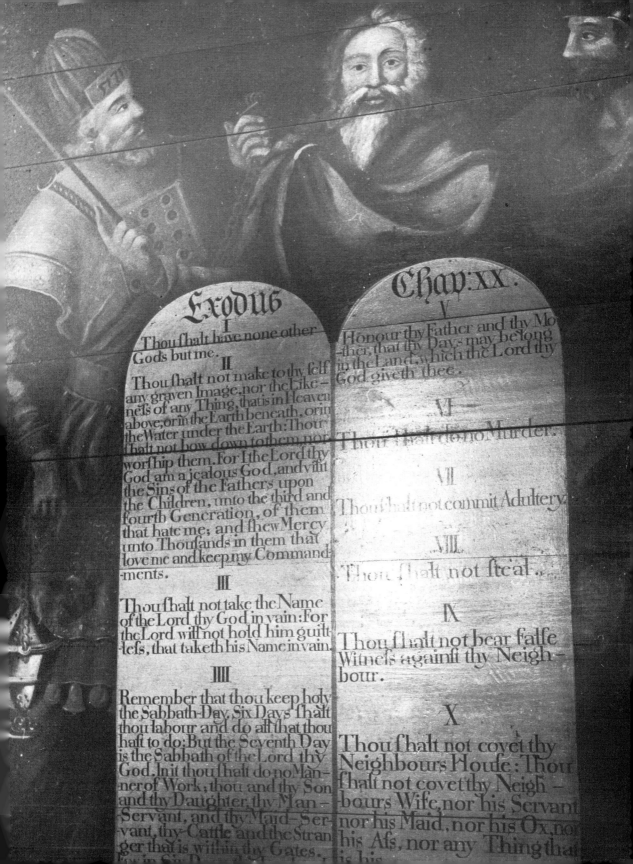

Exodus

I

Thou shalt have none other
Gods but me.

II

Thou shalt not make to thy self
any graven Image, nor the Likeness of any Thing, that is in Heaven
above, or in the Earth beneath, or in
the Water under the Earth: Thou
shalt not bow down to them, nor
worship them, for I the Lord thy
God am a jealous God, and visit
the Sins of the Fathers upon
the Children, unto the third and
fourth Generation, of them
that hate me; and shew Mercy
unto Thousands in them that
love me and keep my Command-
-ments.

III

Thou shalt not take the Name
of the Lord thy God in vain: For
the Lord will not hold him guilt-
-less, that taketh his Name in vain.

IIII

Remember that thou keep holy
the Sabbath-Day, Six Days shalt
thou labour and do all that thou
hast to do; But the Seventh Day
is the Sabbath of the Lord thy
God. In it thou shalt do no Man-
-ner of Work, thou and thy Son
and thy Daughter, thy Man-
Servant, and thy Maid-Ser-
vant, thy Cattle and the Stranger that is within thy Gates,

Chap: XX.

V

Honour thy Father and thy Mo-
-ther, that thy Days may be long
in the Land, which the Lord thy
God giveth thee.

VI

Thou shalt do no Murder.

VII

Thou shalt not commit Adultery.

VIII

Thou shalt not steal.

IX

Thou shalt not bear false
Witness against thy Neighbour.

X

Thou shalt not covet thy
Neighbours House: Thou
shalt not covet thy Neighbours Wife, nor his Servant
nor his Maid, nor his Ox, nor
his Ass, nor any Thing that

Pillaton Hall

esting Victorian church, with long lofty nave, lofty chancel, spacious aisles and transepts. It was designed by J. M. Derick, who built St Saviour's, Leeds, for Dr Pusey—and indeed the tall, narrow proportions here have something in common with the tall, narrow proportions of St Saviour's. The SW spire was never completed, but the interior is rich and rewarding.

Pillaton [11] Down a long farm drive, and across rough fields, stands Pillaton Hall, home of the Littletons (*see* Penkridge and Hatherton) from the 15c until 1740—when they built the new large mansion at Teddesley Hay. Pillaton is romantic and mouldering, but still the property of the family; indeed it is now (1976) being restored for family occupation, and will become once again the principal home of

the Littletons. Originally quadrangular, only the N front survives, with its Henry VIII Gateway Tower. To the W of this is a residential wing; to the E the little chapel of St Modwena, known to have been built by Richard and Alicia Littleton, whose tomb is in Penkridge church, *c.* 1480. This has always been maintained, and is beautifully furnished; there is a rare and lovely carved wooden statue of a saint (early-14c?). The Great Hall would no doubt have occupied the range opposite the Gate Tower, but of this and the E and W sides of the quadrangle there are only fragments standing, and the moat is overgrown and silted. But it is a remarkable and precious gem.

Rangemore [12] A Victorian village, where Needwood Forest

comes closest to Burton-on-Trent. Church, school, club, cottages all display the munificent hand of the Bass family. The small church with broach spire by Butterfield (1866) was enlarged by the later S aisle, and the chancel and sanctuary by Bodley. Many Bodley features: elaborate reredos and altar furnishings, choir stalls, screen and pulpit, painted roofs, marble flooring. The S aisle is of 1885, the chancel of 1895. Forest scenery: oaks, ferns, long straight roads.

Ranton [10] The little village is spoiled by an estate of smart villas of the 1970s. Even modern council houses need not spoil a village, if judiciously planned and sited; but these with their towny front gardens seem out of place in rustic little Ranton.

The small medieval church has

Hamstall Ridware

an 18c brick chancel, and an extra-ordinary Gothick screen at the W end. A mile to the W in a wooded private park are the remains of Ranton Abbey, an Augustinian house founded here in the 12c by Robert and Celestia Noel, of nearby Ellenhall. The first Earl of Lichfield built a shooting lodge here in 1820, but the 15c tower of the monastic church survives. It is visible in the trees from the road to Knightley.

Reaps Moor [2] Solitary hamlet S of Longnor. Close to the road is the church: half church, half school, a stone building of 1842.

The Ridwares [11 & 12] In the right angle formed by the river Blythe and the Trent are Hamstall Ridware, Pipe Ridware, Hill Ridware and Mavesyn Ridware. 'Ridware' appropriately means 'river folk'. Although the cooling-towers of Rugeley power station are only a few miles across the fields, this is rural England.

Hamstall Ridware is the most northerly: the village street climbs gently to church, manor house and rectory. To the E the meadows fall away to the river Blythe, where children bathe on summer days. The church is approached by a path across a field: to the left is the square red Georgian rectory; behind the church looms the gaunt ruined watch tower of the manor. The church is long and clerestoried. W spire with tower window at present oddly blocked with brick. Inside, nave and chancel under one roof; 14c arcades; fragments of 14c glass in S aisle (nine of the twelve apostles); 16c parclose screen (S aisle) and 17c screen (N aisle) with curious carvings; medieval painted panels depicting the life of Our

p 138 **14th-century glass,** ▷
Hamstall Ridware
p139 **Incised alabaster,**
Mavesyn Ridware

IOCOSA·FIL·THO:
CAWARDEN
ARM: ·VXOR
JOHIS CHADWICKE
ARM:
27 MAII 1594.

Mavesyn Ridware

Lord form the reredos; 16c altar tomb (chancel) and late-15c brass (S aisle) to Cotton family.

Behind the church stand the battered remains of the Elizabethan manor house, built by the Fitzherberts who came into the property by marriage with the Cottons. They are of brick with stone dressings, and comprise a quadrangle enclosed by a wall, entered on the N by an imposing gateway set between twin pepper pots; the tall watch tower; and a gabled wing of the house itself with fanciful stone balcony. What else remains is patched up to form a large farmhouse: runner beans and cabbages grow incongruously close to these grand remains, and hens run everywhere.

At *Pipe Ridware* is a little church of 1842, with simple bellcote and 'Norman' features. The interior is a surprise: a triple chancel arch leads into a later chancel by J. Oldrid Scott. An old photograph in the vestry shows the church as it

originally was. Two 18c tablets in chancel. Grand circular Norman font, adorned with pattern of interlacing bands. Variegated sycamore in churchyard. No village.

At *Hill Ridware* is a collection of houses and a pub; and a narrow lane, hard to find, leads down to Mavesyn Ridware.

Mavesyn Ridware, secluded and mysterious, is close to the Trent. There is not much village: the lane leads to the church and the Hall. The church is a curiosity: most of the medieval building, apart from the tower and N aisle, was pulled down in 1782. In its place was built a square preaching box. It is well worth getting the key from a local house: the interior is charming and unusual. The walls of the 'box' have, alas, been denuded of their plaster, but below the cornice is an elegant frieze of shields. The building hovers between Classical and Gothick. A few steps lead down to the medieval N aisle, where there is an array of alabaster slabs and

bas reliefs lining the walls: some are medieval, some 19c. All commemorate members of the Mavesyn, Cawarden and Chadwick families, who in turn held the manor, with quaint doggerel verse inscriptions. Table tomb of Sir Robert Mavesyn (killed at Battle of Shrewsbury, 1403), and other curious souvenirs.

To the S stands the gatehouse: like a great barn, with an arched opening, it bestrides the approach to the Hall. The ground floor is stone, and probably 15c: the upper floor of brick and timber is 16c, and contains a large chamber. Through the archway, on the site of the medieval manor, stands an elegant red-brick house, built by Charles Chadwick in 1718.

Rocester [9] The large village is set between the Churnet and the Dove, and the surroundings are delightful. In spite of its Roman name, and the fort which lay to the E of the village, there is nothing visible of the Roman settlement.

The church was largely rebuilt by Ewan Christian in 1870, though the tower is medieval. The interior glistens with polished marble pillars, and there is much Victorian furnishing. E window by de Morgan. Well-preserved 13c churchyard cross.

There are modern flats and houses in the village, and the large cotton mill was founded by Sir Richard Arkwright in 1782. But the most conspicuous thing is the vast new factory of Messrs J. C. Bamford. This lies to the SW, and the surroundings—acres of grassland—have been landscaped, and lakes formed, by the J.C.B. excavators manufactured here.

Rolleston [9] The village is close to the Dove and the Derbyshire border, and too close to Burton-on-Trent. Although there are several good houses, there have been many suburban villas built in the village. The Hall was pulled down in the 1920s: it was the home of Sir Oswald Mosley's family, who first acquired property here at the beginning of the 17c. The gabled Jacobean house was Georgianised and enlarged by Thomas Gardner (see Uttoxeter) in the second half of the 18c, and partially destroyed by fire in 1870. Photographs survive of the sugary stuccoed Italian house built in 1871—but some of Thomas Gardner's work was preserved.

The church of Norman origins is chiefly Dec; 14c tower and spire; N chapel of 1892 by Sir A. Blomfield. The interior is dark with excellent Kempe glass: many monuments to Mosleys, including the 17c tomb of Sir Edward Mosley (1638), tablets to the later baronets, and a number of inscriptions on black slate. Recumbent effigy of Bishop Sherburne of Chichester, a native of Rolleston, to whom there is also a monument in the cathedral there.

Rowley Regis [17] There is nothing very royal or smart about Rowley Regis. Indeed there is great un-certainty as to what king was ever connected with it, though Charles II had a horse called Rowley. For years the parliamentary seat of Rowley Regis and Tipton returned a Labour member with a large majority: a former Cabinet Minister, Arthur Henderson, was for many years its member, and was created Lord Rowley of Rowley Regis. But the title is now extinct.

Of all the towns in the Black Country Rowley Regis seems hardest to find. Where does it begin, and where does it end? What is more, what is does it comprise? There is a steep hill, crowned with a very red-brick church: from here there are views across the Rowley Hills, half cut away by quarrying, for the very hard 'Rowley Rag' or laccolith is quarried here; and the rest it is either a vast housing estate, or a stretch of semi-derelict country. The church, too, seems to have been unlucky: the original building, a chapel-of-ease to Clent, was founded in 1199. This was rebuilt in 1840, but condemned as unsafe in 1900. A new church was built in 1904, only to be burnt down in 1913. So the present building is of 1923, in the somewhat subdued Gothic of the twenties, with a W tower. Only the raw red brick is unsubdued.

Rudyard [5] The lake was formed in 1831 as a reservoir to feed the Macclesfield Canal: lakeside village with hotels and guest-houses. It was here that J. L. Kipling, architect of Stoke, and his wife became engaged; their son, born in India, was named Rudyard after the spot.

Rugeley [11] Rugeley might well be an attractive little town, were it not for the brutal presence of the enormous power station, which now overwhelms and almost envelops it. Here the gentler country of the Trent Valley meets the wilder wooded slopes of Cannock Chase. But now all is overwhelmed by the power station, which broods over the town like some gargantuan pagan temple—where the smoke of the sacrifices goes up day and night.

There are small streets with few buildings of special note, and a Market Square with Victorian Gothic Town Hall and Market Hall. Of the medieval church the tower and chancel survive, linked by the two-bay N arcade of the ruined nave. The chancel is still used, and there is a gruesome later-17c monument (to Thomas Lauder, 1670), with his corpse swinging as it were in a hammock, below the incription. The new church is of 1822 by Underwood, with galleries, like the Commissioners' churches; but the chancel is more elaborate, by Pearson, 1905. The R.C. church is by Hansom (1849), with tall spire and long narrow nave.

Rushall [14] Now in the NE suburbs of Walsall. Long residential roads on the edge of open country. Victorian church (1856) with imposing broach spire. Inside, dark nave and chancel; the crossing with its rood and wall paintings is lit by the cross light from the clear glass of the S transept—an effective contrast. SE of the church stand the 15c ruins of Rushall Hall, with high curtain wall and mutilated gatehouse. At the outbreak of the Civil War the house was held for Parliament by Colonel Leigh, but was captured in 1643 by Colonel Lane of Bentley for the King. Recaptured by the Parliamentary forces the following year, it was dismantled at the end of the Civil War; in the early 19c the stone house we see today was built close to the ruins.

Rushton Spencer [2] The main road from Leek to Macclesfield follows the line of the defunct railway, and at the river Dane, a mile to the N, crosses the frontier into Cheshire. Along the main road are the houses of the village, and a

Sandon Hall

Gothic railway station—but no sign of a church. Cross the railway, however, climb the hill, and follow the twisting lane to the S, and the quaint little church will appear across the fields at the end of its gated track. With its odd little wooden bellcote and heavy sloping roof, the outside walls and dormers are stone: above the E window is the date 1690, above the S doorway 1713. Inside, the original medieval timber-framed church reveals itself: low beams tie the massive roof together; oak piers, like solid tree trunks, divide nave from N aisle; a heavy W gallery crosses the back of the church; 17c pulpit and enclosed family pew, hatchments and Commandment boards adorn the E end. It is a church of rare charm and interest.

The hatchments of those of the Traffords of Swythamley, and their successors the Brocklehursts:

Swythamley, in its high moorland park, was first granted to the Traffords by Henry VIII in 1540. The house was burnt in 1813, and rebuilt by the Brocklehursts in the middle of the 19c. Handsome 18c iron screen and gates. Close to the park gate is a church of 1905, and across the moorlands to the NE is the extraordinary chasm called Ludchurch. The chasm winds between great walls of rock, only 20 ft apart, and was used as a secret place of worship by the Lollards. Dense overhanging trees enclose the 'Lollard church' from the outside world.

Salt [8] Many modern villas along the village street: at the end stands the church, of uncompromising 19c outline. The double bellcote is so tall that the already lofty church seems even taller than it is; the porch, again, is enormously tall. It

was built in 1842 by Thomas Trubshaw, and the interior is the kind of interior that brings you to your knees. The nave is lofty (as was to be expected from the outside), and the effect of the short but lofty vaulted sanctuary (there is no chancel proper) enclosed by its tall screen, and the altar dignified with its six candlesticks and sanctuary lamp, is solemn, mysterious and moving.

The village takes its name from the ancient salt pits here.

Sandon [8] The wooded slopes of Sandon Park, the home of the Earl of Harrowby, overhang the A51 NE of Stafford. At the S end of the park stands the Pitt Column, erected by the 1st Earl to the memory of the younger Pitt, Prime Minister. The earl had been Pitt's Foreign Secretary.

The original Sandon Hall stood

142

Sandon: churchyard *(top)* and monuments▷

Seighford: gamekeeper's cottage

close to the church, and was the home of the Erdeswick family, including Samson Erdeswick (d. 1603), the antiquary and first historian of Staffordshire. Richard, Samson's son, sold the place to his half-brother, George Digby, whose daughter and heiress married Lord Gerard of Gerard's Bromley. It was his grand-daughter who married in 1698 the 4th Duke of Hamilton. Lord Archibald Hamilton (later 9th Duke) sold Sandon in 1777 to the first Lord Harrowby.

The present Sandon Hall was built in 1852 for the 2nd Earl by William Burn, to replace a classical house designed by Joseph Pickford for Lord Archibald in 1770. It is in Burn's favourite Jacobean style, gabled and turreted, with imposing but comfortable interiors. There are beautiful gardens, and in the park a shrine to the memory of the murdered Prime Minister, Spencer Perceval, and the top stage of Barry's Italianate belvedere tower of Trentham, re-erected here as a

folly when that house was demolished in 1910–12.

Sandon village was also originally close to the church: when the park was formed, it was moved to the main road close to the park gates, and now comprises an attractive group of cottages, village hall, and inn, all designed early this century by Sir Guy Dawber. A short distance away is a grand little railway station, built in 1849 in Jacobean style: the present earl bought the house to preserve it when the station was closed. Alongside the railway runs the Trent and Mersey Canal, and beyond that the Trent.

Sandon church stands by itself in the park, up the lane by the park gates. The oldest part is the 13c S aisle (the original church), to which the nave and chancel were added in the 14c. Perp SW tower. The beautifully furnished interior makes an immediate impression—with its bleached oak pews (some of them 17c), 17c pulpit, chancel screen with gallery over, and the

sight of more 17c furnishings and tombs in the chancel. The commodious gallery over the screen is the Harrowby family pew; tombs with incised tops to the Erdeswick family in chancel, and enormous monument to Samson the antiquary (1603) with a great display of heraldry; white marble tomb to George Digby (1675). Samson filled the windows with heraldic glass, and on the N wall painted an entertaining sham window with more heraldry—with a family tree on either side. Later tablets and inscriptions to Harrowbys in Victorianised N aisle; font of 1669; seven Harrowby hatchments in nave; Stuart Royal Arms.

Sedgley [14] stands on high ground, on the W edge of the Black Country, looking towards Wolverhampton to the N, to open country to the W. At its centre it has the character of a small old-fashioned town, but there are spreading

Sheen vicarage (Butterfield, 1852)

modern housing estates all round. The church is of 1826, and an extraordinarily interesting example of early-19c Gothic. Tall, pinnacled S spire; the impressive interior has the character of a late Perp church—such as St Andrew Undershaft in London—with lofty aisles and windows, and no chancel arch. Plaster vaulted ceiling, gaily decorated. The R.C. church also should not be missed: it stands at the corner of Catholic Lane, along the road to Dudley. It was built in 1823, and the sanctuary, vaulted in plaster, is a masterpiece. The presence of so grand a Roman church here, built at so early a date, is explained by the fact that Sedgley Park was for so long a R.C. college. The house, which is now an hotel, is really in Wolverhampton (approached by Ednam Road, off

the A4039). The N front of this early-18c house has a centrepiece of three tiers with attached columns, possibly of Jacobean date. It was an old seat of the Dudley family.

Seighford [8] The long village street leads at one end to the 18c brick Gothick tower of the church; and the brick S wall with its Gothick windows prepares you for an 18c interior. Not so: apart from this S wall of the nave the church is all medieval, with Norman N arcade, and Norman chancel arch. Late-16c alabaster tomb of William Bowyer and wife; later monuments (and hatchments) of the Eld family; 17c pulpit and altar rails; 18c family pew of the Elds.

At the far end of the village is the Hall, the home of the Eld family though now used as an hotel—a 16c

black and white house, tall with gables and cupola, with tactful 19c wings in matching style. At the end of the stable block is an 18c brick tower, built to resemble a church. It was the gamekeeper's cottage.

A mile S is Clanford Hall, an engaging black and white house with three-storeyed brick porch.

Shareshill [14] The village is becoming suburbanised: Wolverhampton is uncomfortably close. But one or two old and attractive houses survive.

The church is an 18c building of brick with stone dressings, attached to a Perp stone tower. The S porch is semi-circular with Roman Doric columns; there is balustrading in the parapet above each window in the nave, and at the E end an apse with Venetian window. Inside there are box pews, pulpit and altar rails of the period, and the sanctuary is separated from the nave by a triple-arched screen. Beautiful domed ceiling above the altar with IHS in the plasterwork—a holy place. Royal Arms of George I. The two alabaster effigies of Sir Humphrey Swynnerton (1560) and his wife lie uncomfortably on window sills, relics of the old church. The charity board was erected by W. H. Havergal, the hymn-writer.

Next door is the modest early Victorian Gothic vicarage.

Sheen [3] Lonely village in Dovedale. The Victorian church with pyramid tower was built in 1852. The work was begun by C. W. Burleigh of Leeds, who, under the aegis of Alexander Beresford Hope (who had inherited Beresford Hall, and the patronage of the living), was replaced by Butterfield. Beresford Hope was a rich Anglo-Catholic layman, and the church reflects his taste. Restrained, dignified interior. Reredos, font, pulpit, altar candlesticks—all by Butterfield. Stained glass by O'Connor. The village school (by Burleigh) and the vicarage (by Butterfield) complete the picture.

The Light Railway Hotel at Hulme End, a mile or so S, commemorates the Manifold Valley Light Railway. It was opened in 1904, but closed in 1934. For thirty years this narrow-gauge line (2 ft 6 ins) plied its way from 'Hulme End for Hartington' to Waterhouses—where it connected with the normal gauge line to Leek. The little engines, with glorious burnished headlamps—of enormous size, but apparently never used—pulled carriages painted in primrose yellow livery through some of the most lovely and remote Peakland countryside, to such evocative stations as Butterton, Wetton Mill, Thor's Cave, Beeston Tor, and Sparrowlee. When the track was pulled up, a public footpath was formed, so the line can still be followed; a few station buildings still exist. Alas, the Manifold Valley Railway 'arrived too late, and left too early'; what a boom might the line not enjoy today!

Shenstone [15] The hill with two church towers is a landmark from the A5. The village, close to the Warwickshire frontier and only a few miles from Sutton Coldfield, is becoming a resort for Birmingham commuters. The tower of the medieval church survives; alongside, an imposing Victorian church (1852 by John Gibson) has been built. Tall tower, somewhat cold interior—the atmosphere is more that of a town church. Shenstone Court was pulled down before the Second World War, but close to the A38, well protected by high walls, stands Shenstone Hall, an intriguing Jacobean house, whose gables were done up in Gothick at the end of the 18c. The garden façade was even more gloriously Gothickised with porch with elegant clustered columns.

Shugborough [11] There are many delights to be savoured at Shugborough. First to be mentioned must be the setting. The road N from Rugeley makes its way through lovely country: as soon as Wolseley Bridge is past, the steep fern-covered slopes of Cannock Chase accompany the traveller on his left; on his right the long wall and plantations of Shugborough Park rouse his expectations. At Milford the scene opens out into a great wide village green; and here are Samuel Wyatt's square lodges and iron gates to mark the entrance to Shugborough.

Or approach Shugborough on foot from Great Haywood: the little street with its classical cottage terrace leads under the railway bridge to the river and the Essex Bridge. Across this beautiful reach of river, where Trent and Sow join, with the Trent and Mersey Canal running alongside, it is possible to pass through a garden gate into the garden itself, close to the spot where Moses Griffith painted the 18c scenes which still hang in the house. These and the oil paintings by Nicholas Dall evoke so splendidly the setting of Shugborough, and the glories of its classical landscape park.

The house, of course, is different now—or, rather, looks different. It is the same house. The tall commanding centre block with its engaged pediment and balustraded roof, as it appears in the 18c paintings, now appears so much less tall because Samuel Wyatt removed the balustrade in 1794, placed it instead along the attendant wings to increase their importance, and across the front added the great eight-column portico, which at once united wings and centre, and emphasises the horizontal in this façade. The top storey of the house, once so dominating, now seems merely incidental above the portico.

Stand in front of the portico: the columns themselves are of wood, faced with slate and painted; the capitals are of Coade stone. The centre of the house is the house built by William Anson in 1694, to replace the earlier house bought by his grandfather in 1624. The wings with their bows and domes, connected by what were originally one-storey links to the main house, were added about 1748 by Thomas Anson, William's elder son, and are attributed to Thomas Wright of Durham. Twenty years later these links were heightened by Athenian Stuart, and the final remodelling completed by Samuel Wyatt in 1794.

The oval Entrance Hall, by Wyatt (1794), makes the ideal introduction to the house: beyond is the Saloon, added by Wyatt in 1803, with its twelve scagliola pillars down its long walls, and the view of the lawns sloping down to the river Sow. To the right the Bust Gallery and Ante Room lead to the Dining Room (1748). This is a

Shenstone: the Gothick porch

room of great atmosphere: the in-
spiration is Palladian, the tempera
panels of architectural phantasies
are by a Dane, Nicholas Dall, and
were painted for Shugborough in
Bologna. The chimneypiece is by
Scheemakers; overmantel, tables
and picture frames are Kentian, the
coved plaster ceiling by Vassali.

To the E of this room is the Red
Drawing Room, added by Wyatt
behind the Dining Room in 1793,
and a room of equal magnificence;
the chimneypiece is by Richard
Westmacott, the coved ceiling by
Joseph Rose. Blue Drawing Room,
Swallow Passage and Staircase
Hall, all rooms of charm, lead back
to the Entrance Hall, on the S side
of which is the Library. This is a
fascinating room: it is partly in the
main house, partly in the link
building, and the thick outer wall
of the 17c house has become a
screen between the two parts of the
room, composed of little Ionic

columns supporting a flattened
coffered archway. There is rococo
plasterwork by Vassali, and the
proportions are so cleverly worked
out that what is in fact not a large
room seems wonderfully spacious.
An amusing feature is the use of
mirrors on each side of the Ionic
screen, giving the impression of
continuous bookshelves behind the
columns.

The Library is particularly interesting, evoking as it does the attractive character of Thomas Anson, its
creator. He had succeeded to the
property in 1720: he was a
romantic bachelor and member of
the Society of Dilettanti, M.P. for
Lichfield, and a squire of moderate
means. His younger brother
George, however, was the celebrated Admiral, Commander-in-
Chief, First Lord of the Admiralty
and circumnavigator, to whom is
due the great revival of the Royal
Navy in the mid-18c. When he died

childless in 1762, he left his great
fortune to his brother, who inherit-
ing this sudden windfall was able
to transform the house at Shugborough, remove the old village,
create the glorious classical landscape, and thereby commemorate
the fame of his Admiral brother.
This he did with the help of James
(Athenian) Stuart, his friend and
fellow dilettante.

Thomas Anson died in 1773, and
was succeeded by his sister's son,
George Anson, M.P., of Orgreave
(near Alrewas), who assumed the
name of Anson. His son was created
Viscount Anson in 1806; and it was
he who employed Samuel Wyatt in
succession to Athenian Stuart who
died in 1788. The 2nd Viscount was
created Earl of Lichfield in 1831; it
was on the death of the 4th Earl in
1960 that Shugborough was transferred to the National Trust.

The S wing has always contained
the private apartments, and it is

Shugborough: East front

here that the present Earl lives. Beyond this is the kitchen block, and next to that the long façade of the Stables (1765). These now house the Staffordshire County Museum, where there are attractive displays representing the county's agricultural and industrial life and achievements.

After the delights of the house, the delights of the Park: most conspicuous is the Arch of Hadrian. Built between 1761 and 1765, and designed by Stuart, it is a remarkable memorial to the Admiral and his exploits. The triumphal arch itself is a copy of the Arch of Hadrian at Athens, and the superstructure contains busts of the Admiral and his wife, flanking a triumphal *aplustre*, or naval trophy. The sculptor was Scheemakers. Nearby, on a knoll overlooking the river Sow, is the Lanthorn of Diogenes, a copy by Stuart of the Choragic monument of Lysicrates (1764ff). Further to the E, close to the junction of the drives, is the Tower of the Winds, also by Stuart (*c.* 1765), an octagonal two-storeyed tower, with two Corinthian porches, and a coffered dome in the upper room.

The delights of the garden are perhaps the greatest delights of all. To the E of the house runs the river Sow, and along its bank are level lawns. Almost on the axis of the Saloon are the Ruins, a fragment of the earlier house which had belonged to the bishops of Lichfield. Unfortunately Stuart's colonnade and Orangery, which accompany the ruins in Moses Griffith's painting, have disappeared. But smooth lawns lead to Stuart's Doric Temple, almost a facsimile of his Temple at Hagley—which is the earliest building of the Greek Revival in England (1758). Round the corner is the Shepherds' Monument: set in a Doric entablature is Scheemakers' relief of Poussin's painting *Et in Arcadia Ego*. On the island, between the two streams of the Sow, stands the Cat's Monument, an urn to the favourite pet of the Admiral, which sailed round the world with him; and perhaps choicest of all, at a romantic corner where the river makes a deep bend, and where the Chinese Bridge crosses to the island, is the Chinese House. The bridge is of cast iron (1813); the Chinese House, with its wide overhanging roof, painted

pink outside, the interior decorated with red lacquer fretwork, gilded pillars, gilt monkeys, and rococo scrolls, has all the *joie de vivre* of the 18c cult of Chinoiserie. It is Thomas Anson's earliest garden work (1747), and in its idyllic setting perhaps the greatest delight of all—the embodiment of the paradise which he set out to create here in his beloved Shugborough.

Slindon [7] Close to the main road from Eccleshall to Newcastle stands a little church of rare beauty. It is by Basil Champneys (1894), and built for J. C. Salt, the Stafford banker. Small central tower, nave, chancel and short transepts. Inside, the tower and chancel are vaulted in stone; reredos, sedilia, furnishings are all by Champneys; stained glass by Kempe.

Smallthorne [5] The A53 from Burslem descends the hill to the railway. Close to the level crossing is Ford Green Hall, an attractive 16c timbered house, with an 18c addition to the E, and dovecote in the garden. The house is now a museum, and has been beautifully restored.

148

Shugborough: the Library ▷

Shugborough:　　　Doric Temple　　　Tower of the Winds

◁ Arch of Hadrian　　　The Ruins　　　Lanthorn of Diogenes

Stafford [11] is unlucky now in its landmarks: from whatever direction a visitor may come, the first things he sees are monstrous skyscraper blocks of flats. Stafford could have done without these.

For the scale of Stafford is domestic, charming, ancient; it is the county town, dignified and personal; it is the 'staithford', the ford by the landing place, agreeably set in a fold of the river Sow. To the S there are wide water meadows, where the Penk flows in to join the Sow—and these meadows come close to the town; to the W are the low hills on which Stafford Castle stands; to N and E is the quiet, gentle country of which no one knows.

The town itself can be seen and enjoyed on foot: from the S, Bridge Street leads into the delightfully named Greengate Street, Greengate Street into the Market Square. This is the heart of Stafford, the heart of Staffordshire. The Shire Hall is a splendid late Georgian building by a little-known architect, John Harvey, a pupil of James Wyatt (1795), and there are other decent 18 and early-19c houses around, such as the Lloyds' Bank House, which was originally the bank of Stevenson, Salt and Co., to different members of which family we owe the William Salt Library (of which more later), and Slindon Church (q.v.).

The charm of this part of Stafford is in the narrow streets, the number of good 18c houses, and the later 19c public buildings which jostle so happily with them. H. T. Hare's County Buildings (1893 onwards) in Martin Street are a case in point; reminiscent of the Oxford Town Hall (also by Hare), but less monumental and more varied in detail, this Baroque-cum-Arts and Crafts building is a delight. The Borough Hall in Eastgate Street is by Henry Ward (1875), and a pleasant Gothic neighbour. The William Salt Library occupies a decent early-18c house in this street: this

remarkable collection of deeds, drawings and books relating to Staffordshire history and buildings, made by William Salt the banker, was given to the county by his widow, and opened in 1874.

In Greengate Street itself the most prominent building is the timbered High House, bearing the arms of Sneyd and the date 1555. It stands four storeys high, and is a triumph of the timber-builder's skill. At the beginning of the Civil War, Charles I and Prince Rupert stayed here with Captain Richard Sneyd (17–19 September 1642) on their way to Shrewsbury. Its next-door neighbour is of much the same date and style, but plastered. Next door again is the Swan Hotel with its bow windows: the hotel is now given over to steak bars.

St Chad's Church, opposite, is a precious Norman church, though the impressive W front is a reconstruction by Sir Gilbert Scott (1873): old shops originally stood in front of it (as at St Ethelburga's, Bishopsgate), and one almost regrets their disappearance. Inside, magnificent round Norman columns in the nave, with Norman clerestory, much-decorated Norman arch at W of crossing, and Gothic arch at E; the aisles and N transept had collapsed and the arcades had been filled in—so all this is a sympathetic rebuilding. Norman intersecting arcading in chancel; Perp central tower. The quick-eyed visitor may notice that the Norman carvings have a strangely oriental look; the tradition is that the church was built by the Biddulph family (*see* Biddulph), who were great crusaders and employed Saracen carvers in building the church. With its gilded rood-beam and other appropriate furnishings the interior is calm and numinous.

At the end of the street is Chetwynd House, an early-18c brick house, with projecting wings, giant Corinthian pilasters at the angles,

sash windows, bold cornice and hipped roof, all enclosed by iron screen and gates—now somewhat oddly used as the Post Office, but once the home of R. B. Sheridan, when M.P. for the borough, 1780–1806.

The great pleasure, however, is to walk through the narrow passage by the High House, and discover the parish church. So often great medieval churches are screened by houses or gateways (a point which might be remembered by modern town-planners with their itch to 'open up' medieval buildings): St Mary's is a case in point. Here we have a great cruciform church, set in its own peaceful enclave. Many of the features are EE or Dec (the E end, the choir aisle, the S transept); but some are Perp (the nave clerestory, the octagonal central tower, the N transept); the whole church was thoroughly restored by Gilbert Scott in the 1840s, when he not only cleared out Georgian fittings, but also replaced later Gothic features, of which he did not approve, with more 'correct' earlier features. It is a large church; even so, the spaciousness of the interior comes as a surprise. Wide nave and aisles, separated by early-13c arcades. Grand EE crossing under the tower, with elegant arcading above the arch—and above the arcading the outline of the original steep-pitched roof, which was replaced by the present flat roof when the Perp clerestory was added.

The chancel, too, is spacious, with its five-bay arcade separating the equally impressive chapels; so are the transepts. The N transept is clerestoried, and contains interesting monuments, such as the alabaster tomb of Sir Edward Aston of Tixall (d. 1568) and his wife, and the 18c monument to their descendant Barbara, wife of the Hon. Thomas Clifford; she died in 1786, and it is interesting to find these Roman Catholics buried in the Anglican parish church in the 18c (*see* Tixall). The lancets in the S

transept contain medallions of dark stained glass. There is much colourful Victorian glass throughout the church. Other things to be noted must be the Norman font, with its very unusual crouching figures and monsters at the base; the 18c organ with contemporary case; and the bust of Izaak Walton, native of Stafford (1593), in the N aisle.

St Mary's **Stafford**

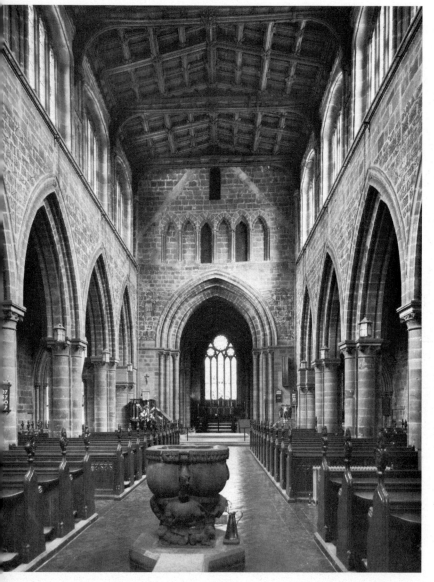

Leave the church and walk W. Adjoining the W end of the church there originally stood the little Saxon church of St Bertelin, an 8c local saint (*see* Ilam), which was wantonly pulled down in 1800; the vandals were with us then, as now.

On the left of the churchyard is a little curving alley, Church Lane; beyond is Mill Street, with the almshouses known as the College—a little 17c open court, with six little houses on either side of the chapel, founded by Sir Martin Noel, *c.* 1660 (*see* Chebsey and Ellenhall). To the W again is the railway station, rebuilt in the early 1960s. Will anybody ever come to love buildings like this?

Outer Stafford will need to be visited by motor car: beyond the railway, Newport Road leads out to Castlechurch. St Mary's is a red sandstone church with a Perp tower, the rest rebuilt by Gilbert Scott (1842) or his son Oldrid (1898), and embowered in yew trees. Above, on its low hill, is what remains of the castle. The original castle here was built by Ralph, 1st Lord Stafford *c.* 1350: most of this was destroyed in the Civil War (1643). But Sir George Jerningham of Costessy, Norfolk, who inherited (in the female line) the ancient barony of Stafford and the property here in the early 19c resolved to rebuild the castle; the plan of the building had been rectangular, with towers at the four corners. Two of these he rebuilt in entertaining castellated style, but the scheme was never finished; what had been built began to crumble, and most has now, alas, been demolished. The base remains, and with its rather sinister profile appears to crouch upon the top of the wooded hill. The castle, together with the barony of Stafford, subsequently descended to the Fitzherberts of Swynnerton (q.v.).

Returning to Bridge Street, and turning right into Lichfield Road (the Public Library, 1914, on the corner), a number of early-19c stucco houses are worth noting; one is incorporated in St Joseph's Convent, with its chapel and other buildings in 1930s baroque. Opposite, a grand stucco mansion is now used as Council offices; a little further S is St Paul's Church (by Henry Ward, 1844). The road leads on over the Penk and the Staffs and Worcs Canal to Weeping

Stafford: up and down Church Lane

Cross. Here turn left into Baswich Lane. At the far end, now set among new houses, is Baswich church. This has been a delightful conglomeration of medieval and 18c, filled with rare Georgian fittings. The base of the tower is medieval, the top 18c. A handsome red-brick nave of 1740, with heavy doorway and round-headed windows, leads up to a late Norman chancel arch, beyond which is the Georgian chancel. This was occupied by magnificent family pews: on the S side, on stout pillars, the gallery for the Chetwynds of Brocton (q.v.); on the N a similar gallery, but on slender pillars, for the Levetts of Milford (*see* Walton-on-the-Hill). The former was of 1740, the latter of 1812. Only a few

feet divided them above, and both were approached by elegant staircases. Alas, two long transepts have recently been added to the chancel, of the most unfeeling design, one gallery has been banished to the N transept, the other seems to have vanished. Only the three-decker in the nave remains; the poorest of flimsy furnishings fill the new transepts, and a very unusual period interior has been lost. Could not a harmonious addition have been built on to the church, and could not the beautiful fittings have been retained *in situ*? The tactful addition to the Georgian Church at Norton-in-the-Moors (q.v.) is a case in point.

The road leads on across the railway, across the canal, and fin-

ally across the river. Beyond stands St Thomas's Priory: fragments of the medieval buildings are incorporated in the charming group of farm buildings, and behind is a tall late-17c brick farmhouse. Altogether a delightful ensemble.

Standon [7] Long, straggling, hillside village; wide views over the rolling countryside S towards Eccleshall. At the lower, E end of the village stands the church. From the NW the oddly 'engaged' 14c tower built into the earlier NW corner of the church presents a strange appearance, with curiously placed windows. The whole building was much rebuilt by Gilbert Scott in 1846. The interior is dark and devotional: EE arcades. Early-

16c tomb in recess in chancel. Fragments of 16c brass close to the prominent Victorian pulpit.

At the upper (W) end of the village is Standon Hall, built of red sandstone in 1910, by Francis Doyle of Liverpool; a large Tudor revival house, now a hospital.

Stanton [6] Small, remote village of stone cottages and farms on the Weaver Hills W of Ashbourne, and the birthplace, in 1598, of Gilbert Sheldon, Archbishop of Canterbury, donor of the Sheldonian Theatre at Oxford. There is an endearing little church of 1847 in magnificent position: all Staffordshire seems to lie below you.

Sheldon's father was steward to Lord Shrewsbury, and the stone house in which he was born still stands in the middle of the village. In July 1664 Bishop Hacket went to take a Confirmation at Uttoxeter, and afterwards came out here to venerate his Archbishop's birthplace. While the rest of the party were partaking of ale and oatcakes downstairs, Bishop Hacket repaired to the bedroom upstairs where the Archbishop had been born, and sat there for some time meditating. Here he composed some rough-hewn Latin lines on a piece of paper which he pinned to the wall. These were subsequently painted on a board—which still hangs in the room today. And Hacket wrote a letter to the Archbishop telling him of his visit; the letter, dated 6 July, is preserved in the Bodleian, and the Latin lines run:

Sheldonus, ille praesulum primus
    pater
Hos inter ortus, aspicit lucem,
    lares;
O ter beatam Stantonis villae
    casam!
Cui celsa post haec invidebunt
    atria.

Statfold [12] Across the gentle park, which here borders the Tamworth–Ashby road and the Warwickshire frontier, stands Statfold Hall, the home of the Pipe-Wolferstan family, who first came here in 1465. The house appears late Georgian, with its canted bays and sedate sash windows; but the little polygonal tower standing up behind is 17c, and the bones of the house are earlier still. And at the back is a medieval private chapel in the garden. The W door is Norman, the rest 13 and 14c. Two 14c tombs; many later monuments to the Wolferstans. The large late-17c tablet to Francis Wolferstan (1676) is specially notable. 14c font, with 17c inscription. One small window with medieval glass; 17c continental glass in E window.

Stewponey [16] The strange name of a lock on the Staffs and Worcs Canal, N of Stourbridge. The Foley Arms keeps alive the name of the Foleys, early pioneering ironmasters in this district—who were later to build the great baroque church at Witley in Worcestershire. Their house here, Prestwood, was burnt and demolished in the 1920s: it was a 16c house, given a Gothick dress in the early 19c; an ugly but fascinating building, according to old photographs. The gardens were landscaped by Repton. A hospital occupies the site. Stourton Castle is in origin a 14c brick house, and former royal hunting lodge; it was the birthplace of Cardinal Pole. It was much rebuilt by Sir Robert Smirke in the early 19c, and is surrounded by castellated walls and gateway. It has recently been sold for offices.

Stoke-on-Trent [5] Stoke-on-Trent is the name given to the six Pottery towns of Tunstall, Burslem, Hanley, Stoke, Fenton and Longton. Architecturally they are disappointing, scenically they are interesting, atmospherically they are compelling. The six towns were united under the name of Stoke-on-Trent in 1910: as will be seen, each town has its character and its features. Together they represent the fourteenth largest city in England. Individually they form a straggling group of haphazard communities which stretch for almost eight miles along the North Staffordshire moorland.

The earliest pottery found in Staffordshire dates back to the Neolithic period (*c.* 2000 B.C.): fragments have been found in the caves of the Manifold Valley. Excavations at Trent Vale (S of Stoke) have revealed a Roman pottery of the first century A.D., with a kiln and examples of bowls and pots, plates and urns and flagons.

Pottery was made (as indeed it still is) in various parts of England—in places where suitable clay is available. Here in north Staffordshire the presence of clay so close to coal was decisive: pottery was made in the towns and villages in the Middle Ages; the name 'le Potter' occurs at Audley in 1280, 'le Throwere' at Biddulph in 1327, and so on. Dr Plot in his *Natural History of Staffordshire* (1686) gives a detailed account of pottery manufacture in North Staffordshire. Burslem he rates as 'the greatest pottery'.

It was at Burslem that Gilbert Wedgwood, great-great-grandson of John Wedgwood of Horton (q.v.) is recorded as the first Master Potter of his family in 1640. There are many great names in the history of the Potteries: Adams, Elers, Whieldon, Astbury, Twyford, Bentley, Davenport, Littler, Minton, Copeland, Spode. The greatest of all is Wedgwood: there have been members of the family in the Wedgwood firm until a few years ago. It is sad to record that there is now none.

The potteries themselves are changing too. The bottle kilns are disappearing as the potteries change over to gas or electricity for firing; at the end of the Second World War, there were 1,000 bottle kilns: now there are less than fifty.

A tour of the Potteries from N to S will start at *Tunstall*. Tower

Square is the centre of the town. There are few buildings to note: a red Victorian Town Hall of 1883 (by A. R. Wood); a small clock tower of yellow tile (1893) in the middle; the Sneyd Arms, with a friendly early-19c face; and a few shop buildings in the High Street, such as Barclays Bank Chambers. Christ Church is the parish church (by Francis Bedford, 1830) up the street N, an undistinguished Commissioners' type building; further N, St John's Goldenhill is of 1840, Norman Revival in brick!

The finest building in the town is undoubtedly the R.C. church of the Sacred Heart: with its two towers, of different shapes and sizes, and its three copper-covered domes, it is the only building which is in any way a landmark; with its imposing Romanesque interior it looks late Victorian, but in fact was built between 1925 and 1930, by the Catholic architect Sidney Brocklesby.

The A50 leads on through unbroken housing to *Burslem*, the 'Mother of the Potteries'. At the beginning of the 18c Burslem was a collection of farms dotted irregularly round a bleak, flat-topped moorland village green, with the village church in the valley below. The farmers made pots, and each house had its oven and outbuildings. By the middle of the century there were over twenty small potteries here, and coal was readily available in the pits near by. So the town grew up: the streets, higgledy-piggledy around the centre, which had formed the village green, are still there and hard to disentangle. There are more Georgian buildings in Burslem than in any of the other Pottery towns.

So Market Square has atmosphere and size. At the corner of Wedgwood Street is Midland Bank House (dated 1751, with the initials of Thomas and John Wedgwood; Thomas was the father of Josiah). The Old Town Hall is undoubtedly splendidly Baroque

(1852 by G. T. Robinson of Leamington), with its palazzo-like portico and clock tower, magnifical hall and staircase. In Queen Street (parallel to Market Square) is the Wedgwood Institute (1883–9, by R. Edgar and J. L. Kipling), of red brick and terracotta, in a kind of Venetian Gothic, with pointed arcading, much sculpture, and a statue of Josiah above the richly decorated porch. It was established to house Museum, Library and Picture Gallery. NW of the Market Square in Westport Road is the Burslem Sunday School (originally a Methodist church) of 1836, with grand Tuscan columns. Next door is the Wade Heath Pottery, placed prominently at the corner, with archway, Venetian window above, and pediment with date-plaque (1834)—a real Georgian façade, typical of so many throughout the Potteries. In Hall Street near by is another of Sidney Brocklesby's Italianate R.C. churches: St Joseph's, looking like a Franciscan basilica in Tuscany.

St John's Square (SW of Market Place) leads down odd hilly lanes to the parish church—the old village church in the valley as it was. The Perp W tower is the only piece of medieval architecture standing in the Potteries. The church itself is of 1717 and of brick, and it stands in what looks like a large country churchyard; any of the lanes around seem likely to turn into country lanes with hedges, at any minute. Instead they lead down to the Trent and Mersey Canal, to the wharves and 'ports' of Longport, Middleport and Newport. Close to the E end of the church are bottle kilns, as there still are close to the Market Square.

The A50 from Burslem to *Hanley* is Waterloo Road, a long straight road formed in 1817. At the Burslem end are older, drabber houses: at the Hanley end grander Victorian villas and terraces. Half-way along is the America Inn, with its large bow window (1830). In a Vic-

torian brick terrace at Cobridge (205 Waterloo Road) is the Arnold Bennett Museum (*see below*), and Christ Church, a yellow-brick Gothic church of 1838. The road descends into Hanley.

Hanley has, more than the other five towns, a big-town atmosphere: the best shops are here, or at any rate the big stores, jazzy and uninteresting. There is no market place. The Town Hall was built in 1867 as an hotel—and it looks it. It is by Robert Scrivener, and French inspired, of brick with stone dressings. The parish church, on a poor site (like so many churches in the Potteries), is an imposing Classical church of brick with W tower (1788). Just below, at the corner of Hope Street and Hanover Street, is the Five Towns Restaurant, Arnold Bennett's birthplace. But the grandest church is St Mark's in Snow Hill, the finest and largest Commissioners' church in Staffordshire, built in 1832 by Pickersgill and Oates of York. The church has recently been cleaned externally, and looks magnificent with its tall, pinnacled tower, long, embattled nave and apsidal chancel.

The road descends to the SW to Etruria, the model village established by Josiah Wedgwood in 1769. Here were his potteries in a rural setting, here were the houses for his workers, here his own house, Etruria Hall, designed for him by Joseph Pickford in 1770. Wedgwood encouraged Brindley to build the Trent and Mersey Canal; Wedgwood cut the first sod in 1766, and five years later Etruria (the name inspired by Etruscan vases) had been established on the banks of the new waterway. In 1939 Wedgwoods moved their pottery to Barlaston, and Etruria was sold. The Shelton Iron and Steel Works took over, and in the last two decades the British Steel Corporation have demolished all Wedgwood's kilns and buildings. There is nothing to see but Etruria Hall itself, now the local offices of the

Stone

B.S.C. and greatly altered. Instead of the sylvan scene portrayed in old prints there is now a purely industrial scene of blast furnaces, railway sidings and concrete roads. Few seem to care.

It is not easy to find one's way from Etruria to Stoke itself: it may be easier to retrace one's steps to the centre of Hanley, and take the main road. *Stoke* is a surprise: apart from the parish church, the Town Hall and the railway station there is very little to see; indeed the surroundings of these important buildings seem almost village-like.

The Town Hall has a long impressive Classical façade—upon the street itself, so difficult to appreciate fully. It was designed in 1834 by Henry Ward, but not originally for civic purposes. If not originally an hotel (as the Hanley Town Hall) it was at any rate a market, and only became the Town Hall in 1885. Almost opposite is the parish church of St Peter-ad-Vincula.

A fragment of the arcade of the medieval church stands in the wide, spreading churchyard. The new

church, built in 1826–9 by Trubshaw and Johnson, is a battlemented and pinnacled Gothic box with W tower—an attractive variation of the Commissioners' type. Large galleried interior, with wide, comfortable, pewed nave, and narrower chancel. Here is a gallery of memorials to some of the most distinguished potters. First is the monument with portrait by Flaxman to Josiah Wedgwood: 'He converted a rude and inconsiderable manufactory into an elegant art and important part of the national commerce.' Near by are the monuments to two Josiah Spodes, father and son (1827 and 1839); to William Taylor Copeland (1868), son of Spode's partner and eventually successor in the pottery; and to William Adams (1829), whose epitaph records his descent from William Adams, Master Potter in 1617.

Best of all, perhaps, is to turn into the railway station (left under the bridge near the Town Hall). Here is a charming small square, with statue of Josiah Wedgwood (by

Edward Davis, 1863) as its centrepiece. Here is the headquarters of the old North Staffordshire Railway. On one side is the station; opposite, the hotel. The other two sides comprise the little houses for the company's employees. All was built together (by H. A. Hunt of London, 1847) in domestic Elizabethan style. The station, with its big upper window (the company's boardroom), might be inspired by Charlton House in Wiltshire, the hotel by Blickling in Norfolk, the lower sides by the Whitgift Hospital at Croydon. All have recently been cleaned: the red brick with blue diapers, the stone dressings, shapely gables, finials and chimneys evoke delightfully the romance of the early railway age.

Across the valley the A50 rises to Hartshill: from here there are fine views across the city, and a grand Gilbert Scott church (Holy Trinity) built in 1842 at the expense of Herbert Minton. Imposing clerestoried exterior with tall spire: imposing vaulted interior, resplendent with Minton tiles which form a colourful dado all round. A tablet 'sacred to Herbert Minton, Esq' records that 'A highly refined taste and unwearied perseverance placed him at the head of the ceramic art'. This road leads on to Newcastle (q.v.), so it will be best to turn back and follow the A50 to *Fenton*.

Here there is really very little to see. Potteries and houses line the road all the way until an imposing church tower beckons into Albert Square, just off the main road, to the right. As the centre of a town, this is both sad and funny: on the S side is the large parish church (by Lynam, 1890), on the E a grim red Town Hall (by Richard Scrivener, 1888)—also of some magnificence. For the N and W sides there are merely the backs of cottages in the adjacent streets, with their garden walls and washing lines! Fenton seems to have aspired to grandeur late, and never quite made the grade.

The main road leads on to *Longton*. Here there are many good pottery façades along the main road—such as the Boundary Works—and indeed along the narrower side streets to left and right. In Uttoxeter Road (the A50) is the Gladstone Pottery Museum, established in 1974 as a working Pottery Museum in the former Gladstone Pottery.

The pottery is named after Mr Gladstone's visit to Burslem, to lay the foundation stone of the Wedgwood Institute, in 1863, though there has been a pottery here since the end of the 18c. The ovens were last fired in 1960, and the bottle kilns and buildings were on the point of demolition when it was decided that this was the ideal site for a pottery museum, to tell the story of the Staffordshire Potteries, and to show how pottery was made and decorated by demonstrating the actual processes. Now it is possible to tour this working pottery, to visit the engine house, the slip house, the clay preparation rooms, the casting

shop and one of the bottle kilns. It is possible to watch potters at work, and admire a display of Staffordshire pottery in the museum.

Otherwise, Longton is not rich in buildings. There is an imposing Classical Town Hall of 1863 in the space known by the impressive name of Times Square, but the square is cut in two by a railway bridge. On the far side is the parish church, a brick building of 1792, with W tower and galleried interior. There is a grand Commissioners' church (St James the Less) in Uttoxeter Road, with clerestoried nave and tall W tower (by Thomas Johnson, 1832). And on the skyline, up Anchor Road, is SS Mary and Chad, a red-brick Gothic church of 1898 by J. M. Brooks.

To the S Longton has suburbs with the romantic names of Dresden and Florence; and so the Potteries with their seemingly endless, shapeless sprawl come to an end. The Six Towns are no longer covered, as of old, with a pall of smoke: the air is cleaner now, and many buildings have been cleaned. Yet the disappearance of so many hundreds of the old bottle kilns must be a cause for regret. Where they appear, as they still do in Burslem and in Longton, behind those long façades that resemble Georgian stable blocks, they provide a shapely landscape feature unique in England.

Stone [8] The most prominent building in Stone is Joule's Old Brewery, which stands in the High Street. Until 1974 smoke puffed out of the tall chimney behind the Georgian house which served as the company's office, and a pleasant aroma of beer would hang around the town. Now the building is merely a distribution depot for Bass Charrington. The Brewery was first established here in the early 18c, and Francis Joule gave it his name in 1785. The Crown Hotel is the best building in the High Street: it was designed by Henry

Holland in 1778, and indeed would adorn any High Street. Alas, anybody entering in the expectation of a distinguished 18c interior will be disappointed: it has been made olde-worlde with sham beams and rough-cast plaster; a disaster.

The parish church is of interest as an early example of 18c Gothick—designed by William Robinson of the Board of Works in 1753. It is a large formal preaching box, with galleries and box pews which have miraculously survived. The chancel has been Victorianised, and the many excellent windows by Kempe cast a certain gloom over the interior. The original altarpiece by Beechey has been relegated to the N gallery. At the W end of the nave is the tablet with long inscription to Admiral John Jarvis, Earl St Vincent (d. 1823), surmounted by his bust by Chantrey. He was a native of Stone, and his family's home was Meaford Hall, to the N of the town, now demolished. At the E end of the church stands the Jervis Mausoleum, also designed by Robinson—a small, handsome, pedimented, Palladian building—where the Admiral and many members of his family are buried.

At the other end of the High Street (corner of Margaret Street) is a large Roman Catholic settlement, with Dominican Convent by Hansom (1852), and a big church alongside—unexciting outside, but imposing and brightly decorated within, and spacious with its long chancel and transepts. This is also by Hansom, with the E extensions by Blount (1856). Christ Church is the Evangelical parish: a large brick church by Lynam (1899).

To the N and close to the site of Meaford Hall is a power station: these erections are always intimidating, but this one, sited in a valley, is less overbearing than some. To the W the open country is soon reached, but the by-pass and the M6 intersect it. The Trent and the Trent and Mersey Canal also pass close to the town, as does the impor-

Stowe-by-Chartley: Hereford tomb

tant railway line to Stoke, with its gabled brick station of 1848.

Stonnall [14] The church stands solitary on the hillside overlooking the straggling village—towards the great suburban sprawl of Brownhills. The nave and W tower are of 1822 and of brick and faintly Gothick; heavier stone Gothic chancel of 1843 by Joseph Potter.

Stowe-by-Chartley [8] The lane from the main road leads across the disused railway track of the Uttoxeter–Stafford line: deep in undergrowth a little wooden station

building survives. Some old houses in the village. The church has a solid Dec W tower, but was enlarged and over-restored by Habershon and Pite of London in 1875. Norman doorways in nave; much restored Norman chancel arch. Table tomb to Sir Walter Devereux, 1st Viscount Hereford, with finely preserved early Renaissance details. Monuments by Lutyens to General Sir Walter Congreve, Governor of Malta (d. 1927), and his son William, V.C., D.S.O., M.C., killed in 1916, aged 25. Royal Arms of George I.

Stramshall [8] Suburbanish village NW of Uttoxeter. Typical mid-Victorian church by the local architect Thomas Fradgley (1852), with turret and lancet windows.

A mile to the NE and close to the Rocester road (B5030) stands Crakemarsh Hall, an elegant two-storeyed late Georgian stuccoed house of *c.* 1815: the main house is a square block, with Roman Doric portico and (on the adjoining façades) polygonal bays; there is a long lower wing at the back. Inside is a magnificent 17c staircase, with long panels of carved foliage, and urns—perhaps by the same hand as the great staircase at Sudbury, near by across the Derbyshire frontier. Crakemarsh in the 18c belonged to the Cotton family, and passed by marriage to the Sheppards: Sir Thomas Cotton Sheppard Bt built the present house; he died in 1822, and there is a monument to him in Thornton church in North Buckinghamshire—his grandmother was daughter and heiress of Sir Charless Tyrrell of Thornton.

Stretton (near Penkridge) [11]

Small village in delightful isolation a mile or so N of Watling Street, clinging to the gardens and park of the Hall—which is one of those serene and perfect country houses built around the turn of the 17 and 18c. It was built by John Congreve, of Congreve—the hamlet which lies a mile or so to the NE (*see* Penkridge); the Congreves had acquired Stretton by marriage in the 14c, and made it their principal home.

The present house stands on the site of an earlier predecessor: old pictures show it a house of two storeys, with long sash windows, the decided cornice of the period, and central pediment enclosing a carved cartouche of arms, the whole surmounted by a cupola—with a service wing extending to the N. So it stands today, only with a top storey added in 1860, and a *porte-cochère* on the W side, which then became the entrance front. The Congreves sold Stretton in the mid-18c to the Conollys, who in turn sold it to the Moncktons of Somerford (*see* Brewood), who still own it. Good period interiors, and a very fine staircase.

The Staffordshire Moncktons descend from the fifth son of the 1st Viscount Galway, who married the daughter and heiress of the 1st (and last) Lord Pigot of Patshull (q.v.). Few families have given longer service to Parliament than the Moncktons, generation after generation.

One represented Stafford continuously in nine parliaments in the 18c; another served under Disraeli. Stretton continues its beneficent role today.

The little church has a Norman chancel, but the 18c nave was disapproved of in 1860, when the Victorian nave and transepts were built. It contains a few fragments of ancient glass, a few monuments and a few 17c fittings.

Swindon [14]

Canal village, on the Staffs and Worcs Canal. With its locks to N and S, its old warehouses, even with its small ironworks, and with its red-brick church of 1854, it has its charm.

Swynnerton [7]

A trim estate village: from N and S the road leads through wooded park country into Swynnerton—and you are face to face with two grand churches, one the parish church, one the Roman Catholic; and between them and

Swynnerton

close to the road the austere back of the great stone mansion of Swynnerton Hall. Like Petworth in Sussex, and other ancient houses, Swynnerton Hall is in the heart of its village and dominates the scene: like Petworth it presents its grandly forbidding back to the public gaze.

Swynnerton has been in Catholic hands since the Reformation. The property passed by marriage from the Swynnerton family into the hands of William Fitzherbert, younger son of Sir Anthony Fitzherbert of Norbury, Derbyshire, in 1562. It was the widow of an 18c Thomas Fitzherbert of Swynnerton who was the celebrated Mrs Fitzherbert, wife of George IV. Today it is the home of Basil Fitzherbert, 14th Lord Stafford.

The present house was built in 1725, and probably designed by Francis Smith of Warwick. It is a severe classical house of three storeys, with heavy cornice below the top storey, and the protruding centre emphasised by giant Roman Doric pilasters. Additions and internal alterations were made by James Trubshaw in 1810; some of these have recently been pulled down. From the terrace there is a sweeping view across the park to the grand prospect to the S—Cannock Chase to the SE, Stafford castle and the town of Stafford to the S, and the hills of Shropshire to the W. The house is not open to the public.

The R.C. church of the Assumption stands to the W of the house, and is a sumptuous Victorian Gothic building of 1868. The parish church is to the N of the house. The base of the tower is Norman, the upper part 16c. Nave and chancel were rebuilt in the 14c. 15c chancel screen. Stone effigy of (probably) Sir John Swynnerton, *c.* 1264, in chancel. E window by Powell (to a design by Sedding). In the SE chapel is the great possession of the church: the statue, 7 ft high, of Christ, sitting and pointing to the wound in his side. It is 13c in date,

and of the finest workmanship. Its presence here is a mystery: it was discovered under the floor of the chapel, presumably buried at the time of the Reformation.

The 18c (former) rectory stands to the E of the church; the brick stable buildings of the Hall, facing the S side of the church, are worth noting.

Talke O' Th' Hill [4] Mining village: the strange name is derived from the Welsh word for 'high place'. Quaint little brick church of 1794 with apse; larger Victorian stone N transept, and bell turret. Modern church hall and outbuildings attached to W end. Views from hilltop over industrial scenery and villas. On the main road below are the decayed and forlorn lodges (early 19c) to Clough Hall. The house, the home of the Kinnersleys, whose grand monuments are in Ashley church, is demolished, and the land built over.

Tamworth [15] Tamworth is the SE outpost of Staffordshire: to the visitor entering the county from the S the town stands as an impressive bastion above the river Tame, at the point where it is joined by the river Anker, above an ocean of factories and industrial villages which border Watling Street and the frontier of Warwickshire. Indeed until 1890 Tamworth castle was in Warwickshire, just as Dudley Castle always has been in Staffordshire, the town of Dudley being nevertheless in Worcestershire.

Tamworth has a distinguished history as the early capital of the kingdom of Mercia. Here King Offa of Mercia, 'overlord of England', established his residence (757–96), and he encircled the town with a ditch. A royal mint was established in the town, which continued to issue coins until the reign of Henry I. And Tamworth remained the residence of the Mercian kings until the town was destroyed by Danish invaders in 874.

In 913 Tamworth was refortified, but by then Mercia had ceased to be an independent kingdom. Alfred the Great nominated his son-in-law Ethelred, who had married his daughter Ethelfleda, as Ealderman (or Deputy) of Mercia; on Ethelred's death Ethelfleda herself undertook the government, and the mound on which the castle stands may date from the time of Ethelfleda.

Ethelfleda died in 918. When her nephew Athelstan became king in 924, he made Tamworth one of his royal residences. His sister Editha married Sigtrygg, the Danish king of Northumbria, but the marriage did not last, and Athelstan gave her the royal residence at Tamworth, where she established a convent, and devoted the rest of her life to charity. Tamworth church is dedicated to her.

In 943 Tamworth was again destroyed by Danish invaders, and never again became a royal residence. After the Conquest the castle and manor were granted to Robert le Despencer, and subsequently passed to his nephew Roger le Marmion, together with the manor of Scrivelsby in Lincolnshire, and the right of acting as King's champion at the Coronation. Scrivelsby and the Championship later passed through a younger daughter to the Dymokes (who hold it still): Tamworth through an elder daughter to the de Frevilles, Ferrers, Shirleys, Comptons; finally, in 1751, to the Townshends of Raynham. The Corporation bought the castle from the 5th Marquis Townshend to celebrate the Diamond Jubilee in 1897.

The castle stands well. Lawns occupy what once was moat, and a steep and narrow path with many steps climbs up the mound to the small entrance beside the tower. The castle itself is a circular keep of Norman date, the lower part 11c, the upper 12c—the work of the Marmions upon the 10c mound. The great surprise on entering the

Hic Situs est

JOHANNES FERRERS de TAMWORTH Comitatu Armiæ.
Filii HUMFRIDI FERRERS Equi auri unicus;
Johan: e: FERRARIIS et FERRARIORUM stirpis,
pro quibus quidem FERRARIORUM familiæ ferminus, ultimus.
de FREVILE MARMION, MONTFORT et BOTETORT
(quorum hujus Regni Baronibus) oriundus,

EX ANNA conjuge,
DUDLÆI CARLETON Equi aurati,
Serenissimo nuper Regi CAROLO, ab intimis consilijs
unius Clericorum,
filium unicum, HUMFRIDUM Equi auratum,
ac DOROTHEAM filiam,
venerabili RICARDO ARRANIÆ (in HIBERNIA) Comiti
(filio nobilissimi ORMONIÆ Ducis IACOBI)
natu selectim, enuptam, suscepit
Diem obijt XIII Augusti an. MDCLXXXX Ætatis suæ, 82.

Iuxta heic pariter situs est
HUMFRIDUS FERRERS Eques auratus,
filius unigenitus,
de THRUMPTON

keep is to find a Jacobean manor house squeezed inside. The porch bears the arms of the Ferrers, to the right is the large mullioned and transomed window of the Great Hall. Inside, Great Hall, Drawing Room, Oak Room and other rooms are adorned with 17c wainscot and chimneypieces. On the top floor is a long Gallery. The whole building owes its survival to the fact that it has been continuously lived in, until our own day. It is now a museum, and among much else to see is a collection of coins minted at Tamworth.

The church, as has been said, is dedicated to St Editha. A collegiate foundation with Dean and six Canons was established here by King Edgar in 963, but most of this early church was destroyed by fire in 1345. So from the outside it appears a large Perp church, with imposing W tower. Dignified spacious interior. Dec arcades to the nave; no chancel arch; long clerestoried vista to High Altar. What comes as a surprise is to find opening into the transepts two great Norman arches, which originally carried a central tower. After the fire the arches to nave and chancel, together with the tower itself, were swept away; the new tower was then built at the W end. A unique feature of this tower is the double spiral staircase in the SW turret; only the base of a spire was built. Crypt of four bays under S aisle. St George's Chapel (N chancel aisle) is separated from chancel by the arched recesses of de Freville and Ferrers tombs. Tomb in chapel itself to Baldwin de Witney, the Dean who rebuilt the church. Burne-Jones glass (1874), and later Morris glass in chapel. E window by Wailes. First World War Memorial windows by Holiday (N aisle). High Altar reredos by Gilbert Scott. The finest object inside

the church is perhaps the splendiferous baroque monument under the tower to Sir John Ferrers (d. 1680): two kneeling figures support the base, cherubs adorn the sarcophagus with luxuriant garlands of fruit and flowers, and an urn stands above. It is by Grinling Gibbons.

As for the town, much of its real but unpretentious charm has been ruined in the last few years by so-called modern development. Market Street, which still contains a number of 18c houses, leads to the Town Hall, a delightful building, cupola-crowned, with open arches on Tuscan columns. This was built

in 1701 by Thomas Guy, founder of Guy's Hospital, and M.P. for Tamworth, who made a fortune in the South Sea Bubble. He also founded the Almshouses (rebuilt in 1913) in Gungate. In front of the Town Hall is Matthew Noble's statue of Sir Robert Peel (1853). But a soul-less, anonymous 'shopping precinct' has been built to the S of the parish church; with the usual shop-fronts of the all too familiar multiple stores the scene might be anywhere: thus is local character destroyed. Worse still are the blocks of tower flats on the other side of Holloway. These change the scale

Town Hall, **Tamworth**

◁ Ferrers monument, **Tamworth**

Tatenhill

of everything in the town, make a desert of Lichfield Street, and stick up everywhere like proverbial sore thumbs. Who ever inflicted these on poor Tamworth? One or two decent houses linger in Lichfield Street, but the setting is gone; at the W end, lying withdrawn down a wide avenue, is a long gabled brick house of the 16c, with wings, sash windows and a little gazebo overlooking the river, called Moat House. It is now a restaurant. In Wigginton Road is the small Norman Spital chapel, originally the chapel of a 13c hospital founded by a Marmion, long decayed, recently revived. The finest 18c house is Bole Hall, with its tall pilastered front, in an unlikely position close to the railway viaduct in Amington Road.

Tatenhill [12] Despite the proximity of Burton, Tatenhill preserves its village character. Large aisleless church with big Perp windows, and sturdy W tower. The interior is light and spacious. Some earlier features of the EE period (such as the S doorway) survive below the later windows. The church was restored by Bodley in 1890, and the reredos, pulpit and choirstalls are his work. Mural monument to the wife and daughters of Sir Henry Griffiths in chancel (1641).

Next to the church stands the particularly handsome early Georgian Old Rectory. It is of brick, and has a formal façade with stone dressings and doorway with Doric pilasters.

Tean [8] Old industrial village on the A50, S of Cheadle. The Philips family (later of Heath House) established tape mills here in the mid-18c. There are great tall mills dated 1823, 1833 and 1885; and these dominate the street in a grimly attractive way. But adjoining the mills somewhat surprisingly is a gabled black and white house of the 17c, and next to that, and built on to it, an imposing early-18c brick house (for the manager), with pilasters and sash windows. There are terraces of weavers' cottages in the village, two early-19c chapels, and a church of 1843 by Thomas Johnson. It is a typical early-19c Gothic building with bellcote and lancet windows; the interior is gaily decorated and devotional. The modern altar seems clumsy and incongruous.

On the high ground to the E in a beautiful wooded setting stands Heath House, home of the Philips family. Imposing Tudor revival house of 1836 by Thomas Johnson, with symmetrical gabled front to the S, and tower and *porte-cochère* to the W. Grand staircase hall inside, and much contemporary decoration. In the garden a classical orangery by Thomas Trubshaw survives from the earlier house.

Thorpe Constantine [12] Thorpe Hall, home of the Inge family since 1651, stands splendidly erect surveying from its low rising ground the wide scene to E and W, close to the Warwickshire borders. The centre is the tall 17c house, shown in an old plan, but it lost its gables in the 18c when it was Georgianised; and in the early 19c lower wings were added on either side, and the whole rendered in stucco. Inside there is an imposing early-19c staircase with iron balustrade, some plasterwork in the Wyatt style, and oak panelling adorned

Tean Mills: The Manager's House

with heraldry removed from Drakelowe (across the Derbyshire border) when that great house of the Gresleys was demolished in 1934. The families had intermarried in the 17c. William Inge, Provost of Worcester College, Oxford, and his son W. R. Inge, the celebrated Dean of St Paul's, were descended from a younger son; the Provost's grandfather had held the living of Thorpe in the 18c. The little church of St Constantine has a medieval spire; nave and chancel were rebuilt by Oldrid Scott in 1883, to replace an 18c building.

Tipton [14] The quintessence of the Black Country. In spite of its great population, its industries, its railways and canals, its main street is like that of a small and undistinguished country town. At each end there is a canal filled with murky water, with works overhanging bank or tow path, the street itself narrow with crowded early Victorian houses and shops—and at one end the red-brick pinnacled tower of St Paul's church (1837 by Robert Ebbles) close to the street. With its buttressed nave

Tixall gatehouse

and long, narrow lancet windows, this is a building characteristic of its date. In the Dudley Road is St Matthew's of very red red-brick (1876 by J. H. Gibbons), among very red streets of Victorian terrace housing. St Martin's, the parish church, is a plain Georgian church of brick and stucco (1797), three-quarters of a mile from the town proper, close to the enormous new gasworks.

With its canals and its locks, its railways and sidings, its chimneys and factories and strange abandoned sites, its odd stretches of rough and scrubby countryside, its little cottages, its great forbidding warehouses, its sounds and its smells, there is no place more redolent of the Black Country than Tipton.

Tittensor [8] Main-road village on the southern approach to Stoke-on-Trent. Strange late Victorian church by T. Roberts, a local architect (1881), built of stone, brick and tiling—as though rubble from a demolished building had been used. Timber-framed top to NE tower; timber-framed gable to the W end, perhaps inspired by Whitmore.

Tixall [11] The great gatehouse stands magnificent but roofless above the lane from Ingestre to Milford. Built in 1570, it is the largest and grandest Tudor gatehouse in England. An engraving in Dr Plot's *Natural History of Staffordshire* (1686) shows it standing in front of the half-timbered mansion built by Sir Walter Aston in 1580,

where Mary Queen of Scots was housed for a fortnight in 1586. This was burnt down in the 18c, and a new house was built in 1780, on a new site to the side of the gatehouse. The 6th and last Lord Aston died in 1720, and Tixall went by marriage to the Cliffords, who became the Clifford–Constables of Burton Constable, Yorkshire, and sold Tixall to Earl Talbot of Ingestre in 1840. The long Catholic connection with Tixall so came to an end, and the chapel was moved to Great Haywood (q.v.). In 1926 the 18c house was pulled down.

But the gatehouse remains, noble and erect: of three storeys, with domed turrets at the four corners and balustraded top, the mullioned windows are framed by pairs of columns, Roman Doric on the ground floor, Ionic on the first, and Corinthian on the second; the spandrels of the archway are richly carved with figures, and one Tudor fireplace remains in a floorless upper room. The great shell varies in its mood, according to the light and time of day: sometimes it is stern, pensive and forbidding—sometimes light, elusive and fairy-like. It has recently been acquired by Mr John Smith for his Landmark Trust, and the building is being restored and made habitable once more (1977).

Behind the gatehouse stand the stables, a great Gothic crescent designed by Joseph Ireland for the Cliffords in the early 19c. They have been used as farm buildings, but are now to be restored and converted into several houses under the direction of Mr Lawrence Bond, the architect. Up the slopes behind, on the edge of the Deer Paddocks, are two little stone deercotes.

Along the lane to the E lie magnifical brick farm buildings of the early 19c, and a little pepper-pot lodge with domed roof, coeval with the gatehouse. In the village is the small parish church of 1849 (by Wyatt and Brandon); on the little green at the intersection of the roads stands an 18c obelisk milestone; while at the end of a young lime avenue a rotunda, recently moved from Ingestre, makes a new focal point in the meadows.

Trentham [8] Travellers along the A51, on their way to Stoke, must be puzzled by the sight of the imposing gates to Trentham, just where the suburban sprawl begins, with the strange, squat, somewhat sinister shape of the Mausoleum, close to the pavement on the opposite side of the road. Such is the first sight of Trentham, until 1907 a ducal palace—now, albeit still the property of the family, a playground for the populace. The palace is gone: the gardens, the lake, the church, a fragment of outbuildings, survive.

Trentham was originally a

Trentham: The Mausoleum

priory of Augustinian monks; in 1540 it was acquired by James Leveson, a member of an old Staffordshire family with property chiefly in or near Wolverhampton (q.v.). A century later the Leveson heiress married Sir Thomas Gower, 2nd Bt. The family became Leveson-Gower (pronounced Lewson-Gore), acquired in time a barony, an earldom, a marquisate; the first marquis married the heiress of the Duke of Bridgwater, the 2nd married the greatest heiress of her time, the Countess of Sutherland (in her own right), and was created Duke of Sutherland.

The house, too, achieved a similar transformation. The Caroline manor house, which appears in Dr Plot's *Staffordshire* (1686), was replaced in the early 18c by a classical

house by Francis Smith. This was enlarged by Capability Brown and Holland towards the end of the century, and Capability created the great lake. Finally Sir Charles Barry in the middle of the 19c doubled the size of the house, transforming it into an Italian palazzo, with grand entrance semi-circle, *porte-cochère* and tower; rebuilt the church, and with the aid of Nesfield created the Italian gardens. In 1907 the place was abandoned, upon the threat of pollution from the approaching Potteries; in 1910 the house was pulled down.

Now the place is open to the public: there are the gardens to enjoy, there is boating on the lake, golf, swimming, eating and dancing; there is a 'garden centre'—but for all the magnificence that survives in the layout there is a great emptiness on the terrace where the house once stood. The chief building there now is the dull S side of Barry's church (never meant to be exposed), and it proves a poor centrepiece. What is much worse, a terrible utilitarian Exhibition Hall has been erected near the *porte-cochère*; and the tarmac paths and cast-iron seats give the air of a municipal garden. But the lake, coming right up to the gardens, with its overhanging woods, and the column commemorating the 1st Duke on the high ground opposite, are unquestionably magnificent.

The church is better in than out: Barry re-used the 12c arcades, the 17c screen, the 18c gallery. The S chapel has interesting Sutherland monuments, from the Elizabethan Sir Richard Leveson to the Victorian 1st Duke and Duchess by Chantrey and Noble.

The Mausoleum is the work of C. H. Tatham (1807): it is grim, even a little frightening in its solidity and severity. A description of it written in 1808 describes it 'situated on the road-side: the Ancients usually built their tombs near the highways, which reminded them of their ancestors. . . .' So the Trentham Mausoleum speaks to us of the glory that once was here.

Trysull [13] (pronounced Treesul). The village, attractive and intact, is close to the Shropshire border, watered by the Smestow Brook and by the Staffs and Worcs Canal: there are impressive locks at Awbridge. Good-looking houses in the village: the Croft is a tall late Georgian house of red brick, built in 1808 by 'Gentleman Perry', whose tomb is so prominent by the S door of the church; the Red House is half a century earlier, with Venetian windows; the Manor is of plaster and timber, dated 1633:
Stranger, should this catch your eye
Do a favour, passing by
Bless this house . . .

runs the inscription on the porch. Dr Johnson's aunt lived in this house, and he stayed here at least once. The church has solid Dec tower, and one Norman arch outside; otherwise early 14c. Good woodwork: 15c screen, Jacobean pulpit, impressive roof timbers.

Tutbury [9] Tutbury stands on the S bank of the river Dove, which is here the frontier between Staffordshire and Derbyshire; and from the main road from Derby to Uttoxeter the jagged ruined towers of the castle on the wooded hillside are a familiar silhouette. The little town lies below to the S. High Street and Castle Street contain several Georgian houses, and the Dog and Partridge is a tall 16c timbered house with overhanging upper floors.

Tutbury Castle was originally built by the de Ferrers family (*see* Chartley), but after various forfeitures and restorations it finally passed to the Crown; in 1361 it was bestowed on the fourth son of Edward III, John of Gaunt, Duke of Lancaster. It still belongs to the Duchy of Lancaster today.

The castle was besieged in the Civil War, and after its capture by the Roundheads in 1646 much was demolished. The ruins now comprise a loose and somewhat odd assemblage of buildings. Steep grass banks climb to broken walls interspersed with ruined towers. The entrance is through the NE gateway (14c), and opens into a great grass sward, called the Tilting Ground. Here it is possible to survey the inner court. On the S side stands the 17c block of the King's Lodgings: Mary Queen of Scots had been imprisoned here three or four times between 1569 and 1585 under George Earl of Shrewsbury (Bess of Hardwick's fourth husband), who leased the castle; James I and Charles I used the castle as a hunting lodge for Needwood Forest, and this range of buildings was formed here in the 1630s. One bastion-like corner with sash win-

dows survives, and there are rooms on the first floor which are still habitable. From the ruined wall adjacent large gaping square windows look down on to the town and country to the S. Adjoining is the 15c South Tower; next along the E wall is the decorative John of Gaunt's Tower. To the W of the King's Lodgings, on the site of the original Keep, stands Julius' Tower, a round tower built in the early 19c by the then Lord Vernon, who leased the castle. In the centre of the Tilting Ground are the foundations of the Norman chapel.

From all sides there are grand views over the valley of the Dove and the Trent—across to power stations, and the breweries of Burton. The atmosphere is delightful: the castle is well looked after by the Duchy of Lancaster, but the place has escaped being smartened up. An unsophisticated little tea room occupies the King's Lodgings, and children play on the grass in front.

The church, at one time the church of a Benedictine priory (of which nothing else survives), stands to the E below the castle, but above the town. Even in its truncated form it is a grand Norman church. The W front has a great sumptuous doorway, richly carved window above between interlaced arcading, and round windows in the gable. The S doorway is smaller, but surmounted by a carved lintel of a boar-hunt. Inside, a nave of considerable splendour, with great Norman columns. The present clerestory is the Norman triforium, with Perp windows inserted. The transepts and central tower have disappeared, and the present chancel with apsidal E end was built by G. E. Street in 1866, and is extraordinarily successful. Furnishings by Street. Early-19c monuments in N aisle. Royal Arms of Queen Victoria (metal in frame) over W door. Unique in England must be the collection of no fewer than 39 Glastonbury chairs to be found about the building.

The Staffs & Worcs Canal, **Trysull**

Uttoxeter [9] (pronounced 'Uxeter' or 'Utcheter' or 'U-toxeter') A frontier town: the river Dove here forms the frontier between Staffordshire and Derbyshire, and a very good stretch of country it is. To the S is the wooded land of Needwood Forest, to the N the Peak District, to the W the unknown countryside that leads to Stafford. Uttoxeter is in itself an agreeable small market town. Approaching it across the Dove Bridge (partly 14c, partly 17c), narrow streets lead into the town, and the Market Place at the centre comprises two somewhat irregular squares, with 18c and Victorian brick or timbered houses and shops, and the little domed and pedimented Classical building—the Weighing House—of 1854, designed by Thomas Fradgley, the Uttoxeter architect, who also designed the Classical Town Hall in the High Street (1853).

Many of the streets have pleasant Georgian houses: the White Hart Hotel in Carter Street has an engaging white-painted front with prominent porch, and Tudor panelling in the Dining Room from Beaudesert. The finest house in the town is Bank House, NE of the parish church, designed by Thomas Gardner, a pupil of Joseph Pickford, in 1776, with its central pediment crowned with magnificent tall urns, and elegant doorway.

The church has a solid medieval W tower with recessed spire: the rest was rebuilt in 1828 by Trubshaw and Johnson. Long galleried nave, with lofty arcades and aisles, and tall pulpit to command the attention of congregations above and below. 16c tomb of Thomas Kinnersley of Loxley, and later monuments and tablets—the whole church redolent of the comfortable and delightful atmosphere of an early-19c small country town at worship. The R.C. church is by Pugin, but much altered by later additions; the Methodist church is of 1812, and the Congregational church of 1827, both with Classical features.

The Market Place was the scene of Dr Johnson's penance: at the age of 70 he stood bareheaded in the rain on the spot where his father's bookstall had stood, and where on one occasion, which he afterwards bitterly regretted, he had refused to help him. 'In contrition I stood, and I hope the penance was expiating' he wrote afterwards. There is a bas-relief of this incident on Johnson's monument at Lichfield.

SE of the town is the race-course, and a mile or so to the SW on rising ground above the road to Stafford stands Loxley Hall. The S front is eleven bays long and two and a half storeys high, with wide central portico of Roman Doric columns; an impressive late-18c stone façade. It was the home of the Kinnersleys and Sneyd-Kinnersleys; the spacious early-18c staircase, and the hall with still earlier painted panelling, suggest a much older core, and there are legends connecting the place with the haunts of that 're-doubtable freebooter, Robin Hood'. It is now a County Council school.

Wall [15] A Roman settlement on Watling Street: the village takes its name from the fragments of the Roman walls of Letocetum, the

Tutbury

settlement of forts established here in the first century A.D. At the foot of the hill, by the side of the old main road, are well-preserved remains; beyond, are the remains of a bath house excavated in the last century, with hot bath, tepid bath, and cold bath. There is a small museum, with tiles and urns found on the site.

A steep lane leads up to the village, past an early-19c Classical stuccoed house. The church is of 1843, an early work of Scott and Moffatt, with nave, small chancel and little steeple. Further to the E, at the foot of the hill, is an early-17c stone house with dormers and mullioned windows.

Walsall [14] is a place of very considerable character. The town itself has its attractions, and the steep hill with the parish church on top, cobbled streets and alleys climbing up its side, is a splendid place to stand and view the surrounding Black Landscape. So climb first to the parish church.

From the outside this appears a building of the early 19c, with its prominent SW spire, thin and lofty pinnacles, and silvery stone. In fact the medieval nave was encased by Francis Goodwin in 1820, and it will soon be seen that the chancel is original; a vaulted passage runs under the E bay. The tracery of Goodwin's windows is iron. Splendid interior: lofty, elegant nave, with graceful arcades of cast iron, and galleries—the *tour de force* being the flat plaster fan-vaulted ceiling with its rich pendants. The rood screen leads into the lower, darker, mysterious Perp chancel, and many

steps lead up to the elevated High Altar, beneath which runs the arched outside passage. 15c stalls, with set of eighteen misericords. Under the chancel a crypt of the 13 and 14c.

Opposite the S door are the Memorial Gardens, enclosed by brick walls with clair-voyants, designed by G. A. Jellicoe. These are delightful, and very unlike the conventional municipal public garden; from the little galleries there are magnificent views over the town. To the SW will be seen the outline of the R.C. church by Joseph Ireland (1825) in Vicarage Walk—an imposing Grecian design, with giant Doric pilasters. Further to the SW will be seen, beyond the motorway, the hilltop of Wednesbury, crowned with its two church spires. All around and

below you are the chimneys and factories and teeming streets of Walsall and its neighbours. To the NW are the great cooling towers of the Walsall power station, and tall blocks of flats. Closer at hand is the baroque tower of the Council House, whose blackened Italianate outline gives an undoubted air to Walsall.

Now it is time to descend: it is a pity that many old houses round the hill are being torn down to make way for yet another 'shopping precinct'. Walsall could do without this: the narrow streets and cobbles give the town character which cannot be replaced. The Council House, and adjoining Library, are by J. S. Gibson, a grand baroque composition of 1905. The Art Gallery contains an interesting collection of paintings left to the town by the wife of Sir Jacob Epstein, a native of Walsall.

One of the pleasant surprises of Walsall is to find here shady streets lined with great plane trees, early-19c stucco houses and terraces, and especially to discover the great Doric stucco portico of the County Court, which was built for the Walsall Literary Society in 1831. A visitor here might be forgiven for thinking that he was in a corner of Cheltenham. Round the corner is St Paul's church (by Pearson, 1891), Dec in style, in stone, with Pearson's favourite lofty apse. Near by is the statue of 'Sister Dora' (sister of Mark Pattison), who devoted her life to nursing in Walsall and died in 1878. In Lichfield Street are the buildings of Queen Mary's Grammar School (1849-Tudor, in red brick: an attractive building) and, opposite, the Arboretum. The railway station in Park Street has a good façade to the street with handsome iron canopy.

To the NW, St Andrew's, Birchills, with its gabled brick pinnacles, long red roof and *flèche*, stands in its own little enclosed garden with Calvary and parish buildings forming an attractive

enclave off Birchills Street. Designed in 1894 by J. E. K. Cutts, a local architect, it is a church with a devout Anglo-Catholic interior. And beyond is Bloxwich, now a suburb of Walsall, but an ancient parish. All Saints, prominent from the motorway, stands on a wide green: red-brick, with W tower with pyramid roof and galleried interior, it is a Victorian rebuilding of an 18c church. The green, with its sprinkling of older houses, gives Bloxwich character. The Roman church, with its brick twin-towered façade by Edward Kirby, is further up the High Street.

Walsall grew rich and prosperous on leather. It is an ancient borough, having received its first charter from Edward III. Jerome K. Jerome was born here in 1859: there is a tablet to record the fact on his birthplace in Bradford Street.

Walsall Wood [14] In the built-up countryside between Brownhills and Walsall; suburban, but still retaining its village atmosphere. Strange-looking church beside the high road, partly early, partly late Victorian; partly built of purple, partly of very red red brick. Well-furnished, devotional interior, with incredible cast-iron Gothic arcades, and pillars with near-Corinthian capitals. Intimate memorials include a miner's lamp and marble pulpit—'this pulpit was the gift of those confirmed at Walsall Wood, 1877–1884'.

Walton-on-the-Hill [11] On the E outskirts of Stafford, with modern houses along the main road, but something of the old village around the church. This is by Thomas Trubshaw (1842), in an elementary Gothic, with N tower and spire of unusual outline. Memorials to the Levett family of Milford Hall, including the recumbent effigy to Richard Byrd Levett, killed in 1917: the canopy and chapel are by Cecil Hare. Mil-

ford Hall is a three-storeyed, stuccoed, late-18c house; Milford village is set round a wide and spreading green, at the far end of which are the gates to Shugborough.

Warslow [5] A well-built 'estate' village in Peakland: glorious countryside and views. The church is late Georgian (1820), with chancel added in 1908 by Charles Lynam. Attractive interior with bleached pine furnishings, two-decker pulpit, box pews, and a larger pew for the squire and his family. Stained glass by Morris, and much *art nouveau* decoration and mosaic work in the sanctuary.

The Hall is behind high walls along the road to Longnor—a Georgian shooting box in a fine position looking towards Hartington, belonging to the Harpur-Crewes of Calke Abbey, Derbyshire.

Waterfall [5] Moorland country watered by the river Hamps, which here disappears underground through crevices in the rocks. Stone-built village. Georgian church (1792), incorporating a Norman chancel arch of somewhat squashed aspect. Norman tympanum over 18c S door. 'The river of God is full of water' runs an inscription on the altar; 'Let the floods clap their hands, and let the hills be joyful before the Lord' runs another, appropriately.

Wednesbury [14] is a town with some odd and ancient character, which sets it apart from the amorphous mass of urban conglomeration that makes up so much of the Black Country. First, there is the prominent hill, crowned with the spire of the medieval parish church, and—next it—the thin copper spire of the Roman church. This hill, with its two rival spires, is a landmark across the built-up wastes. Below the hill to the S, separated by a wide and unexpected stretch of grass, lie the streets of shops and the market place; but it is a shapeless, straggling town, and there are few buildings to note.

The parish church was somewhat rebuilt in 1827, and again (by Champneys) in 1890. It is Perp with polygonal apse and transepts, with 16c lectern and 17c pulpit, glass by Kempe, and many monuments. It has a civic air. The Roman church next door is by Gilbert Blount, prominent with its long nave and apsidal chancel. Below the market place is St John's, with its heavy blackened Victorian features, and—again—a spire; it is of 1845, by Dawkes and Hamilton.

Main roads and roundabouts cut the town in bits; the Holyhead Road is the turnpike laid out by Telford, and in St James's Street, a murky side street, is St James's (of 1847). With its wide, aisleless nave, and richly decorated apsidal chancel and attendant chapels, it has all the atmosphere of a beautifully furnished and much loved Anglo-Catholic church of a slum parish. St Paul's, Wood Green, to the NE of the town, was built by the Elwell family of Wednesbury Forge in 1870. The architect was Edward F. C. Clarke of London; it has a devout Tractarian interior, and gives Wednesbury one more lofty, blackened, spire.

This is old industrial countryside: Wednesbury Forge was first established in the reign of Elizabeth I: in the 18c it was making gun barrels; for a century and more it was owned and managed by the Elwell family, and is still an active centre of the iron trade. Close to the Darlaston road are Old Park Works, another ancient site where industry has persisted. Here today are made electric locomotives, and underground trains for London. New housing estates are rising all round to take the place of the old industrial cottages, and bulldozers are levelling the old waste ground.

Wednesfield [14] Now caught up in the NE suburbs of Wolverhampton, the town grew tremendously in the 19c on the manufacture of vermin-traps—as well as other local industries. Handsome 18c church: W tower, pedimented doorways— all in brick with baroque stone quoins and dressings. Galleried interior. The church was burnt in 1901, and admirably restored by F. T. Beck in 1903.

Weeford [15] James Wyatt, the architect, was born here in 1746. He was the sixth son of Benjamin Wyatt, a farmer who also practised locally as a builder. The small village lies under the lee of Watling Street, in a pretty valley watered by the Black Brook. Imposing quadrangular farm buildings with dovecote lie beside the church, an unpretentious late 18c cruciform Gothic building, with later chancel. The window in the S transept is filled with old French glass—of Pilate washing his hands—which came from the Chapel of the Duke of Orleans at the time of the French Revolution. One monument to James Wyatt's brother, a surgeon of London, and other tablets to the Swinfens of Swinfen Hall, and the Manleys of Manley Hall.

Manley Hall, whose 'towers and pinnacles rise majestically' over its wooded park (Kelly's *Directory* 1936) was 19c Elizabethan, and has been destroyed. Swinfen Hall, the work of Benjamin Wyatt, is now a prison. It was built in 1755 and resembles the kind of house built in the early years of the century (such as Venn House, Somerset) with stone pilasters and a bold top storey above the main cornice. It was the home of the Swinfen family. Packington Hall, which looks so salubrious in 18c prints, stands stark near the A51, and is used as a factory.

West Bromwich [14] is certainly disappointing. For all its size, its fame, its great population and achievements, there is very little to see. It is like a vast overgrown hamlet. There is one long wide street, made up of undistinguished houses and cottages, with a large red Victorian Gothic Town Hall of 1874 (Architects: Alexander and Henman), an Edwardian baroque Public Library next door (by Stephen Holiday, 1907), and Christ Church of 1821, by Francis Goodwin in his Perp style, standing in an overgrown churchyard opposite. That is all there is to see in the centre of the town.

The fact is that the town grew up suddenly and rapidly in the early 19c, on a stretch of heath and open common 'where rabbits burrowed in great numbers' as William White commented in 1834, and which had by then become 'a chain of villages and streets'. Coal and ironstone were discovered, collieries and factories opened, and the population soared.

The old parish church, the old village church of All Saints, is a mile to the N, on the A4031; the W tower is medieval, the rest rebuilt by Somers Clarke in 1873, and not one of his outstanding achievements. Monuments to the Whorwoods of Sandwell, their successors the Dartmouths, and the Turtons of Oak House.

One almost incredible treasure, however, there is: the Old Hall or Manor House of West Bromwich, in Hall Green Road, half a mile W of the parish church. What had become by 1950 a group of decayed 19c tenement dwellings standing in a derelict plot of land awaiting demolition, turned out to be the medieval manor house of Bromwich, long forgotten and buried in a casing of brick and stucco. The land was to be 'developed', the derelict buildings destroyed— when it was discovered that beneath the later additions a timber-framed 14c Great Hall survived intact, approached by an Elizabethan gatehouse. Great Hall, gatehouse and attendant buildings were rescued and restored (under the architect Mr James Roberts), and the moat dug out and filled with water.

Originally held by the Devereux and Marnham families, the place passed by marriage to the Stanleys, was subsequently purchased by Sir Richard Shilton, solicitor-general to Charles I, and in the 18c was bought by Sir Samuel Clarke. The Clarke-Jervoises (as they became) inherited property in Hampshire, and lost interest in Bromwich Hall—which, ancient and decayed, became submerged and forgotten. It is to the eternal credit of the local council that it was saved—and has now been opened as a most interesting restaurant by Ansells the brewers.

There is another house of note: the Oak House, in Oak Road (Lodge Road leads from the Town Hall into Oak Road). This is a remarkable 16c gabled, timbered house—which has survived in a sea of Victorian terrace houses. There is an imposing gabled front with porch, and at the top a timbered, gabled prospect tower: at the back it is partly timbered, partly early-17c brick, with twin-shaped gables. The home of the Turton family, a Staffordshire branch of the Turtons of Turton Tower, Lancashire (*see* Alrewas), until the early 19c, the house was saved by Alderman Farley, Mayor of the town, and presented to the borough as a museum: it contains a good collection of period furniture.

To the E of the town the M5 motorway roars past, to join the M6 at 'Spaghetti Junction'. There is much new housing everywhere, with terrifying towerblocks of flats. One oasis remains, close to the motorway: Sandwell Park. The site of a Benedictine priory, Sandwell Hall was built for the Legges, Earls of Dartmouth, by William Smith in the early 18c, and appears in old pictures as a handsome house, with corner pavilions. The family removed to Patshull (q.v.) in the later 19c, and the house was demolished in 1928. The park the family presented to the town, and it remains almost unbelievably countrified. A fragment of the 18c gateway survives in the middle of the roundabout at the S end of the High Street.

Weston-on-Trent [8] A busy village, intersected by two main roads, the railway, the Trent, and the Trent and Mersey Canal. The church possesses an exceptional early-13c tower: sturdy and buttressed, the upper stage is decorated with graceful lancet windows, and arcading on either side. The tower is crowned with a plain Perp spire, tactfully rebuilt in 1830. Most of the church was rebuilt in the 19c, partly by Gilbert Scott, partly by Butterfield.

Opposite the church is a solid Jacobean-Gothic house by Gilbert Scott; on rising ground near the Stafford road stands Weston Hall, a tall, awe-inspiring, early 17c house of four storeys, with mullioned windows and many gables.

Weston-under-Lizard [10] The 'Lizard' is the Lizard Hill, two miles to the SW across the Shropshire frontier. Terrible traffic on the A5 bisects the patriarchal village. Good-looking estate cottages stand along the road: the great house, the church in its shadow, lies half hidden behind high protecting walls to the S.

The estate was held in the Middle Ages by the Weston family, who were followed by the Myttons. The last of the Myttons, Elizabeth, married in 1651 Sir Thomas Wilbraham, a Cheshire squire, and took the property to his family. Again it passed by marriage to the Newports, Earls of Bradford, and so to the Bridgemans; it is the sixth Earl of Bradford (of the second creation) who is the present owner of Weston.

The special interest of the house as a building is that it was designed by Lady Wilbraham herself: she was one of that interesting line of amateur architects, and her annotated copy of Volume I of Palladio's *Quattro Libri dell' Architettura* is preserved in the house. Building began in 1671.

Weston is a large square brick mansion: the S front is distinguished by a stone centrepiece and big segmental gables, the E front by a pediment—to which has been added a tactful 19c *porte-cochère*. The roof-line of the whole house is crowned with stone balustrade and noble chimneys. The low E wing is a Victorian addition, and the long façade is continued by the 17c stable block, with its central pediment, weather vane, sundial, and carved cartouche of arms. Behind the stables stand magnifical 18c farm buildings. It is an attractive ensemble, and now that the Victorian stucco has been removed from the house, the pink brick glows.

Inside, nothing survives from the 17c. The most notable 18c room is the Tapestry Room—companion to similar rooms at Osterley and Newby—lined with rose-pink Gobelin tapestries (dated 1766). The Dining Room is a grand creation of the mid-19c: the marble staircase redolent of the splendours of the late 19c. But the most notable feature of the house is the important collection of pictures: there are portraits of the successive owners of Weston, and others, by Holbein, Gainsborough, Hoppner and Reynolds, in addition to impressive Dutch, Italian and French pictures. Of special charm are the many small and early portraits in the Breakfast Room. Everything is in first-class condition, thanks to the enthusiasm and energy of the present Lord and Lady Bradford, who have rescued the house, and opened it to the public.

The park was landscaped in the 18c, and there are many 'features' to give delight. The Temple of Diana by James Paine (1770) is an

Weston-on-Trent: Hall and church

Near Wetton

orangery of singular beauty. The Roman Bridge, with its sentry-box ends, at the head of the Temple Pool, is also by Paine. Close to the terrace on the S front of the house stands a magnificent plane tree, coeval with the house: the guide book to the house speaks of its having always 'realised' what was expected of it'; it must be the finest and grandest plane tree in the country.

The church was built by Lady Wilbraham in 1700: the tower and E wall survive from the earlier building, and there are Victorian additions by Ewan Christian (1876). Pulpit with tester, 1701. Early-18c wrought-iron altar rails.

19c stained glass by Hardman and Kempe. Many monuments.

Wetley Rocks [5] Moorland village on the main road from Leek to Cheadle; above the road a forbidding outcrop of millstone-grit rocks. The church was built in 1833, by the Sneyd family of Ashcombe Park: it has an interior of some style. George Mason Mills, the Victorian painter, lived at Wetley Abbey, the early 19c Gothic house which stands S of the village, off the main road.

Wetton [6] Exhilarating Peak countryside. Lonely roads lead to Wetton, from Ilam, from Alston-

field, from Grindon—and all around are the green fields enclosed by stone walls. The Manifold Valley Light Railway made its way up the valley of the Hamps and Manifold, and had a station at Wetton Mill, NW of the village. The site of the station is now used as a car park, for those wishing to explore one of the best parts of the valley. Half a mile SW of the village is Thor's Cave, a spectacular cave overlooking the steep bank of the river, used in distant times by the local moorland tribes. Thomas Bateman of Hartington and Samuel Carrington of Wetton excavated this and other caves and barrows in the mid-19c, and discovered multi-

Wetton

tudes of pots and coins. These are now in the Sheffield Museum.

Wetton church has a medieval tower; the rest was rebuilt in 1820, and is a solid and unsophisticated Gothic box, with enormous quoins clasping the E wall. George IV Royal Arms.

Wheaton Aston [10] A large village of many lanes and many modern houses just N of the A5. Small Victorian church, with little turret and spire, of 1857; somewhat grander chancel (by Lynam) of 1893. At the E end of the village the Shropshire Union Canal passes by, and the Hartley Arms provides for travellers and navigators.

Whiston [5] Main-road hamlet in the high country N of Cheadle. Pretty little stone church of 1910 (by J. H. Beckett), Arts and Crafts inspired.

Whitgreave [8] Tiny village above the M6 S of Stone. Humble little early-19c brick church with pointed windows and bellcote.

Whitmore [7] Rolling agricultural country. To the W are the frontiers of Shropshire and Cheshire: to the E a high ridge of ground, upon the slopes of which lie the plantations of Swynnerton Old Park, protects the village from sight and sound of Newcastle and the Potteries.

Spruce estate village. Small medieval church with timbered bell turret and W gable. Aligned on the W porch a broad avenue of ancient limes leads up to the Hall, with its delectable S front, built in 1676. But this façade, two storeys in height, of richly-coloured brick with stone dressings and balustrading, in fact conceals an earlier timbered house, and the Mainwarings who live here can trace their descent, and tenure of the manor, back to John de Whitmore who died in 1208. The estate has changed hands only by inheritance, never by sale. Early 17c stable block. Beautifully landscaped lake and park behind the house. Incised

Wightwick Manor. Great Parlour: *left* The Gallery with 'Love Among the Ruins' by Burne-Jones. *right* The window with glass by Kempe

alabaster monument to Edward Mainwaring (d. 1586) in the church.

(The house is not open to the public.)

Whittington [12] Whittington Barracks are on the Heath close to the A51; the village lies to the N. The church is 18c, a building of brick, with stone spire, and interior glorified by the great 17c pulpit from Lichfield Cathedral. This dates from Bishop Hacket's restoration after the Civil War, and was thrown out to make way for the Victorian Gothic furnishings of Gilbert Scott. Victorian chancel by Ewan Christian (1881): fragments of medieval glass.

The Hall is in part a 17c brick house; but it was greatly enlarged at the end of the 19c by Holding of Northampton for Samuel Lipscomb Seckham (creator of Park Town at Oxford). Past the Hall, the road to Elford crosses the railway, and is bounded on the left by a long brick wall. This was Fisherwick Park. Here in 1774 Capability Brown built a great mansion for the first Marquis of Donegal, and laid out the grounds 'in the most exquisite taste, so as to entitle it to rank among the finest seats in the country'. But in 1810 the place was sold to the Howards of Elford, the house pulled down, the park divided into farms. Now no trace survives of Capability's layout—except for a lodge near the road, and a pair of great gate piers which can be spotted across the fields near the level crossing. According to tradition, the bricks for the park wall were the bricks bought by Sir Charles Pye for his great house at Clifton Campville—the house that was never built.

Wigginton [15] is now very close to Tamworth, but preserves some of its village character. Attractive little Georgian church (1777) of brick—nave and N aisle with gallery, and tall round-headed windows. Two Doric pillars at the W end support the little tower. It has all been delightfully redecorated recently. Victorian Gothic chancel.

Wightwick Manor [14] The house stands just off the Wolverhampton–Bridgnorth road (A454: the approach is signposted), on the outskirts of the town. It was built in two halves, the first in 1887, the second in 1893, for Theodore Mander, the paint and varnish manufacturer, and its architect was the Liverpool architect, Edward Ould. It is an interesting example of the taste of a rich and cultivated late Victorian, and of the influence of William Morris and John Ruskin. The scale is domestic, human—a far cry from the somewhat forbidding grandiose houses

◁ **Wightwick Manor.** Drawing Room fireplace with tiles by William de Morgan

sometimes built by the Victorians, and the atmosphere is one of great charm. Standing on the garden side it is easy to see how the house was built. The W half, more conventionally Victorian, displays a fine array of timbered gables, but the ground floor is built of hard red Ruabon brick, as are the chimneys, and (on the entrance side) the low tower which contains the front door. The E half is much more freely timbered; it is more decorative, and built on a low plinth of local stone, with chimneys and other features more obviously copied from (or inspired by) famous Elizabethan houses of Shropshire or Cheshire. It is altogether mellower. The ensemble is delightful.

Inside, the front door leads into a long spacious corridor: in the older part of the house are Drawing Room and Library; in the newer, the Great Parlour, Dining Room and Billiard Room. Every room displays distinguished decoration by C. E. Kempe, Morris wallpapers or Morris tapestries, de Morgan tiles, stained glass (again by Kempe), Pre-Raphaelite pictures and a splendid collection of furniture of different periods, including a settle designed by Bodley, a cupboard painted by Treffry Dunn, and the Swinburne folding bed from The Pines at Putney. The most impressive room is the Great Parlour, which is like a Great Hall and rises through both floors. Dining Room and Billiard Room have many period fittings, such as the built-in sideboard in the Dining Room, and the raised recess in the Billiard Room, by the fireside framed by blue and green Morris tiles. Perhaps the most beautiful room is the Drawing Room, a room of unusual shape, with an Italian Renaissance chimneypiece. With its rare collection of china, its little pictures, Kempe glass, Morris damask and richly-coloured rugs, the room glows; here, as in several other rooms, there is an elaborate

plaster ceiling by L. A. Shuffrey.

The house, which was presented to the National Trust by Sir Geoffrey and Lady Mander in 1937, is surrounded by gardens, formal and informal, which descend to a lake. These were designed by Alfred Parsons and T. H. Mawson. There is no hint that the great sprawl of Woverhampton is so close.

Willenhall [14] lies in the great built-up area between Wolverhampton and Walsall. But off the main road there is a withdrawn little market square—a reminder that Willenhall is in origin an ancient town. There are brass and iron foundries, where locks and keys and bolts are made, and a few older Victorian and Georgian houses. The parish church was rebuilt in 1867 by W. D. Griffin, a Wolverhampton architect: tall pinnacled W tower.

Closer to the motorway is Bentley. Here stood Bentley Hall, illustrated in Dr. Plot's *Staffordshire* (1686), in the mid-17c the home of Colonel John Lane and his sister Jane. It was here that Charles II arrived in the early hours of 10 September 1651, on his flight from Worcester. The Lane family moved from Bentley to King's Bromley (q.v.) in 1748; the old stables here survived into this century. On a fine site overlooking the motorway and a sea of council houses stands the church designed by Lavender, Twentyman and Percy in 1951. Impressive in size and furnishings, and surrounded by spacious parochial buildings, an inscription within records that it was built to the memory of Alfred Ernest Owen, of Rubery Owen and Co., the Darlaston engineers.

Willoughbridge [7] Remote, on the borders of Shropshire and Cheshire. In the late 17c Lady Gerard of Gerard's Bromley (*see* Ashley) discovered warm springs here, and built a bath house. The place was in a fair way to becoming

a spa, a Tunbridge Wells of Staffordshire, and only just missed becoming fashionable. The house called Willoughbridge Wells, beautifully set against the woods and beside the little lake, preserves its memory. Willoughbridge reverted to hamlet status.

On a lonely hilltop near by stands Willoughbridge Lodge, an intriguing 16c (or early 17c) hunting lodge, built by the Gerards. The N front has a central porch tower with staircase turret, the stone cap oddly decorated with scale pattern. It has long been a farm, and gazes N across the Cheshire plain.

A signpost points to Eld's Wood, where an unusual wild garden has in recent years been created in an old gravel quarry. In this woodland garden grow daffodils and a whole host of azaleas and rhododendrons; it is regularly open to the public throughout the spring and summer.

Wilnecote [15] Industrial village on Watling Street, close to the Warwickshire border. Reliant Scimitar motor cars are made here, in a factory on the A5. Little church of 1821, stone on the street front, brick at the back, with plain Gothic features and entertaining little W tower.

Wolverhampton [14] is an ancient town, and has always been a place of importance. In the shadow of the parish church is the Wolverhampton Cross, dating probably from the 9c; the church itself is a noble medieval town church. In the Middle Ages Wolverhampton grew rich on wool, and wool remained its great industry until the town turned to iron in the 18c. Prints of the late 18 and early 19c show a place of solid houses and a few chimneys, surrounded by green fields and undulating hills, dominated by the great medieval church, with an elegant Georgian church in the foreground. There is a charming print of the race-course in 1825, with the town compact and attractive on its hill, the race-course in front filled with the smart carriages and horses of the local gentry.

What remains? From the E and the S murky streets lead into the town from the Black Country—from Coseley and Sedgley, from Bilston, Darlaston and Willenhall. Newer suburban housing accompanies the traveller from the N. Pleasant countryside, the Shropshire border country, lies to the W, and the approach from Tettenhall is pleasant: along the Tettenhall Road and Compton Road are agreeable Victorian mansions, and a few terraces of Regency brick or stucco houses.

The best way to see Wolverhampton is to start at the parish church. Close to the S porch is the Anglo-Saxon cross: tall and blackened, its carvings hard to decipher, it is none the less remarkably well preserved; it dates probably from the middle of the 9c. Behind looms the impressive mass of the church, built of red sandstone, cruciform, embattled and pinnacled, with tall Perp central tower and long Victorian apsidal chancel. Inside, the crossing with its low arches is 13c, the nave 15c. Note specially the panelled stone pulpit, contemporary with the nave and structurally all part of the arcade; a seated stone lion is perched on the staircase handrail, and an angel carries the shield of the Swynnerton family, donors of the pulpit. The S chapel is the Leveson Chapel (see Trentham): table tomb of John and Agnes Leveson (1575) with effigies; splendid bronze standing figure of Admiral Sir Richard Leveson (c. 1634) by le Soeur—'He died without progeny, but not without the lamentations of many: worthy of gold, but content with bronze.' The N chapel is the Lane Chapel: alabaster table tomb of Thomas and Katharine Lane (1582), and perhaps most touching of all, the wall monument (by Jasper Latham) to Colonel John

Lane, protector of Charles II—'His remains the King would have interred with great funeral pomp in the Royal Tombs at Westminster, had not the hero's modesty in his dying moments refused so great an honour.' The Lane arms, however, are resplendent with the special canton bearing the royal lions of England, as conferred on the family at the Restoration. Note, too, the unusual 17c windows in this transept; the ancient screens, especially that in the S transept; the medallions of 16 and 17c Flemish and German glass in the chancel; and the 15c stalls from Lilleshall Abbey, presented by the Leveson family in 1546. The chancel is a rebuilding by Ewan Christian (1867) in the Dec style, and replaced a 17c building. There are many other memorials: of special interest are those to the Mander family, and to John Marston who died in 1918 'developer of the cycle, motor cycle and motor industry' in the town.

'Wolverhampton' means Wulfrun's Heanton (or High Town): it was the Lady Wulfrun, sister of King Edgar, who endowed the collegiate church of Wolverhampton in 994 with Dean and Prebendaries. Edward IV in 1479 united the Deanery with that of Windsor, and this Royal Peculiar continued until 1846. Until fifty years ago the old Deanery stood at the E end of the church.

From the steps at the W end of the church there is a view across the Old Market to the Town Hall, a French-inspired building of 1869 by Ernest Bates; next door, the Civic Hall is a 1930s Classical building with giant Ionic portico. But of most interest is the 18c brick Giffard House in the NW corner. This was the town residence (1728) of the Giffards of Chillington (q.v.) and was given by them to the R.C. Vicar-General of the Midland District. The house contains a remarkable staircase, and attached to the back the Roman church of SS Peter and Paul was built in 1825 (Joseph

Ireland, architect). Stuccoed, with shallow domes, high lunette windows and distinguished Soanian interior, this is a precious and historic early Roman church. To its right stands the Molineux Hotel of the mid-18c, which was originally the residence of the Molineux family. At the E end of the parish church stands the Museum and Art Gallery (1883 by J. A. Chatwin) with its coupled Ionic columns and long sculptured panels; next to it, on the site of the Deanery, is the College of Technology (1926).

Descending the steps from the S porch, Queen's Square contains the equestrian statue of the Prince Consort by Thomas Thorneycroft (1866), and an entry into a new 'shopping precinct' called the Mander Centre (what it is the centre of seems uncertain), as anonymous as all these 'precincts' are. But it is possible to walk down Victoria Street (which contains one 16c timber-framed house, dated 1300!) and Worcester Street into what remains of St John's Square. This poor square, which contained good if somewhat dilapidated town houses, has been torn apart, and the new ring road driven through it. But in the centre stands St John's church, built by William Baker in 1725—the Classical church of the prints. Noble W tower, lantern and spire, the whole composition is reminiscent of St Martin-in-the-Fields. Interior with galleries, elaborate reredos and organ by Renatus Harris (1682). There are still some Georgian houses in George Street (E end of St John's), which leads into Dudley Road. Here the R.C. church of SS Mary and John is not to be missed: High Victorian Gothic, the interior is deeply devotional with its apsidal sanctuary and colourful Hardman glass. The church is by Charles Hansom (1851).

Cleveland Road leads to St George's Parade, where stands St George's, a Classical Commissioners' church of 1828 by James

Willoughbridge Wells

Morgan. W tower and spire, galleried interior with all the atmosphere of a High Church slum parish. Cross Walsall Street, and up Piper's Row: on the corner of Horsley Fields is the old railway station, and in Lichfield Street is the Grand Theatre, with its magnificent Victorian baroque interior; but Queen Street is the street to walk down—the best street in the town. Here there are a number of delightful late Georgian façades, and the best of all is the County Court, with its two-storeyed, pedimented portico, built originally as the Library and Assembly Rooms, by Vulliamy, 1829.

All this can be seen on foot.

Further out, to the NW, St Andrew's is of 1965 by Twentyman, Percy and Partners, to replace a Victorian church destroyed by fire. (The church is in New Hampton Road West—first turning off Waterloo Road N of the ring road.) This is a simple square brick block, which gains its effect from bold massing and shafts of light from four side windows at roof level to N and S; the only other window is the great rectangular W window filled with glass by John Piper, depicting the Sea of Galilee—whose strongly-patterned blues are thrown up on to the E wall by the western sun.

Parallel to New Hampton Road,

Tettenhall Road leads out to Tettenhall, attractive with its Upper and Lower Greens. The parish church was destroyed by fire in 1950, and rebuilt by the architect Bernard Miller. The medieval tower survives: the nave and sanctuary (the chancel has become the Lady Chapel) and cross-gabled aisles are designed in what may be described as latest *art nouveau*—Gothic in spirit, 20c in detail. Upon the skyline rises the Gothic silhouette of Tettenhall College—founded in 1863, the school buildings by Bidlake, 1865. The school has absorbed the adjoining Tettenhall Towers, the stuccoed late Georgian house with its odd

St Peter's **Wolverhampton**

polygonal turrets. Mount Road leads to the Mount, now the Mount Hotel, built in 1870 for Charles Benjamin Mander, cousin of Theodore who built Wightwick Manor. Like Wightwick it is (in part) by Edward Ould, but the older part of the house is as early as 1870. Its chief interest is the magnifical Ball Room (added by Ould). For Wightwick Manor *see* separate entry.

To the SW is the submerged village of Penn; the church lies S, off the main road (A449), and from here there is an unexpected view of the open country to the S. The church has a Georgian Gothick W front, with tall brick tower of great charm, probably by William Baker (1765). The core of the church is medieval, but dark and Victorianised within. Outside, against the S wall, is the base of the Godiva Cross, discovered in 1912 buried—perhaps buried when the church was built. The inscription records that the cross was erected by Lady Godiva, Lady of the manor of Nether Penn, wife of Leofric, Earl of Mercia, and that itinerant priests were provided by Dudley Priory to take occasional services there until Sir Hugh de Bushbury built the church, *c*. 1200. Penn Hall is an early-18c brick house of two storeys, with projecting porch and carved cartouche of arms, built by the Bradney family, a short distance W of the church.

Further E, close to the A4123, is a church of 1938 which deserves a visit: St Martin's, Ettingshall, by Lavender and Twentyman. The church, with its solid oblong tower, and connected to its vicarage by short cloister, forms an attractive composition from the road. Inside, its long white nave with simple round arches, long windows and low narrow aisles, leads the eye to the altar: it is an impressive yet restful interior.

One more submerged village must be mentioned: Bushbury, to the N. A vast estate of council houses comes close to the church, which is medieval, and (though much restored in the 19c) full of interest. Perp W tower, Dec nave and chancel—the latter impressive with Easter sepulchre and sedilia. And in the S aisle is the monument to Thomas Whitgreave, who secreted Charles II in Moseley Old Hall after the Battle of Worcester. Moseley Old Hall is in the parish—see special entry.

Wombourn [14] Industrial and suburban growth on the W side of the village: the old street survives by the church—the only church in England dedicated to St Benedict Biscop. Medieval tower and spire; most of the church rebuilt by Street in 1862ff. Many furnishings by Street; stained glass by Kempe and by Clayton and Bell. 18c monument to Sir Samuel Hellier, who brought from Italy the small 16c Italian relief of the Good Samaritan. Monument by Chantrey (1820) to Richard Marsh, of Lloyd House. Lloyd House stands on the far side of the A449; and is now a Cheshire Home: a late-18c house of stone, with centre bow and giant Ionic columns. In a secluded spot off the A457 stands the Wodehouse, since the 17c the home of the Hellier family. A Jacobean house, it was sympathetically restored by G. F. Bodley in the 1870s, and decorated by C. R. Ashbee in the 1890s. With his Guild of Handicraft, he was responsible for much of the delightful decoration—weather vanes, sundial and inscription. Delectable grounds watered by a stream. A remarkable oasis.

Woodlane [12] Hamlet on the A515 N of Yoxall, where the road begins to assume the air of Needwood Forest; the surprise here is to find a little late-18c Roman Catholic church, close to the road. It has tall pinnacles and Gothic windows, and is attached to a house—as was so often the case with Roman churches of this date. The church was founded by the 15th Earl of Shrewsbury (*see* Alton), whose father, a younger brother of the 14th earl, had lived at Hoar Cross.

Wootton Lodge [6]
'Wootton-under-Weaver,
Where God comes never.'

In magnificent, remote, wild countryside, bounded by the river Dove, the river Churnet and the Weaver Hills, stands Wootton Lodge, a Jacobean mansion built of local grey stone, dramatic in itself, dramatic in position. The house stands immensely tall, a square porch in the centre, flat three-sided bay windows at either side, and round the corner at either end a deep semi-circular bow; porch, bays and bows rise to the full height of four storeys, the flat roof crowned by a simple balustrade and an orderly phalanx of chimneys. In front is a walled courtyard with flanking pavilions at the outside corners; and a great flight of steps leads with wide welcoming curve up to the front door. Here coupled Ionic columns, crowned with coupled obelisks and a carved cartouche of arms frame the doorway. At the back the house stands above a deep ravine, rougher, almost windowless, like a medieval castle.

Wootton was built for Sir Richard Fleetwood, 1st Bt, in the early years of the 17c: the arms on the porch bear the baronet's hand, and Sir Richard became a baronet in 1611. This may help to date the house. His grandfather Sir John, whose tomb is in Ellastone church (q.v.), bought the property in 1560, and converted the monastic buildings of Calwich into a house for himself. His grandson aspired to something better. Sir John's son Thomas married a Shirburn of Stonyhurst, his grandson Richard a Pershall of Pershall (near Eccleshall)—both recusant families. Sir Richard was himself a fervent recusant, and a fervent Royalist. Wootton was besieged in the Civil War, in 1643, and severely damaged. No doubt the wrecking of the house, coupled with the heavy recusancy fines, led to the place being sold by the 3rd baronet at the end of the century. It was

bought by John Wheeler, wealthy ironmaster of Stourbridge. Perhaps the house was still partly derelict after the siege; at any rate the interior was remodelled and redecorated in about 1700, and nothing of the Jacobean interior survives. Outside, balustrade, steps and pavilions date from 1700 too. The Wheelers and their descendants the Unwins continued to live at Wootton until the Second World War. The place has changed hands once or twice since.

But who designed this romantic house? Its great height and its great array of enormous mullioned windows recall Hardwick; the porch with its attendant bays Caverswall and Barlborough, the bows Burton Agnes—all houses built at much the same time. Though but scanty evidence exists, these houses must all be by the same hand, the hand of Robert Smythson. Smythson died in 1614 at Wollaton, outside Nottingham; he is described on his monument there as 'architect and surveyor unto the most worthy house of Wollaton, and divers others of great account'.

Such a house is Wootton: a house of 'great account'. The design of its front is of simple perfection, and, set as it is in its remote park and on the edge of its precipitous ravine, it seems enchanted and mysterious, a house of dazzling, almost unreal beauty.

Wordsley [17] Landscape of old industries, N of Stourbridge: there are all the ingredients—glass works, iron foundries, small factories, terraces of Victorian villas and cottages for the workers, and one or two grander late Georgian houses, once the homes of early captains of industry. Dominating church by Lewis Vulliamy, 1829. Long clerestoried nave; pinnacled W tower; the interior specially grand and spacious, with lofty arcades, galleries, flat ceilings, Perp windows. It might be a prosperous church in Kensington.

Wychnor

Wychnor [12] From the main Lichfield–Burton road Wychnor church is clearly visible, standing lonely above the meadows of the Trent. A tall brick farmhouse, with bay window on Tuscan columns, stands on one side of the main road; on the other a lane marked 'WYCHNOR ONLY. NO THROUGH ROAD' leads off the dual carriageway—and in turn another track leads off this to the church itself. From this low escarpment there is a wide panorama, across the canal, across the river, to Alrewas church, to the spires of Lichfield, to Cannock Chase beyond. The church is chiefly Dec, but the tower has a 17c brick top. The first lane leads on to Wychnor Park. The manor was originally granted by John of Gaunt to Sir Philip de Somerville on condition that a flitch of bacon was always ready at the Hall, to be offered on certain strict conditions; this comic custom, of course, lapsed, but a wooden flitch is preserved at the house—now a square 18c mansion which replaced the earlier, moated, hall. The property passed to the Levett family, and so to the present owners. Two cream stuccoed lodges guard the entrance beside a lake; it is an ancient park, withdrawn from the world, private.

Yoxall [12] A large village on the A515, on the southern edge of Needwood Forest. The Rookery is a tall 18c brick house in the main street; and there are other decent houses. The church was largely rebuilt by Woodyer, and is large, opulent and attractive. Good late Victorian furnishings, and glass by Wailes. The S chapel contains 18c monuments to the Ardens of Longcroft. Alabaster tomb with effigies, in N aisle, to Humphrey Welles (of the former family of Hoar Cross). Canopied tomb in S aisle, by Baron Marochetti, to Admiral Henry Meynell of Hoar Cross.

To the NE stood Yoxall Lodge, in the 19c home of the Revd Thomas Gisborne, friend of Wilberforce and the Evangelical leaders.

Index